GainManagement

A Process for Building Teamwork, Productivity & Profitability Throughout Your Organization

Robert J. Doyle
Paul I. Doyle

amacom

American Management Association

Library of Congress Cataloging-in-Publication Data

Doyle, Robert J., 1931–
        GainManagement : a system for building teamwork, productivity &
    profitability throughout your organization / Robert J. Doyle, Paul
    I. Doyle.
            p.   cm.
        Includes bibliographical references and index.
        ISBN 0-8144-5052-0
        1. Gain sharing.   I. Doyle, Paul I.   II. Title.   III. Title: Gain
    management.
    HD4928.G34D688   1992
    658.3'225—dc20   91-43630
                                                                CIP

Printing number

10   9   8   7   6   5   4   3   2   1

A.M.D.G.

Contents

vii

Acknowledgments

This book represents the work, the hopes, and the dreams of many people. The thoughts and sentiments of those who have used, criticized, embraced, and questioned the ideas presented here are incorporated as much as possible. To all of you we are very grateful.

There are several we must single out for their direct and important contributions to the book as it is written. Kevin Boyle provided the critical ideas and much of the material for Chapter 12. Kevin is a visionary unionist, and we were fortunate to obtain his insights and assistance.

Ellen Doyle Mizener provided invaluable advice for clarifying the content and the style of the entire manuscript. If you find the book easy to read, you have Ellen to thank for much of that.

For the past five years, Tommy Badley has helped us develop many of our basic ideas, using his wealth of experience, and he also helped us sweat the detail of the first draft. Dick Raymond, John Mancino, Tom Carline, Otto Zach, and Jim Knister provided some excellent refinements to the finished manuscript.

Mary Doyle, working from some very rough drafts, corrected our spelling, our tense, and in many cases our sense to create a coherent manuscript. For her many hours of hard work we offer our sincere thanks.

Finally, we must thank you, the reader. Without you it would not be a book at all.

Thank you!

Introduction

From 1946 through 1960 Drucker, McGregor, Herzberg, Likert, and several other visionaries in the field of management and organizational psychology began to explain a fundamental weakness in the management of organizations. They gave us a clear statement that prevailing theories and practices of management were no longer appropriate to the needs of the emerging workforce and the modern organization. As is the case with prophets their words were believed by a few, misunderstood by others, and ignored by the overwhelming majority of managers and teachers of managers.

In the 30 years since this alarm was sounded, a handful of believing managers and organizations have been hard at work devising new theories and new practices to cope with the new realities. Our work in this area has centered on the gainsharing approach that began with Scanlon plans and progressed with the enlightened approaches of CEOs such as John Fenlon Donnelly. In 1983 we recorded the state of the gainsharing art in our book *Gainsharing and Productivity*. Since then we have continued to learn from the results of gainsharing plans and expand the basic concept.

Our major discovery is that gainsharing bonuses do not make people or organizations perform better. *Management* is what enables organizations and people to perform. This is what Peter Drucker first said in 1946 in *The Concept of the Corporation*, and what many others have since repeated. As gainsharing has been popularized in the past ten years, the emphasis has been too much on gainsharing and not enough on *gainmaking*. Tinkering with gainsharing formulas while organizational performance continues to decline is like rearranging the deck chairs on the *Titanic* as the ship sinks.

The fundamental problem in organizations today is outmoded

management practices. This book presents a process, which has its roots in the early gainsharing models, that addresses this fundamental need for new management practices. We call this new process "GainManagement" because its first priority is the continuous management of performance gains and its keystone is the participation of *all* workers in managing those gains.

GainManagement is comprehensive because the problem is complex. GainManagement is hard work because the problem is urgent and important. There is nothing clever or glitzy or even profound about GainManagement. It is a straightforward management process.

The GainManagement process has three major elements: GainPlanning, GainMaking, and GainSharing. GainPlanning is the work managers do to lead and focus the organization on continuous gains and to organize for a high level of employee involvement. GainMaking is the involvement of all employees in a structured process for making continuous performance improvements. Then, as performance improves, everyone associated with the organization shares in the gains, which is GainSharing.

In GainManagement there are GainShares for all of the organization's constituents, not just for employees. GainShares for customers are better products and services. GainShares for owners and investors are better returns on their investment. GainShares for employees are better work, more promotions, security, personal growth, and financial GainShares. GainShares for suppliers are fair dealings and more business. And GainShares for communities are more jobs, more taxes, and more responsible employers.

The book is organized in four parts. The first part, Chapters 1 through 4, provides the context for GainManagement. It discusses the difficulties and consequences of using obsolete management practices to direct today's workforce in today's more competitive global market. It presents a model for understanding the complex nature of employee participation. Finally, it reviews the history of gainsharing and traces the evolution of these ideas from Scanlon plans to gainsharing to GainManagement.

The second part, Chapters 5 through 7, describes each of the major elements of the GainManagement process: GainPlanning, GainMaking, and GainSharing. There is considerable detail in these chapters. Some of the detail, unique to GainManagement, is of the *how-to* variety. Some of the detail is of the *should* or *just-do-it* variety because the how-to already exists in many excellent books.

The third part, Chapters 8 through 11, covers the procedures and steps that an organization would follow to plan, design, implement, and operate the GainManagement process. There are checklists, guidelines, and step-by-step procedures to guide the organization in its implementation and use of the GainManagement process.

The fourth part, Chapter 12, is a special chapter we wrote with Kevin Boyle of the Communications Workers of America. It describes the role of unions in the GainManagement process.

A note of caution is required here. GainManagement is a dynamic process that must be carefully adapted to the unique needs of each organization that uses it. The guidelines in this book should not be followed or applied like a formula or recipe. Everything about GainManagement must be molded to fit the people, the situation, and the environment specific to each organization. The concepts are very sound, but they require thoughtful adaptation.

More than one design team chided us that our first book did not have any pictures. We have tried to correct that omission by including in this book a series of word pictures. In most chapters you will find short stories that illustrate points presented in the text. All of these stories reflect actual experiences although, in most cases, names and company identities have been changed or omitted.

Many critics today state that U.S. schools are failing to prepare students to be skilled workers with a productive work ethic. Although we agree that the schools should always strive to do a better job, we do not agree that the decline in organizational performance today is due solely to the failure of our schools. Out-of-date management systems use only a fraction of the skills and motivation already available in the workforce. As schools work hard to better prepare future workers, managers must work even harder to use the abundant talents that are now available. Management systems must catch up with the new worker. It is to this end that we offer Gain-Management to managers who need practical guidance about how to set into motion new management systems, and especially to the workers who are ready and want to be more involved.

The concepts and ideas in this book do not come from a classroom or laboratory. They are ideas we have learned as we have worked in and with organizations that are trying to achieve excellence. We consider ourselves to be students of this process as well as authors. Because you are one of our readers and a practitioner of these ideas we would very much like to hear about your experiences.

Bob Doyle
Paul Doyle

I

Background and Context for GainManagement

Chapter 1

The Need for GainManagement

Methexis, Inc., is by all accounts an excellent company. Its customers swear by the company's products: "Best you can buy for any price . . . best quality, best service, and best of all, best price anywhere. I don't even bother looking for another source."

Methexis employees say: "I've never had a job I like so well as working here. We have excellent management. They tell you what is going on, and they listen to you. They treat you with respect, and they are fair with you. I am proud of the company and our products, and most of all, I am proud of the way we serve our customers."

Methexis shareholders, bankers, and other investors are very pleased with the security and return on their investments: "A very healthy company. They are profitable now and have a well-designed, long-term strategy for serving their market. They have a loyal customer base and a solid organization that will ensure their profitability for years to come."

Suppliers fight for their business: "They are a tough customer demanding the highest quality and on-time deliveries, but they are a pleasure to work with. Their business is growing, they never miss a payment, and their high standards are contagious. We are becoming excellent just trying to keep up with them."

The mayor of Rose City had this to say at last year's chamber of commerce awards luncheon: "Methexis is the city's leading corporate citizen. It seems like everybody in town wants to work there, and the lucky ones do. Methexis led the way in cleaning up the pollution in Black Lake, for which the whole town is grateful. . . ."

Methexis, of course, is not an actual company. It is an ideal company, one that serves the needs of all of its constituents in an excellent manner. How many of the preceding quotes can be said of your company or hospital or school or agency? Customers, clients, employees, shareholders, owners, investors, suppliers, patients, parishioners, and communities need organizations that excel in the manner of Methexis. Organizations of this quality must become the standard rather than a visionary ideal. The good news is that this level of organizational excellence is achievable. We know how to create excellent organizations.

Very few organizations are considered excellent by all of their constituents, though many meet the standards of excellence of one or more of them. There are organizations that are highly productive. Some produce excellent products. Others are rated highly by employees or by investors. These successes are proof that the knowledge exists to manage resources, markets, and organizations in ways that will provide excellent results to all. It is imperative that organizations use this knowledge and create new systems of management to compete in today's challenging environment and to lead today's workforce.

Until recently businesses were asked only for the quantities of life: more food, more appliances, more goods of all types. Today we are still asking for those things—even more and better things, in fact—but in addition we are asking for a better quality of life. We want more services, a pristine environment, and, for people at work, achievement and personal fulfillment in addition to good wages. Today's customers demand better quality, value, and service. Today's employees want more participation, achievement, and personal growth. Today's communities want organizations to be more socially and environmentally responsible. The demands that society is placing on its businesses, hospitals, schools, and government agencies call for a major change in the way organizations are managed for performance.

Management systems that were effective a generation or two ago are inadequate today. They are not able to generate acceptable levels of quality, productivity, and performance. Nor are these outdated management systems able to provide effective leadership to a new generation of workers who have much higher aspirations than their predecessors.

This book describes a process by which organizations can achieve new levels of excellence. It is a process for managing gains in productivity and quality of work life on all levels and in all areas. It is GainManagement.

GainManagement is an innovative process for organizational excellence. It is designed to meet both the higher-level personal needs of employees and the higher performance levels required of organizations in today's more demanding global environment. Personal and organizational goals are achieved and continuously advanced through a structured participative management process based on principles of excellence, openness, equity, and teamwork. Much of the GainManagement process is new, yet it is built on a foundation of 50 years of experience with gainsharing and similar programs.

GainManagement is the result of years of learning and discovery, of successes and failures, of effort and results. It is a continuous process rather than a one-shot program or campaign. It is strategic rather than a "quick fix." GainManagement takes time. It requires effort. It requires dedication. It will not produce phenomenal results by the end of the first quarter. However, with courage, patience, persistence, and commitment on the part of everyone involved GainManagement provides the dynamic model an organization needs to become like Methexis, Inc. . . . an excellent performer in the challenging environment of the 1990s and on into the 21st century.

Problems of Productivity and Quality of Work Life

Over the past 50 years a great deal of energy and effort have been spent trying to improve organizational effectiveness and reshape the American workplace. There have been many programs for strategic planning, management effectiveness, and employee motivation. Yet the problems persist, and today the need for excellence is greater than ever. In this chapter we will review three critical performance problems facing organizations and show how the changing workforce is demanding new, more participative management systems. This review will define the context for the new process that we call GainManagement.

First, there are three critical problems confronting organizations today: (1) declining productivity, (2) increasing worldwide competitiveness, and (3) pressure from workers for a better quality of work life. A brief review of these three problems will explain the growing interest in their solution.

Declining Productivity

The productivity of the American economy boomed following World War II but slowed significantly in the 1970s and continued to be a problem through the 1980s. From 1950 to 1970 the U.S. economy grew at a healthy 3–4% per year but dropped off to about 1.5% by 1980. Since then growth has increased only slightly, to about 2%. Many causes were identified to explain this declining productivity, including aging plants and equipment, a slowdown in the introduction of new technology, excessive government regulation, restrictive labor practices, high labor costs, and a general erosion of the work ethic. In response, a variety of efforts were mounted to update plants and equipment, introduce new technology, deregulate, negotiate new work practices, reduce labor costs, and increase employee motivation.

Some industries, including automobiles, began to modernize plants and equipment, but others just walked away from old plants. Many plants in the "Rust Belt" were abandoned as a collection of industrial dinosaurs. U.S. Steel quit the steel business. There was a renewed interest in technology, and for a time there was a robotics craze. CAM (computer-aided manufacturing) became as popular as CAD (computer-aided design), and then CAE (computer-aided engineering) was added to link CAD and CAM.

President Carter started deregulation, but the Reagan administration accelerated it and was responsible for returning the transportation, finance, and communications industries to free enterprise. Inspired by Reagan's success in the air traffic controllers strike, businesses started chopping away at so-called restrictive work practices as labor contracts came up for negotiations. Some contracts were bought out, some were negotiated amicably, and others resulted in fierce struggles that were only resolved by plant closures, hiring replacement workers, union decertifications, and moving operations off shore.

The methods introduced to reduce labor costs included reductions in force, two-tier wage structures, lump sum payments, and a variety of efforts to contain runaway health care costs. It was during this period that more companies began offering gainsharing programs to offset or soften the impact of wage reductions or freezes.

The problem of the declining work ethic proved to be more difficult to address. Studies by government and public interest foundations confirmed the work ethic decline. Other studies indicated that schools were not preparing young people to be productive workers and responsible citizens. A few commendable business-education cooperative efforts were begun and continue, but not on a scale commensurate with the size of the problem.

Increasing Worldwide Competitiveness

The problem of declining productivity went from bad to worse as other countries became more productive and more competitive in world markets. Just as the U.S. economy started to slow, Japan and Western Europe emerged strong and vibrant from their rebuilding following World War II. In Japan and West Germany productivity grew at the rate of 5–7%. Other European countries did almost as well. Exporters were selling autos, electronics, shoes, steel, machine tools, and other capital goods at lower prices and of better quality than U.S. industry could produce. Suddenly, and for the first time in recent memory, America was not competitive.

The impact of foreign competition on U.S. industry was twofold. Automobiles provide a good example. Foreign manufacturers took a large share of the U.S. automobile market. As a result domestic automobile manufacturers found themselves fighting not only the foreign companies but each other for the remaining market. Chrysler teetered and had to be rescued by a massive government loan and union concessions. American Motors did not survive and was acquired by the rejuvenated Chrysler. As competition intensified, U.S. businesses could no longer simply raise prices to cover increasing labor and material costs, and the inevitable profit squeeze followed. This cost, price, profit squeeze was intensified twice in the 1970s due to sudden increases in the price of oil, brought about by political and economic changes in the Middle East.

A presidential commission was convened to study why U.S. industry was no longer competitive and how to remedy the problem. This, and other inquiries into the problem, produced a list of causes quite similar to the list of reasons for declining productivity. These inquiries also led to a discovery that the Japanese, in particular, managed their organizations better than the Americans did. In no time at all several books and a host of journal articles appeared proclaiming the wonders of Japanese management methods. For a while it looked as if all that had to be done to solve the competitiveness problem was copy Japanese management techniques. During the early 1980s there was a flurry of activity to do just that.

Japanese management did not prove to be the easy panacea many expected, so a couple of years were spent looking for reasons why Japanese management did not work in the United States. There was some agreement that cultural differences explained their better management techniques until it was remembered that the Japanese were using ideas developed by Douglas McGregor (Theory Y), W. Edwards Deming (statistical quality control), and other Americans. If the ideas originated in the United States, they certainly weren't unique to the culture of Japan. So U.S. industry started using techniques such as quality circles. "If Japan Can, Why Can't We?"—the title of a 1980 NBC white paper on the subject—became the slogan.

Quality circles sprouted everywhere. Some early successes brought lots of publicity and enthusiasm. But, like the seed that fell among the rocks, quality circles sprang up and withered within two years. The analysis of these failed efforts showed that the roots were not strong. Employees were trained and involved, meetings were held, but the employees' ideas were not used. Studies showed that where quality circles were used only as a technique, they failed. Where they were introduced along with fundamental changes in management processes, they produced good results, and several continue to work very well.

Despite this lack of success with quality circles a fundamental interest in participative management, employee involvement, and labor-management cooperation has continued to grow. Today the dominant belief is that increasing employee participation is the right solution to these problems even though many managers do not yet know how to do it well. This interest reflects a growing awareness that knowledgeable, informed, committed, and motivated employees are an essential requirement in today's competitive environment. Technology, financial resources, and access to markets are no longer sufficient competitive advantages. The only certain competitive advantage a company can have in a truly open market is the people it can attract to do its work. Developing human resources will be the most important strategic organizational objective for the 1990s and into the 21st century.

Pressure for a Better Quality of Work Life

The human needs of people at work is the third problem creating interest in gainsharing and other participative management programs. Employee surveys have shown a steady decline in job satisfaction for at least the past 20 years. As a problem, quality of work life does not receive the attention that productivity and competitiveness do. Employee-satisfaction surveys do not attract the same scrutiny by the decision makers as do the profit and loss statements. Employee dissatisfaction is a problem, however, and will continue to be a contributing cause, if not the principal cause, of declining productivity and noncompetitiveness until it is solved. More consequential than its impact on productivity is the fact that quality of work life is an important human need. Work is important to people for many human reasons: It pays their rent and buys the groceries, of course, but it is also a primary source of learning and growing throughout their adult lives.

That people constantly strive to improve their quality of life is not a new discovery. In 1914 Samuel Gompers, president of the American Federation of Labor, testifying before a Senate Commission on Industrial Relations, was asked if there was a limit to how much improvement in the conditions of labor the workers wanted. Gompers answered that the goal was "to accomplish the best results in improving the conditions of the working people, men and women and children, today and tomorrow and tomorrow—and tomorrow's tomorrow; and each day making it a better day than the one that had gone before."

Mr. Hillquit: Then, Mr. Gompers, if it should get, say, 5 percent more within the next year, will the organized labor movement rest contented with that and stop?

Mr. Gompers: Not if I know anything about human nature.[1]

The need to improve quality of work life comes, as Gompers stated, not from the A.F. of L. but from human nature.

As far as we know, this natural need is insatiable. However, we are discovering that it is shifting from dollars to personal achievement. We are not at the point where every American can blow a million dollars on their birthday bash, but we are at a point where the overwhelming majority of U.S. citizens have their basic material needs satisfied to an extent that was unimaginable 50 years ago. Now that paychecks are reasonably satisfying, interest is turning to the quality of work life, which means such things as challenging work, opportunity for achievement, a chance to learn new skills, career advancement, and personal growth. As the 1990 U.S. Army recruiting slogan says it: "Be all that you can be." As Gompers predicted, this desire for constant improvement in the condition of work continues. The 1914 needs have been met, but there is a new batch of needs for the 1990s. In 1987 Marvin Weisbord, in *Productive Workplaces*, identified some of these new worker goals as dignity, meaning, and community.[2] These are human needs that go well beyond paying the rent. Some of the interest in such programs as employee involvement, autonomous work groups, sociotechnical systems, and gainsharing is occurring as a result of this growing need for a better quality of work life.

GainManagement: A Comprehensive Approach

Despite past efforts, in the 1990s there are still problems of declining productivity, noncompetitiveness, and dissatisfaction with the quality of work life in American businesses and other organizations. In 1990 U.S. productivity, at a 2% growth rate, ranked tenth among 11 industrialized nations. This was down from fifth place during the 1979–1987 period. Employee dissatisfaction continued its gradual negative trend. Past efforts have not adequately solved the underlying causes of these and other problems.

Many of the programs in vogue do not offer a balanced approach to the problems of productivity and quality of work life. They appear to be "either-or" solutions; either productivity or people. Productivity-focused approaches tend to receive strong management support but less enthusiasm from the rank and file. Quality-of-work-life programs are favored by workers, less so by management. When management emphasizes productivity and competitiveness, they raise old fears of exploitation of the workers. Likewise, when consultants, professors, workers, and labor leaders stress quality of work life, it strikes the practical business manager as soft and "touchy-feely."

A better solution must be comprehensive and unifying. It must be comprehensive enough to address the problems of productivity and quality of work life simultaneously rather than favoring one over the other. A better solution must unify management and workers in a common effort to achieve both organizational and human goals. Early gainsharing programs such as the Scanlon plan were adequate and unifying for their circumstances, but two things have happened to erode the usefulness of gainsharing.

First, productivity and competitiveness are much more complex and intense today than they were when gainsharing started. The problem then was mainly blue-collar labor productivity. Today the issue is the total productivity of labor (blue-, white-, and gold-collar), materials, capital, and every other resource the organization uses in its work.

Second, as gainsharing programs have become more popular, employee participation, rather than expanding as it should to meet today's more demanding human and organizational needs, has been dropped from most programs. The popular concept of gainsharing today is that of a group incentive. Quality of work life has slipped into a subordinate role in gainsharing, and in some cases it is out of the picture entirely.

Still, the basic gainsharing concept is sound. Building upon that basic concept, this book presents a new process for creating gains in both total productivity and in the quality of work life. This new process, GainManagement, is in tune with today's complex organizational realities and rising human expectations. It is a process that has evolved from but goes well beyond gainsharing.

GainManagement is based primarily on the principles of employee involvement and participative management. Its fundamental premise is that excellent performance can only be achieved by a highly committed workforce, and that workforce commitment is a direct result of the level of employee participation. Today's employees demand a very high level of involvement in return for their commitment and this requires management systems that are highly participative. Just tinkering with the old programs will not be adequate. The current situation calls for substantive change.

To fully understand the need for the GainManagement process it is necessary to examine more carefully the size and interaction of the changes occurring in organizations, in the workforce, and in management systems.

Changing Organizations

Within the span of a single century the United States has changed from a society of family farms and mom-and-pop shops to a society of organizations. This radical change has transformed every aspect of American culture and society. As recently as the 19th century most families grew their own food and provided their own education,

health care, and other services. When they bought shoes and clothing, they bought from the local cobbler, tailor, and seamstress. Today
organizations and institutions provide goods and services for every
human need from the cradle to the grave. And almost everyone
works as an employee of an organization. Not only have there been
changes of great magnitude, but the rate of change has gone from
normal play to fast forward.

For instance, in transportation both method and speed were
essentially the same for Julius Caesar and George Washington, who
lived 1,800 years apart. Four score and seven years after Washington,
Abraham Lincoln rode in trains powered by steam locomotives. Forty
years after Lincoln gave his Gettysburg Address, the Wright brothers
made their first flight at Kitty Hawk, North Carolina. Twenty-four
years after the Wright brothers, Charles Lindbergh flew across the
Atlantic Ocean. Twenty years later Chuck Yeager broke the sound
barrier, and in another 22 years Neil Armstrong walked on the moon.
Today we are sending space probes to the planets and galaxies. Each
advance in transportation technology creates larger and more complex organizations. Consider the difference between the Wright
brothers' bicycle shop and NASA.

Organizations continue to grow in size and complexity, creating
opportunities and problems. Large manufacturing organizations have
enabled society to achieve a standard of living that would have been
pure fantasy just three generations ago. New organizations have
created many new job opportunities in many new fields of specialization. Marketing and advertising, for instance, are entirely new
fields within the past 100 years. Most of the jobs available today did
not exist in 1900. Large organizations not only serve the social and
material needs of people, they also create employment opportunities
for people to learn, to grow, and to achieve.

Large organizations have also created the need for management
and managers on a scale that has never been seen before. Peter
Drucker calls the emergence of management in the 20th century a
pivotal event of history.[3] Management is that function which makes
an organization perform. Customers and entrepreneurs create organizations, and organizations create management and employees.

These new opportunities are not without their problems of
performance, which are of concern to management, and problems of
quality of work life, which are of concern to employees. There is not
a class of organization without its performance problems. Businesses
have problems of productivity and competitiveness, schools have

problems of declining student achievement, health care organizations have problems of rising costs, and government agencies are criticized for inefficiency and excessive red tape.

Despite this concern about poor organization performance, there are a few organizations that perform very well. In the 1991 Fortune 500 list the median return on equity for all 500 companies was a modest 13%, but ten companies returned more than 50%.[4] There are also some schools, government agencies, and other organizations that perform well above the norm. These few high-performing organizations are creating new standards of performance and excellence, which is causing expectations to rise.

There is not a class of employees without some quality of work life problems. Studies show declining job satisfaction for men and women, for all races, ages, and ethnic groups, and in all types of jobs. At first glance this seems to be a surprising turn of events. Compared to 100 years ago or even 50 years ago, pay, hours of work, safety, and creature comforts have vastly improved. Based on this, job satisfaction should be getting better. Yet it continues a decline that appears to have started in the 1960s. A closer examination of the situation shows that although some conditions of work have definitely improved, employee expectations are growing at a faster rate than are workplace improvements. Contrary to this trend there are organizations where people work not only without conflict but in an atmosphere of enthusiasm and cooperation. Successes such as those reported in the *100 Best Companies to Work for in America* cause quality-of-work-life expectations to rise.

> It can be argued that both conventional managerial techniques and the innovative practices described in this book enhance productivity and create a healthy economy. But the "100 Best" offer an added benefit of such high value that it's difficult to place on the same scale: a working life for thousands of people really worth living and worth looking forward to every waking day.[5]

It would be inaccurate to conclude that the failure of organizations to perform and provide a satisfactory quality of work life is due to a lack of effort and concern. The effort to improve organizations through research, education, union organizing, political action, and legislation over the past 50 years has been enormous. However, the problems do persist, so it is fair to say that the efforts have not been sufficient if only because they have not been completely successful. Though organizations have changed and provide many new benefits, they must continue to change to meet the rising expectations of stockholders, customers, employees, and society.

The Changing Workforce

The changes in the U.S. workforce, which have been even more dramatic than the changes in organizations, are the result of more education, the changing nature of work, and social legislation. The new worker is comparatively well educated. The grandparents of today's workers averaged three years of formal schooling. The parents had about ten years of schooling. Today the average worker is educated to a level of about one year of college. About 80% have high school diplomas, and 60% have attended college. One of every four people entering the workforce has one college degree, and two degrees are becoming common.[6] With advanced education comes greater knowledge and ability and, inevitably, greater expectations. Workers with greater knowledge of how things can or should be done are more demanding. The fit between the workers' expectations and what they actually experience on the job will determine their motivation for work and their commitment to the organization . . . their work ethic.

Formal schooling is not the only source of education today. A few generations ago people were born, lived, and died on the family farm without ever venturing more than 50 miles from home. Today we can sit on the couch and by switching channels go from the Amazon jungle to the White House to Moscow to Hollywood in seconds. All the world was with Neil Armstrong when he stepped on the moon. All the world was in Berlin when the wall came down and in Baghdad, looking out the hotel window, when the first bombs of Desert Storm fell. Workers are learning about life, customs, and occupations all over the world. The media are making them aware of opportunities and raising their expectations and aspirations. People bring these new expectations and aspirations to work with them.

In 1950 almost three quarters of the work in manufacturing was rated as unskilled manual work. By 1989 unskilled work had dropped to less than 20%. The new work is knowledge work. Mechanization and automation have all but eliminated the heavy physical labor that two generations ago was the norm. Digging ditches with a hand shovel, machining a single metal part with a hand-controlled lathe and micrometer, and tightening bolts by hand were all standard operations 50 years ago. Much of this work has been rendered obsolete by new technology. The difference between the old methods and operating a diesel shovel, machining with a computer-controlled jig bore, and pneumatically tightening bolts is that the latter requires more brains than brawn. Most jobs in engineering, marketing, personnel, and research did not exist 50 years ago. These new jobs require theoretical knowledge and analytical skills. Prerequisite education and continuous training are required to obtain and hold these positions. This trend to more knowledge work and less physical labor adds to the rising expectations.

With their specialized education the new workers tend to be more loyal to their ideas than to their company. Peter Drucker relates an old story about three stonecutters. Each was asked what he was doing. The first replied, "I am making a living." The second said, "I am doing the best job of stonecutting in the country." The third looked up with a visionary gleam in his eye and replied, "I am building a cathedral."[7] The second stonecutter represents today's educated knowledge worker. These workers are challenged by opportunities to use their knowledge and skills. They have little interest in being a cog in a wheel and want jobs that use their talents. Under traditional leadership the new knowledge worker will focus on personal skills and knowledge and continue to respond as the second stonecutter. With more participative leadership these workers can become cathedral builders.

Social changes that began in the United States with the New Deal policies of the Roosevelt administration have also had a great impact on the situation of the average worker. The Wagner Act and subsequent labor legislation gave workers the right to organize unions and a power base from which to confront the practices of management. Social Security removed a critical economic fear. Government-sponsored work reduced unemployment, and unemployment insurance reduced the fear of unemployment. FHA, VA, and similar loan programs made it possible for more workers to own their own homes. Worker compensation and OSHA legislation made employers more accountable for workers' safety on the job. In addition to these social benefits (and to some extent because of them) the wage of the average American worker today is four times that of their grandparents in relative purchasing power.

Maslow's Model of Progressive Human Needs

The combined impact of all these changes—education, knowledge work, and social legislation—on the motivation of workers can be best described using a model developed by the psychologist Abraham H. Maslow in the early 1950s (see Figure 1-1).[8] From his research Maslow concluded that there are five progressive levels of human needs that motivate behavior. The first and most basic needs are for the physical necessities of food, shelter, clothing, and health. Denied these needs, people will do almost anything to obtain them—they will be, in Maslow's theory, highly motivated to satisfy their first-level needs.

When the first-level basic needs are satisfied, they no longer function as motivators, and the second level of needs becomes the new motivating force. Second-level needs, called security needs, consist of assurances that the first-level needs are secure. This is the need for economic security, which is satisfied by job security, personal savings, Social Security, and by unemployment, accident, health, and life insurance. Workers with families to support are motivated to satisfy these needs not only for themselves but for their families as well. As long as these needs are not satisfied, people are motivated by them. But when these needs are satisfied, they no longer motivate, and Level 3 needs take over.

Figure 1-1.   Model of progressive human needs.

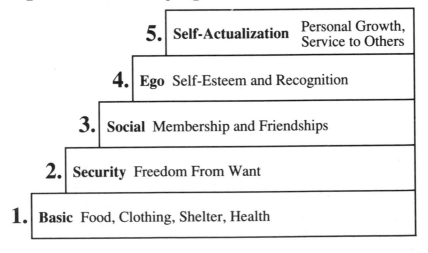

5. **Self-Actualization** Personal Growth, Service to Others

4. **Ego** Self-Esteem and Recognition

3. **Social** Membership and Friendships

2. **Security** Freedom From Want

1. **Basic** Food, Clothing, Shelter, Health

Level 3 needs are social and consist of the needs to belong, to hold membership, and to give and receive love and friendship. The basic social unit, of course, is the family, and people need the love and support that families provide. As people mature and enter the larger society outside of the family, they need to belong to other organizations. Churches and social groups satisfy some membership needs, but workers also bring these needs to work. When companies do not satisfy the workers' need to belong, unions sometimes fill the gap. The very terms *union, association,* and *brotherhood* connote Maslow's Level 3 needs. When these social needs are reasonably satisfied, people begin to reach up to the next level for satisfaction. This reaching up is motivation.

Level 4 consists of ego needs for self-esteem and for the recognition of one's capability. This need motivates people to learn skills in school and on the job and to demonstrate proficiency in using their skills. This need to be competent, and to be seen as competent, is a strong force in the modern worker. This is especially true of knowledge workers, who have considerable knowledge and skills to demonstrate, for which they crave recognition. Beginning at this level needs are not as easily satisfied as at lower levels. People are almost unlimited in their capacity to learn and develop new skills. It is doubtful that these needs will ever be fully satisfied, but, as before, the more they are satisfied, the less they motivate. The next and highest level becomes the motivator.

Maslow labeled Level 5 needs as *self-actualization,* the highest order of human needs. Self-actualization means personal growth for self-fulfillment. At this level the person is motivated by a genuine desire to serve others and not just to obtain recognition. It is Level 5 motivation that makes organizations like the Peace Corps both possible and successful. This level of motivation is also the basis for the best type of teamwork and cooperation.

This constant reaching to satisfy higher-level needs is the key to understanding Maslow's model of worker motivation. In the first half of the 20th century workers were motivated primarily by Maslow's Levels 1, 2, and 3. In the second half of the century Levels 4 and 5 began to assert themselves and are now gaining strength as the motivating forces of the new worker. Management practices based on the assumption that workers are motivated only by Levels 1, 2, and 3 are obsolete for most organizations. New management practices that appeal to higher-order human needs are required now to motivate the achieving worker.

Two other pieces of research confirm this change in worker motivation. Herzberg[9] in 1959 and Yankelovich and Immerwahr[10] in 1983 studied worker motivation and came to very similar conclusions. Both studies showed that there are some features of work, called *satisfiers,* that make work pleasant but do not motivate employees to work harder or more productively. Satisfiers (Herzberg called them hygiene factors) do not influence how well or how hard people work. When these features are present, workers are satisfied, and when they are missing, they are dissatisfied. Both studies also showed another class of features called motivators for which workers will work better and harder. The lists of satisfiers and motivators in Figure 1-2 are derived from the two studies mentioned and from other sources.

These lists add to our understanding of the needs of the new workforce. The satisfiers are primarily needs that occur at Maslow's Levels 1, 2, and 3; the motivators mainly occur at Maslow's Levels 4 and 5. Today, when people come to work, they expect to find the satisfiers in place. If they are, employees say they are satisfied; if not,

Figure 1-2.   Satisfiers and motivators.

Satisfiers	*Motivators*
Low stress	Work requires creativity
Convenient location	Interesting work
Clean work area	Control of work
Friendly managers	Responsibility
Friendly coworkers	Work requires thinking
Being informed	Challenge
Flexible pace	Uses current skills
Flexible work hours	Opportunity to learn
Good benefits	Recognition
Fair workload	Performance bonuses
Fair and adequate pay	Advancement
Good equipment	Teamwork
Job security	Clear goals and standards
Fair policy administration	Achievement

they are disappointed. Workers in both studies said they would not work harder because of these features; the workers simply expect all the satisfiers. Employees say they *are* motivated by the features on the motivator list. They will work harder when they are present and will work hard to get them.

Continuing the theme that workers' needs are changing, the point must be made that these lists pertain to the worker of 1990. It is not likely that the same lists would have occurred in 1930. Many of the items listed today as satisfiers were the motivators for an earlier generation of workers, who were operating at Maslow's Levels 1, 2, and 3. Many of the items on today's motivator list would have been pure fantasy for 1930s workers. Day care is an example that could be added to the 1991 list of motivators but will most likely move to the satisfier list by 1995.

The changes that have occurred and will continue to occur in the workforce are making obsolete many management practices that were effective in the past. The management system required to motivate a workforce striving for Maslow's Levels 4 and 5 is an entirely new process. To motivate today's workforce to excellence, managers must make greater use of motivators in organizing and designing work, in making policies, and in analyzing the success or failure of their personal managerial decisions.

Management Systems

Organizational management as it is practiced today is a relatively new function. It has come about entirely because of the emergence of so many new institutions and organizations in society. Management is the function that provides direction to organizations and causes them to perform.

Management systems, as they will be discussed here, refer to the whole complex array of interacting and interrelated activities and practices of management in an organization. Management systems are composed of values, strategies, structures, policies, goals, standards, controls, communications, feedback, decision-making processes, rewards, relationships, responsibilities, and authority.

Over the past century management systems have been forced to adapt to both the changing nature of work and the changing needs of the workforce. This is an important distinction. Management systems do not shape the workforce; the workforce shapes the management systems. Management does not create worker motivation; the worker does that. Managers can only respond or adapt their systems to the motivation the worker brings to the job. Today's problems of low productivity, noncompetitiveness, and worker dissatisfaction indicate that management systems are not adapting as rapidly as they must. One of the main purposes of GainManagement is to introduce a management process that is appropriate to the people and the work of the modern organization.

For a management system to be *efficient* there must be consistency and coherence among the many elements of the system. For the system to be *effective* it must be appropriate to the tasks, circumstances, and people who work in the system. Management systems have been studied extensively to determine how to make them efficient and effective. Of the many management systems experts the one with the clearest and most comprehensive theory is the late Rensis Likert, founder of the Institute for Social Research at the University of Michigan. By 1961 Likert had found evidence of four distinct systems of management, showing a progression in management practices from authoritarian to participative.[11] In 1976 Likert predicted the emergence of a fifth system within a decade.[12]

Five Management Systems

System 1: Authoritarian

This system is characterized by a top-down chain of command and highly centralized and controlled management practices. Decisions are made only at the top and carried out by workers directed by those with authority. Top management makes all decisions about goals, strategy, standards, and rewards. Management sets controls to ensure compliance and communicates only on a need-to-know basis.

System 1 has its origins in military organizations where, until very recently, it was the norm. It is an appropriate system in situations where highly centralized control is important, as in emergencies. It is also appropriate for unskilled workforces unable to participate in management processes. It is not a highly productive system because it uses only a small portion of the organization's human resources potential.

System 1 was the only system from the beginning of the Industrial Revolution until about the 1920s. In the early 1900s most American industrial workers were uneducated, unskilled immigrants whose prior work experience was on the family farm. Management training was unheard of, so the only leadership or management models available to emulate were parents, teachers, pastors, and the military. These models of top-down, authoritarian management were the basis for System 1.

System 1 does not expect employee ideas and problem solving and so does not encourage them—"theirs not to make reply, theirs not to reason why, theirs but to do and die." Among the workers it produces attitudes ranging from simple compliance to apathy and hostility when its use is inappropriate.

System 1, as a management system for business and other organizations, was tolerable in its time for two principal reasons. Lacking education and training, workers were not capable of much more than unskilled labor. Those who learned quickly on the job were promoted and became part of the authority structure. The second reason is that workers at the turn of the century only expected the satisfaction of Maslow's Level 1 needs from their employment. Under the circumstances they accepted the authoritarian practices of System 1.

As people's needs moved from Level 1 to Level 2, they became dissatisfied with the management practices of System 1 and began to oppose them. This opposition led to the emergence of System 2.

System 2: Paternalistic

Paternalistic, or System 2, management is only slightly different from System 1. It is also a top-down, highly controlled, authoritarian system of management. But in response to the resentment caused by System 1, System 2 is more sensitive to the human needs of people at work. Paternalistic management emerged clearly in the 1930s and became the standard through the 1950s. By 1930 the immigrant American workforce had changed significantly. Workers were no longer driven only by basic needs as were their Ellis Island predecessors. Security and social needs, Maslow Levels 2 and 3, were beginning to replace basic needs as the prime motivators. These needs for security and belonging were the major reasons for the rise of the industrial unions. The principal goal of union organizing efforts was security, as defined by Maslow. Unions sought for the worker those needs not being met by System 1 management, such as job security, better wages, shorter hours, and safer working conditions. Many organizations resisted this pressure in an authoritarian fashion but gradually moved toward paternalistic practices in order to motivate employees to remain productive. Interestingly, it has been said that it was Mrs. Ford who finally persuaded Henry to end his violent opposition to the United Auto Workers in 1938. Perhaps there is also a bit of maternalism in System 2. The human misery brought about by the Depression of the 1930s also caused the U.S. government to enact a number of paternalistic social reforms as part of the New Deal policies.

The evolution from System 1 to System 2 is similar to the change of heart that happens to Scrooge in Dickens's famous Christmas story. System 2 managers provide safer and more pleasant working conditions but still maintain a highly structured, authoritarian culture. System 2 may use simple employee-involvement techniques such as suggestion boxes, though not successfully. System 2 managers do not really expect any great number of useful employee ideas. Suggestion boxes are provided more as a benefit than a serious effort to tap employee creativity. System 2 managers are more interested in keeping people happy and controlled than creative. In fact, System 2 has been shown to be the least effective system in generating creativity among employees ("Things are nice here, so don't rock the boat."). System 2 is about as effective as System 1 but can be slightly more efficient because there isn't quite as much energy lost due to resentment or antiorganizational resistance. It does provide a better quality of work life, but the improvements tend to be limited to physical working conditions, fringe benefits, and security.

Beginning about 1950, as a result of the GI bill and a rising standard of living, young people stayed in school longer and entered the workforce better educated. These new workers brought with them a new set of needs and pressure for the next management system.

System 3: Consultative

In this system managers begin their first tentative steps to involve employees in the work of the organization. In System 3 managers consult with or ask employees for ideas and opinions but reserve final decision making to those in authority. The use of the quality circle program in the United States is an example of how System 3 works. Circles were formed, members and facilitators were trained, problems were carefully analyzed, and solutions were recommended. Managers listened to presentations and gave their approval and thanks but then failed to implement many of the proposals.[13] System 3 managers only commit themselves to listen, not necessarily to respond. This is the weakness of System 3. It uses participative techniques but without a full management commitment to participation. System 3, therefore, is only useful as a transitional step in the evolution to a more complete participative system.

Despite its limitations System 3 produces some favorable responses among employees, leading to improved performance and a more effective and efficient organization. Consultation is a first step toward participative management and in the short run produces favorable employee attitudes. An extended use of System 3 will lead to frustration as employees eventually realize they are not being treated as full partners. Their ideas are filtered through the management decision process, which is still fundamentally authoritarian.

System 3 reflects a beginning awareness in organizations that the needs of the workforce are changing and that management systems must be adapted to these changing needs. The problem with System 3 is that managers don't fully understand the workers' needs for real involvement and participation. These needs reflect a dramatic change and are entirely new phenomena in the workforce as workers strive to reach Maslow's Levels 4 and 5. Never in the history of the world has it been possible for great numbers to expect any more from their work than basic survival. Today, primarily due to their education and a general rise in affluence, American workers and workers in other developed economies do expect to find self-esteem and fulfillment through their employment. These rising expectations are the pressure compelling managers to go beyond System 3. The suddenness and the extent of this change is catching many managers by surprise, causing their response to be awkward and tardy. Many managers today are stuck at System 3, but the taste of participation in System 3 causes workers to want more, which is System 4.

System 4: Participative

System 4 is the major milestone in the evolution toward more open and participative management systems. Top-down, hierarchical, authoritarian management practices give way to genuine participative practices involving employees. System 4 managers expect a fairly high level of participation and actively solicit employee ideas. Managers communicate more fully and delegate more authority to work teams and individuals. The System 4 organization is characterized by teamwork and high performance. Employees are better trained and informed. They know the organization's mission, strategic objectives, products and services, and customers. They understand how their work, as part of a team's work, contributes to the whole. They also know the problems facing the organization and eagerly work to overcome obstacles and help the organization to achieve its excellence.

System 4 management, because it makes better use of its human resources, is more effective and more efficient and provides a much better quality of work life for its members. System 4 management values and encourages employees to strive for self-esteem and fulfillment, Maslow's Levels 4 and 5. System 4 management recognizes the new knowledge worker as the organization's most valuable resource. At System 4 authority of competence begins to replace authority of position and status. In System 4 employees are very much involved in problem solving, in finding innovative ways to make and sell the organization's products and services, and in administering internal functions. But participation is mainly concerned with operating issues. The ability and urge to influence strategy and policy and the desire for even greater teamwork are the forces pressuring the move to System 5.

System 5: Partnership

In a 1969 conversation with Rensis Likert we asked him if there was a System 5. Likert, a scientist who was not given to speculation, responded that so far he had not discovered it. By 1976 Likert's studies of evolving management systems began to suggest a system beyond System 4, a system with the promise of being even more successful in terms of effectiveness, efficiency, and quality of work life. He predicted that System 5 would emerge by 1990. He did not, however, provide a detailed description of System 5 because he did not have specific examples. He forecasted that the major feature of the new system would be even less reliance on hierarchical authority than in System 4.[14] It is now clear that there is a System 5; though it is just emerging, it promises to be more effective and efficient than System 4 and more in tune with the expanding needs of the evolving workforce.

The first four systems are characterized by the way in which managers use their power in the decision process: from authoritatively to participatively. System 5 is characterized by the relationships, values, and interaction among all the organization's members; in a word, partnership. A System 5 organization is a network of partnerships working harmoniously toward common goals in an atmosphere of mutual trust and mutual respect. There are partnerships between management and labor; owners and employees; sales, engineering, and production; home office and field; first, second, and third shifts; company and customers; company and suppliers; and the company and its community.

The words *partner* and *partnership* occur more frequently today in all writing about management, usually as adjectives or adverbs modifying a particular structure or action. At System 5 partnership becomes the organizing principle of an advanced management system. There must still be owners, bosses, and decision makers, but at System 5 decisions are made with the understanding that excellent performance is the result of intelligent teamwork among a complex network of players. The level of teamwork required in the System 5 organization cannot be forced on people, no matter how much training is done or what kind of financial incentives are employed. It can only come as a result of a freely given commitment by partners seeking a common objective, a mutual goal.

System 5 is also characterized by a very strong organizationwide commitment to excellence—so strong that everyone understands that it is a continuous process of doing, learning, and doing even better. In a System 5 organization people achieve excellence and immediately set goals for the next level of excellence.

In today's competitive global economy a System 3 company may be temporarily competitive and somewhat secure, a System 4 company will be a strong competitor, and a System 5 company will significantly outperform all of its competitors. The trend in management systems is toward Systems 4 and 5, and those companies and organizations that get there first will be the excellent companies, schools, hospitals, and agencies of the 21st century.

Summary

The ability of organizations to perform is a function of the management systems used to guide the organization. The appropriateness of the management system is determined by the needs and capabilities of the organization's members or workers. Workers' needs and capabilities have changed profoundly in the last 50 years. Greater education and affluence have so changed workers that authoritarian management systems are no longer effective and must be replaced by higher participative systems.

Systems 1 and 2 do not tap the rich problem-solving resources of today's more educated knowledge workers.

System 3 is a start, but it is only a transition system that must, of necessity, be short lived.

Systems 4 and 5 are the highly participative systems that will produce the results organizations need in an increasingly complex and competitive environment.

Notes

1. Final Report and Testimony submitted to Congress by the Commission on Industrial Relations. U.S. Congress, Senate Doc 415, May 22, 1914.
2. Marvin R. Weisbord, *Productive Workplaces* (San Francisco: Jossey-Bass, 1987).
3. Peter F. Drucker, *Management: Tasks, Responsibilities, Practices* (New York: Harper & Row, 1973).
4. Staff. "The Future 500," *Fortune* (April 22, 1991).
5. R. Levering, M. Moskowitz, and M. Katz, *The 100 Best Companies to Work for in America* (New York: Addison-Wesley, 1984).
6. Robert E. Kelley, *The Gold Collar Worker* (New York: Addison-Wesley, 1985).
7. Peter F. Drucker, *Management: Tasks, Responsibilities, Practices* (New York: Harper & Row, 1973), p. 431.
8. A. H. Maslow, *Motivation and Personality* (New York: Harper & Row, 1954).
9. Frederick Herzberg, Bernard Mausner, and Barbara Bloch Snyderman, *The Motivation to Work* (New York: John Wiley, 1959).
10. Daniel Yankelovich and John Immerwahr, "Putting the Work Ethic to Work" (The Public Agenda Foundation, 1983).
11. Rensis Likert, *New Patterns of Management* (New York: McGraw-Hill, 1961).
12. Rensis Likert and Jane Gibson Likert, *New Ways of Managing Conflict* (New York: McGraw-Hill, 1976).

13. Edward E. Lawler III and Susan A. Mohrman, "Quality Circles After the Fad," *Harvard Business Review* (January–February 1985), pp. 65–71.
14. Rensis Likert and Jane Gibson Likert, *New Ways of Managing Conflict* (New York: McGraw-Hill, 1976).

Chapter 2

Worker Participation in Management

The key to a successful GainManagement process is greater employee involvement and participation in the whole process of managing productivity gains. Employee participation in management is anything but a simple one-step process. If participation were so simple, suggestion boxes would be much more successful than they are. Participation is a complicated process of actions, reactions, and interactions that are easy enough to describe but take some hard work to achieve.

The chapter presents a model that describes a series of five steps from participation to experiences, to attitudes, to responses, and finally to performance gains (see Figure 2-1). A thorough understanding of employee participation in management is a prerequisite to understanding the full potential of the GainManagement process. The model will also help in understanding the successes and failures of past gainsharing and other employee involvement programs. More importantly, it demonstrates how higher levels of participation cause improved personal and organizational performance. The model shows that participation, through a series of intervening steps, causes gains. Since more participation is better, as management systems progress from System 1 to System 5, results improve from poor to average to excellent. This model is based on a similar framework described by Marshall Sashkin in 1984.[1]

Step 1 of the model is a matrix that describes five areas of organizational work where employee participation is possible: (1) problem solving, (2) innovation, (3) designing work processes, (4) strategies and goals, and (5) policies. The matrix also shows five levels

Figure 2-1. Participation in management.

Participation In Management

STEP 1: Participation Opportunities

Levels of Participation	Problem Solving	Innovation	Designing Work Processes	Strategies and Goals	Policies
1. Authoritarian					
2. Paternalistic					
3. Consultative					
4. Participative					
5. Partnership					

STEP 2: Experiences of Participating

Achievement   Involvement   Influence   Fairness   Trust

STEP 3: Attitudes and Feelings

Challenge   Security   Loyalty

STEP 4: Worker Response

Creativity and Productivity   Responsibility and Commitment

STEP 5: Performance Gains

Organizational Performance and Quality of Work Life

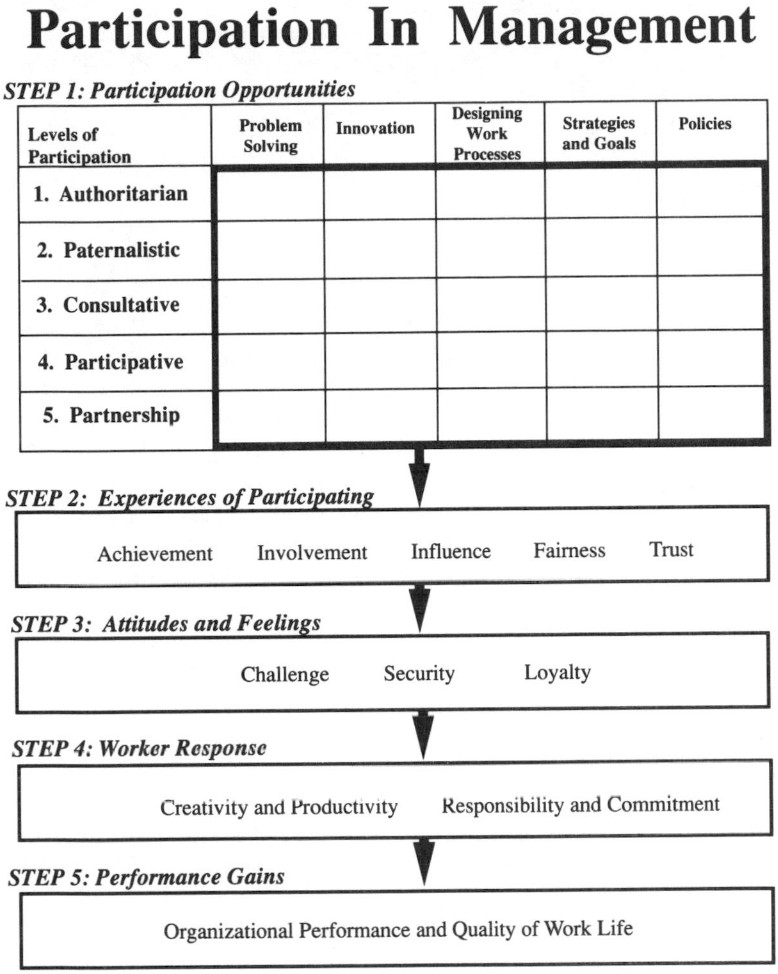

of participation corresponding to the five management systems described in Chapter 1.

In Step 2, as workers participate, they experience achievement, involvement, influence, fairness, and trust. The more they participate, the more of these experiences they will have. It is important to understand that these are real experiences that happen to workers when they participate. This is much more than giving workers a "sense" of participation.

Step 3 shows that the experiences in step 2 lead to attitudes and feelings of challenge, security, and loyalty. When workers experience achievement and influence, they feel challenged. When they experience fairness and trust, they feel secure. And so on. The more favorable experiences workers have at Step 2, the stronger and more favorable will be their feelings and attitudes at Step 3.

The fourth step describes the workers' response to the feelings generated at Step 3. When workers feel challenged and secure, they become more creative and productive. Workers who feel secure and loyal are more responsible and committed to their organization.

The fifth and final step describes the results produced by the workers. The results are gains in personal, team, and organizational performance. More creative, productive, responsible, and committed workers produce more results . . . more gains. The details of each step follow.

Step 1: Participation Opportunities

Participation Opportunities are shown as a matrix of the five areas of work where participation is possible and the five levels of participation.

The Five Areas of Work

Horizontally, the matrix lists five areas of the organization's work where participation is possible: solving problems, innovating, designing work processes, deciding strategies and goals, and making policy.

1. *Problem solving.* Every aspect of work and every operation has standards of performance, usually expressed in terms of time, cost, output, and quality. Whenever the performance of an operation drops below standard or a goal is not met, there is a problem to solve. When this occurs, experts can be brought in to devise a solution, and tell the workers what or how to change.

A more participative approach is to provide the responsible work team with information about the goal or standard and the deficiency. Teams analyze and solve their own problems. Experts are requested by the team when needed to assist them in the process. One advantage to more participation in problem solving is that the insights and

A Midwest glass-manufacturing company needed a machine to cut glass faster and with less scrap. The engineering department was asked to design a new machine. True to the participative nature of the company's gainsharing program, the engineers met with production workers to solicit their ideas—to involve them in the change. Ideas were collected, and the engineers disappeared to their drawing boards. In a few months the new machine was delivered and installed. The operators were stunned. None of their ideas had been incorporated in the machine design. They felt betrayed and angry.

Once the machine was installed, everyone—engineers, managers, and employees—struggled to get it to produce. It would run properly for a while and then suddenly go out of adjustment or break down. Mechanics were constantly working with the machine. The engineers began to accuse the production workers of deliberately tampering with the machine to prevent it from functioning properly. Production workers blamed the faulty design. After a frustrating and unsuccessful year it was decided to scrap the machine and look for a better one.

A better machine was located at a West Coast tool company. Normal company procedure called for the project engineer alone to take a pallet of glass to the manufacturer, try the machine, and make recommendations based on the trial. But as a result of their recent unsuccessful experience, everyone realized that more involvement and participation were required. A team composed of an engineer, a foreman, and a production worker was sent to conduct the trial.

After the trial the team of three specialists returned with a recommendation to purchase the machine. More important, the operator gave a very positive report to the glass-cutting work team. The new machine was installed and within two months ran 140% faster and better than the manufacturer claimed it would. Several jigs and fixtures to facilitate loading and unloading were suggested by the work team and added by the engineers. The new machine rarely broke down or went out of adjustment.

experience of those closest to the problem are used. A second advantage of at least equal importance is that the team will be more industrious in implementing its own solution.

2. *Innovation.* Innovation means the process of finding better ways, better methods, and new ideas. Even when operations are performing to standard and running well, they can be improved. In an employee-orientation film used at Ford Motor Company Henry Ford II encouraged the new hires to innovate. "There is nothing we are doing today that cannot be done better," he said.

Innovation can be viewed as limited to products or to the research department, or it can be made a requirement of every job and every team's charter. Traditional management assigns innovation to specialists and experts. More participative systems expect innovation from everyone. One of McGregor's assumptions for Theory Y is that the capacity for imagination, ingenuity, and creativity is widely distributed in the workforce.[2]

One advantage to greater participation in innovation is that if two heads are better than one, many heads are even better. Another advantage is that when the workers innovate, it is an achievement and a source of pride. When an outsider makes the innovation, it's the outsider's achievement, and the workers tend to resist the change.

3. *Designing work processes.* There is a great variety of work in most organizations—planning, design, manufacturing, assembly, shipping, sales, distribution, administration, and so on. Each of the many tasks must be completed and coordinated with other work to produce high-quality results. How these tasks are laid out and grouped influences motivation and determines the organization's efficiency.

A West Coast specialty food processing company creates 750 to 1,000 unique products each year. For each new product a team of marketer, engineer, production manager, and production worker decides how the product is to be made and what resources are required. Jointly, the team prepares a critical path process sheet. In the first three years using this participative approach to work design numerous process improvements were made that contributed to an increase in profit margins of 300% in each of the first three years.

Work processes and jobs can be designed by experts who tell the workers what to do and how to do it, which is the procedure under authoritarian management systems. On the other hand, work processes can be designed participatively by those who will do the work. When employees participate in designing their own work processes, they have more ownership of the process. Once a work process is in operation, employees will also be more inclined to debug and improve their own designs. Giving the workers more control of their work is a powerful motivator.

4. *Strategies and goals.* Every organization has several strategies and many goals or objectives. There are strategies for marketing, products, financing, and organization development, among others. There are goals and objectives for individuals, teams, departments, functions, products, services, and for the organization as a whole. Traditionally, strategies and goals were always decided by top management and a handful of specialists. In more participative systems workers are involved first in setting goals for their own jobs and the work of their teams. With more information, education, and experience, however, workers can also contribute ideas and enthusiasm to the setting of goals for departments, functions, and the organization as a whole. Even in highly participative systems basic strategies and

---

At a Midwest plywood manufacturer the finishing department work team had historically produced 2,300 panels per day. The first-line manager and the production manager decided an improvement to 2,600 panels per day was needed. This was a 13% improvement. Rather than order the change, the department manager asked the team what level they thought they could achieve. After enough discussion to understand the process and the company's need the team agreed to go for 2,700 panels, a 17.4% improvement. The team spent one hour solving the problem of how they would achieve 2,700, panels, and the day after their suggestions were implemented, the team produced 3,300 panels—a 43.5% improvement. Within two months the standard had reached 3,400 panels per day with no significant decrease in quality. One day during this period the team produced 4,400 panels—a 91.3% improvement.

major goals are top-management decisions. Setting direction for the organization is their primary function. At System 5, however, top management will communicate strategic information openly and solicit and use feedback and suggestions from the rest of the organization.

5. *Policies.* Policies express the organization's values and the way the organization will conduct itself and relate to others in the pursuit of its mission. There are external policies for marketing, customer service, supplier/vendor relations, and public relations. There are internal policies for business development, quality, finance, and stockholder relations. There are also internal policies for employee relations, labor relations, and personnel that pertain to the community of employees at work. The policies of an organization are usually determined by the organization's founding members and changed infrequently unless there is a major change in the direction of the business.

The area of policy making is seldom considered an opportunity for employee participation; it is therefore one of the last to be included. Policies in many organizations are not written down; consequently they are not clearly understood as policies. Most so-called policy manuals don't contain policies at all; they outline procedures for dealing with repetitive or routine decisions. Decisions involving policies, generally important issues, are referred to those who "know" the policies—top management.

Decisions involving policy seem to occur only infrequently, so there does not appear to be much opportunity for employee participation. As management systems become more participative, opportunities appear that were previously overlooked. The first step toward more worker participation in policy making is to educate workers about the policies that already exist. With this better understanding workers are able to make more informed judgments and take actions consistent with the policies. This ability to work more purposefully is an aspect of employee participation. When policies are better known and understood, there is less need for detailed procedure manuals and the red tape that restricts workers' freedom to perform.

Understanding also opens opportunities for employees to suggest policy improvements and refinements. The customer-service work team can participate in improving service and refining customer-service policies. The entire work community can participate in making and improving work community policies. There are many opportunities for employees to participate in policy, from understanding policy to following policy to helping make policy and policy improvements.

The Five Levels of Participation

Vertically, the matrix in Figure 2-1 shows five levels of participation. The five levels of participation correspond to the five systems of management presented in Chapter 1. From Systems 1 to System 5, participation progressively includes more of the work and involves more workers.

System 1: Authoritarian. Active participation is limited to managers and professionals who make all or most of the decisions about problem solving, innovation, work processes, strategies, goals, and policies. For the bulk of the workforce, participation at this level consists of simple compliance.

System 2: Paternalistic. Active participation is still limited to managers and professionals making all decisions, as in System 1. However, System 2 management is more sympathetic to employee needs and is influenced by requests to improve working conditions. There may be a suggestion box where workers can recommend ideas to those in authority. Suggestion box ideas tend to be limited to problem solving and, occasionally, innovation. Work processes, goals and strategies, and policies are seldom the subject of suggestions, as they are considered the exclusive province of management. Where there are unions, workers participate through collective bargaining in some aspects of work-community policy, namely wages, hours, and working conditions. For most of the workforce participation at this level is still limited to simple compliance.

System 3: Consultative. The most active participation continues to be concentrated among managers and professionals. Other employees begin to participate as they are consulted in the areas of problem solving, innovation, and designing work processes. There may be some consultation in goals, but this tends to be limited to personal-performance and some group goals. It is unlikely that management will submit strategy or policy to consultation, but it may be willing to listen to objections when they are raised. Where there is a union, collective bargaining continues to influence some work-community policies. If there is a suggestion box program, it tends to be more active under System 3, and suggestions may be directed to all five areas of the organization's work. Participation by nonmanagement workers at this level consists of compliance, suggestions, and recommendations.

System 4: Participative. Most workers are active participants at this stage. The organization is structured into participative work teams. Management comes to the workers not for consultation but for solutions. Within the work teams there is considerable participation in problem solving, innovation, and designing work processes. Strategies, goals, and policies are considered to be management work; although management is open to influence, participation in these areas is limited. Sometimes special task forces are assigned to work on strategic goals and policy, but active participation by the work teams is not expected and happens infrequently. Participation by nonmanagement workers at System 4 consists of genuine compliance, suggestions, solutions, and action.[3]

System 5: Partnership. Here there is active participation by all workers in all five areas of the organization's work. Participation comes from commitment;[4] everyone is a partner involved in helping the organization to succeed. There are still specific roles for managers, professionals, technicians, clerks, and operators. People work at their assigned roles but in a collaborative way that is highly sensitive to the way their work combines with the work of others and contributes to the whole. People participate in every aspect of the business by being informed and offering suggestions and support in any area where they can contribute. This is *not* management by committee, where every decision must be reviewed by everyone; it is a high-performing system where everyone does his or her job well, cooperates with others, and is open to any and all influence that will improve performance.

Step 2: Experiences of Participating

Participating adds new dimensions to the workers' experience of their jobs (see Figure 2-2). Participating workers experience achievement, involvement, influence, fairness, and trust. The higher the level of participation, the more frequent and rich these experiences will be. Current management literature often advises giving workers a sense of participation. A "sense" is not enough: Participation must be real; there must be the experience of participating.

Figure 2-2.   Experiences of participating.

STEP 1: Participation Opportunities

Levels of Participation	Problem Solving	Innovation	Designing Work Processes	Strategies and Goals	Policies
1. Authoritarian					
2. Paternalistic					
3. Consultative					
4. Participative					
5. Partnership					

STEP 2: Experiences of Participating

Achievement	Involvement	Influence	Fairness	Trust

▲ *Achievement:* Achievement at work is the experience of having completed something as opposed to just being busy or putting in time. It occurs when the worker has a stake in the outcome of work and a real experience of having contributed to that outcome. The worker can look at a result and say, "I did that" or "we did that." The experience of achievement comes from participating in goal setting, problem solving, or innovating. The more participation, the more intense will be the experience of achievement.

▲ *Involvement:* Involvement is the experience of being included, of being a player rather than being on the sidelines while others do all the important work. Workers experience involvement when they participate in designing their work processes and when they participate with their teams in problem solving and innovating.

▲ *Influence:* Employees have a need to influence, to have their ideas heard and used. This need is especially strong among knowledge workers, who constitute the bulk of the modern workforce. Workers experience influence most when they participate in designing work processes, setting goals, and making policy.

▲ *Fairness:* Workers experience fairness in several ways through participation. By being better informed, which is an important aspect of participation, they can see the fairness of decisions made by others. Lacking information, they sometimes see decisions as arbitrary or based on power. By participating in the design of work processes and setting goals and by being better informed about strategy and policy, workers experience the fairness of job assignments, goals, and policies. Inconsistency, favoritism, and unfairness are common employee complaints when participation levels are low. The very process of participating provides the opportunity to resolve issues of unfairness as they occur.

▲ *Trust:* The experience of trust is the experience of being trusted, which occurs when workers are included in solving problems, designing work processes, and setting goals. Higher levels of participation automatically include more delegation of responsibility and greater freedom to act. When workers are given more responsibility and freedom to act, they have the experience of being trusted.

Step 3: Attitudes and Feelings

Experiences produce attitudes and feelings (see Figure 2-3). Good experiences lead to good feelings and positive attitudes. Bad experiences, or the lack of good experiences, cause bad feelings and negative attitudes. As workers experience achievement, involvement, influence, fairness, and trust, they feel challenged, secure, and loyal. influence, fairness, and trust, they feel challenged, secure, and loyal. There is no way to create good feelings and positive attitudes except through good experiences, and participation creates the experiences.

▲ *Challenge:* The feeling of challenge is the desire to do better, to excel. The best examples of this feeling can be observed in the

Figure 2-3.   Attitudes and feelings.

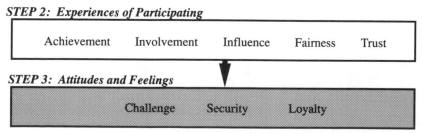

Olympic Games, where it has produced unbelievable performance. This feeling will also occur in workers who experience achievement and involvement in their work. Having achieved once, workers feel challenged to do even better next time. The greater the experience of achievement, the stronger will be the feeling of challenge.

▲ *Security:* The feeling of security is based on confidence in the organization and knowing that one is respected as an important member of the organization. For the worker it means freedom from the fear of losing job and income or of being dealt with unfairly. When workers experience involvement and fairness, they feel secure from unfair treatment. When workers experience achievement and influence, they feel more confident in the future success of their organization.

▲ *Loyalty:* The feeling of loyalty means being responsible to and for others. When workers experience involvement and trust, they feel loyal to those with whom they are involved and to those who place their trust in them. When workers participate actively in work teams, this feeling of loyalty is especially strong. Loyalty that begins with the members of one's work team gradually expands to the larger organization.

Step 4: Worker Response

Feelings and attitudes lead to actions on the job (see Figure 2-4). Positive attitudes cause workers to work creatively, productively, responsibly, and with commitment.

▲ *Creativity and Productivity:* Workers who feel challenged and secure will be more creative and productive. The feelings of challenge

Figure 2-4. Worker response.

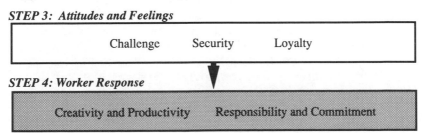

and loyalty prompt workers to be more creative and productive and, because they also feel secure, to take more risks, try new things, and be open to change and new ideas. The feeling of security also gives them the assurance that they will benefit from their creativity and productivity.

▲ *Responsibility and Commitment:* The feeling of loyalty causes employees to act responsibly toward their team members and to the organization as a whole. Similarly, employees with these positive feelings are committed to the organization and its success. When workers are strongly committed to the success of their work team and the organization, they participate more enthusiastically. The effect of this whole process is magnified as each worker realizes that he or she is on a work team where the team members are responsible for and committed to each other's personal well-being. This social bond that occurs in highly participative teams is a powerful source of motivation.

In a Midwest automotive parts manufacturing company, Dale worked in the grinding department stacking parts on carts as they came off a conveyor leading from the big surface grinder. He would then push the loaded carts to the molding departments, where the parts were fed into the injection molding machine. In the monthly team problem-solving meeting Dale observed that his job would not be necessary if the two machines were closer together. The molding machine operator could take the parts from the conveyor and load them directly into the molding machine.

This was a fairly obvious improvement and undoubtedly would have been discovered by the engineers in due time. In this case it was the operator who suggested the elimination of his own job. This happened because the worker felt challenged to improve productivity and because the company's personnel policy protected workers' employment when they were displaced by technical changes. Dale assisted in moving the equipment to implement his suggestion and through the job-posting procedure was retrained and placed in a new job.

Step 5: Performance Gains

The gains produced by creative, productive, responsible, and committed workers may take many forms: higher profits, better quality, increased market share, new products, improved customer service, lower costs, better utilization of capital resources, higher levels of satisfaction with the company and the job, more job security, bonuses, better work methods, fewer acidents, better working relationships, and lower turnover and absenteeism. Performance gains (see Figure 2-5) refer to the effectiveness and efficiency with which the organization achieves its goals. Effectiveness means the organization does the right things for employees, customers, shareholders, and the community. Efficiency means doing things right: honestly, economically, responsibly, and with regard for high quality. Improved results or gains come from greater participation of the organization's human resources in accomplishing the work of the organization.

As the model demonstrates, the process begins at the top with participation. The secret to success is simple to describe: More participation leads to continuous performance gains. Participation is not an easy path, but it is the best path to managing gains—to excellence.

Summary

Worker participation in management is not a simple suggestion box or one-step process. It is a five-step process beginning with greater participation and leading to greater performance results.

Figure 2-5.   Performance gains.

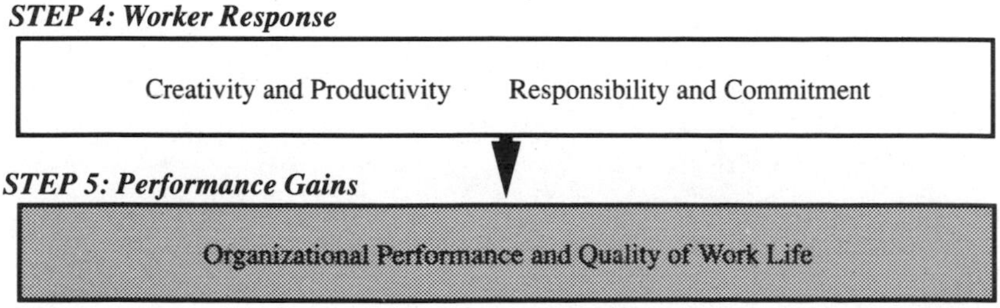

STEP 4: Worker Response

| Creativity and Productivity   Responsibility and Commitment |

STEP 5: Performance Gains

| Organizational Performance and Quality of Work Life |

We are learning that all management systems are participative—more or less. We are also learning that for today's worker, in the United States and in other developed countries, more participation is better and that there are many opportunities to increase worker participation in problem solving, innovating, and designing work, strategies, goals, and policy.

Notes

1. M. Sashkin, "Participation Is an Ethical Imperative," *Organization Dynamics* (Spring 1984), pp. 5–22.
2. Douglas McGregor, *The Human Side of Enterprise* (New York: McGraw-Hill, 1960).
3. Peter M. Senge, *The Fifth Discipline: Mastering the Five Practices of the Learning Organization* (New York: Doubleday, 1990).
4. Ibid.

Chapter 3

History of Gainsharing

Gainsharing is an important development in the evolution of management systems. For the past hundred years this evolution in the management of people has proceeded along three separate tracks. First there were incentive plans, used extensively to encourage greater effort and to control labor costs. The number and variety of incentive plans used in American businesses have been countless. The most common are individual production incentives, sales commissions, and management bonuses. It would be hard to find a business that hasn't tried several of these incentive plans.

On a second track there is participative management, which has not been used quite as widely or in as varied forms as incentive plans. Nevertheless, there have been many different approaches to participative management, from suggestion boxes to quality circles to the standard course on delegation in every basic management program.

The third track is gainsharing, which combines incentives and participation. As management systems moved toward more participative processes, a natural outcome was for employees to share in the productivity gains brought about by their ideas, suggestions, and better effort.

Early Gainsharing Experience, 1935–1975

Profit Sharing

The earliest gainsharing programs were profit-sharing plans, whose origins go back to 19th-century France and Germany. In one French example a painting contractor paid house painters a share of the profits instead of an hourly wage. This was popular with the workers, and the business was very successful. In Germany one large farmer deeded plots of land to long-term farmworkers for their retirement sustenance, providing the first example of a deferred profit-sharing plan. The records don't mention participative management, but as both businesses were reported to have been successful, we can surmise that the employees were satisfied with these plans.

By the 1920s there were a handful of very successful profit-sharing programs in the United States, most notably at Procter and Gamble, Eastman Kodak, and Sears Roebuck. These early models were based only on financial incentives. They were designed to encourage better work by providing a financial reward that was contingent upon the performance of the company. The express purpose of these programs was to encourage employees to help increase company profits in which they would share. Managers encouraged good effort and quality work by constantly reminding employees of their potential profit shares.

A point to keep in mind about the success of these early programs is that they provided a type of financial security to employees that was unavailable from any other source. They provided a retirement fund for employees where none existed. It was not common in the first third of this century for companies to provide retirement funds or pensions for workers, and there were no federal old-age benefits. Workers either had to save for their own retirement, which was difficult to do at the prevailing wage levels, or depend on their children for assistance.

So when Procter and Gamble introduced a profit-sharing program in 1912, the response was very positive. The company had met a critical employee security need (Maslow's Level 2), and people responded. This was a System 2 paternalistic benefit appropriate to the times and to the needs of employees—and it worked. There is no evidence from these early programs of any formal employee participation. Nor was it necessary; because employees needed this type of economic security, they were motivated by the profit sharing alone.

In 1939 Congress passed a law permitting companies and employees to defer federal income taxes on profit shares contributed to a retirement trust. Within a few years thousands of companies had started profit-sharing plans to take advantage of this tax deferment. At about this same time Social Security payments started providing basic old-age income security. These new company profit-sharing plans lacked motivational punch for two principal reasons. First, the employees' need for this deferred benefit was significantly reduced by Social Security. Second, management did not provide the benefit as a part of a management strategy but only to take advantage of the tax avoidance opportunity presented in the new law. To employees, the benefit of profit sharing did not come from management but from the government. And, because management did not explain profits to employees or involve them in profit making, profit sharing became just another entitlement with no motivational impact whatsoever.

In the 1970s, however, as experience and success with other gainsharing programs became better known, a few companies began to experiment with modifications to their profit-sharing plans. Some made quarterly or year-end cash payouts to encourage and reinforce employee profit-making efforts; it is difficult to maintain a high level of interest in improving productivity today when the payout won't occur for 20 years. A few companies also introduced popular employee-participation programs such as suggestion systems and quality circles to encourage employee ideas. This trend to reconstitute profit sharing as a more motivational program has been actively promoted by the Profit Sharing Research Foundation in Evanston, Illinois, with some success.

Scanlon Plan

The gainsharing plan developed by Joseph N. Scanlon and made famous by Douglas McGregor is the best known gainsharing plan of all. It was started by Scanlon at Empire Steel and Tin Plate Company in Mansfield, Ohio, in 1938, when the mill emerged from bankruptcy. Joe Scanlon, then president of the local steelworkers union, withheld demands for higher wages because the company's worn-out facilities were not sufficiently productive. Keeping the business open and people employed took precedence over wage hikes.

Scanlon was a scrappy leader with a background in both cost accounting and steelmaking. He knew firsthand that employees could contribute considerably to the mill's productivity. He persuaded the workers to rebuild some of the equipment without pay. Then, he persuaded management to restart the mill and share productivity gains with workers as gains were made. He also convinced management to listen to and act upon employee ideas for productivity improvement. Then, with some help from United Steel Workers vice-president Clinton Golden, he developed employee productivity-improvement committees to solicit and process employee suggestions for improving operations.

And so the first Scanlon plan was created with participative management practices, structured employee participation, and a method for sharing productivity gains between the company and the employees. The success of this program prompted Philip Murray, president of the United Steel Workers, to appoint Scanlon as the union's research director. From this base Scanlon encouraged other companies with USW contracts to try his plan. By the 1940s word of his plan reached Douglas McGregor, who invited Scanlon to join his pioneering industrial relations department at the Massachusetts Institute of Technology.[1]

M.I.T. gave Scanlon access to the leading participative management thinkers of the time and a national base of operations. Scanlon plans were installed with some frequency in and around New England as the postwar economy grew. Russell Davenport further publicized the Scanlon plan in two *Fortune* magazine articles, "The Greatest Opportunity on Earth," October 1949, and the classic Scanlon plan case study, "Enterprise for Everyman," January 1950.[2] Then in 1960 Douglas McGregor immortalized Scanlon's work in the history-making classic, *The Human Side of Enterprise.*[3]

In Chapter 8 of his participative management bible McGregor states: "The Scanlon Plan is not a formula, a program, or a set of procedures. It is a way of industrial life—a philosophy of management—which rests on theoretical assumptions *entirely consistent with Theory Y*" (italics added). McGregor's book was and continues to be very popular, but interest in Scanlon plans declined during the 1960s. Many experts who claimed intimate knowledge of McGregor's Theory X and Y seemed unaware of his endorsement of the Scanlon plan. Other programs and techniques such as T groups, management by objectives, sociotechnical systems, and job enrichment became the new interests.

It was about this time that interest in participative management began to increase. Building on the early work of Elton Mayo, Rensis Likert, McGregor, and others, participative management was pursued as its own goal. There was such a strong interest in the social needs of people at work that participative management deliberately distanced itself from material concerns such as incentives.

Although interest in Scanlon plans declined as the experts pursued pure participative management, it did not die out. In fact, a vigorous new interest began to grow in western Michigan. In 1949 Dr. Carl Frost emigrated from M.I.T. to Michigan State University with the news about the Scanlon plan. Two companies, Herman Miller and Donnelly Mirrors, embraced the idea and eventually developed two of the most successful and enduring of the Scanlon plans. Considering the short life span of many new management ideas it is significant that these two plans and several others are still going strong after 40 years. These two companies in Zeeland and Holland, Michigan, respectively, are virtually a mecca for gainsharing pilgrims. The leadership and commitment necessary to support this new way of industrial life at Herman Miller is well documented in Max De Pree's 1989 book, *Leadership Is an Art*.[4] John F. Donnelly left a tremendous legacy of enlightened industrial leadership.[5] The Donnelly Scanlon plan today is not just as good as it was when it was installed in 1952—it is many times better. Using experience as the good teacher it is, several major content and process innovations were added to the Scanlon plan under John Donnelly's leadership. Donnelly was also the major force behind the creation of the Scanlon Plan Associates, a group of Scanlon plan companies that meets regularly to share experiences and improve the application of their plans. They also provide information and guidance to companies newly interested in pursuing the gainsharing idea.

The Scanlon plan, as McGregor points out, is more than a formula—it is a way of industrial life. Others saw the Scanlon plan in similar far-reaching terms. A 1952 Life Magazine editorial[6] praised the Scanlon plan as one of the most hopeful developments in labor-management relations. John Chamberlain's *Life* magazine feature about the Scanlon plan at Adamson Steel Company in East Palestine, Ohio, concluded with the thought that East Palestine was in the direction of New Jerusalem.[7] At a time when the world was embracing communism and socialism, many saw participative approaches such as the Scanlon plan as a major tool of democratic capitalism. Russell Davenport started his two-part series on Scanlon plans in *Fortune* magazine with the title: "The Greatest Opportunity on Earth." Clearly there were great expectations for the Scanlon plan in its early years. Just as clearly the Scanlon plan has not lived up to those early expectations. While there have been a few significant successes, the number of genuinely successful programs is still rather small.

The key difference in the very successful programs has been the extent to which they formalize the practices of participative management. Many Scanlon plans include participative management but have not progressed beyond a System 3 consultative application of participation. In other cases employee-participation structures and processes have been installed but not fully used. As happened with quality circles in the United States, employee ideas were asked for but not implemented. When participation is talked about but not delivered, employees lose interest in so-called participation and become cynical about the intentions of management. An Alabama employee, complaining about management's failure to fully implement the company's participative management program, summed it up this way: "They talk the talk, but don't walk the walk."

In the successful programs management has moved beyond System 3 and made a major commitment to involve all employees in the management process. In these cases managers have made the break from authoritarian thinking. They realize that good ideas can and will occur throughout today's more skilled workforce. They believe completely in the Theory Y principle that creativity is not limited to managers or specialists with college degrees. They follow the rule that what is right, not who is right, is what matters. Managers of successful Scanlon plans have taken to heart their responsibility to build and develop an effective organization of committed and involved people. They do not limit their role as managers to building a better mousetrap, opening a new market, or acquiring another company.

The second feature of the Scanlon plan is a formal structure and process for employee involvement. Scanlon plans typically include a two-level committee structure to solicit and process employee suggestions. Every department has a productivity committee made up of the department manager and two or more department employees elected by their peers. There is also a plant or company screening committee made up of key managers, union leaders, and representatives from each of the department productivity committees.

The function of the Scanlon plan committee structure is twofold: (1) processing employee suggestions and (2) communications. The committees' first function is to solicit and process employee suggestions. When employees have ideas for improving quality, productivity, or quality of work life, they write them up and give them to their productivity committee representative, who brings it to the next meeting. Department committees meet monthly and review all suggestions received during the month. These committees discuss and approve or disapprove each suggestion. Ideas that cost more than the first-line manager can approve or that require approval and/

or coordination with other departments are forwarded to the proper authority or to the screening committee. All disapproved suggestions are also forwarded to the screening committee for their information and review.

The screening committee meets monthly with an agenda consisting of several items. First, they act on all suggestions forwarded for approval by the department committees. They also review all disapproved suggestions as an automatic appeal process. Sometimes the senior committee will see potential in a suggestion that is not visible lower in the organization. They may approve a suggestion that was denied in the first step. The reasons for disapproving a suggestion must be explained to the employee who submitted the idea, and this second review makes that process all the easier.

The second function of the screening committee is communications. The committee screens the monthly productivity results and sends information back to the organization through the representatives about the productivity results and other matters of interest to the business. The screening committee also announces the gainsharing information for the month. They will include information about why a bonus was earned or not earned, and what factors or suggestions caused one month's bonus to be higher or lower than the previous month's. The purpose of this information is very straightforward: Continue to do those things that caused productivity to go up, and eliminate or discontinue those things that caused productivity and bonuses to go down.

The screening committee is pivotal in a cycle of communications: Suggestions come up the chain and are evaluated, and information is passed down for another round of suggestions. Success in Scanlon plans and in other forms of participation is closely related to the effectiveness of this cyclical communications flow and to the speed with which employee ideas are resolved. Fast resolution of employee suggestions stimulates more suggestions, creates more favorable employee attitudes about the program, and ties management practices and the participation process together.

The third element of a Scanlon plan is the way in which productivity gains are measured and shared. The Scanlon plan pays gainshares on improvements in labor productivity only, measuring labor cost as a percentage of the sales value of production. So a typical Scanlon plan has as its productivity base labor cost in the range of 25% to 35% of the sales value of production. In those months when labor costs are less than the Scanlon base there are gains. The employees receive 75% of the gain, and the other 25% goes to the company.

In months when labor costs exceed the base there is a loss. To offset losses a part of gains earned in positive months is set aside in a reserve fund. Any losses that occur are deducted from this fund. Reserve funds are closed at the end of each year by paying out any surplus or writing off any deficits. A new reserve fund is started each year.

This basic approach was unchanged for the first 20 years of Scanlon history. In 1954 John Donnelly introduced a modification to the base productivity measurement to include the cost of tools and materials in addition to labor. The basic concept was the same except that he used a broader, more inclusive productivity measurement that covered 75% of the sales value of production. With this broader measurement the sharing of the gain was also adjusted because the company could not afford to pay out the same share of the gains made on this broader base. A new sharing ratio was calculated to provide the employees with the same amount of dollars they received under the former labor-only plan. This new sharing ratio paid 40% of the gains to the employees and 60% to the company.

Most Scanlon plans pay gainshares monthly, although a few pay quarterly. In most cases employee gainshares are paid as a percentage of each employee's actual pay earned during the gainshare month or quarter. A few companies pay the gainshare in equal amounts to employees regardless of pay level.

The Scanlon plan still has a strong and loyal group of followers, but few plans today conform to its original design. Most have been modified to meet changing business conditions by using different participation structures and broader productivity measures. It is very common today for a company to describe its gainsharing program as a modified Scanlon plan.

Rucker Plan

Allan W. Rucker, an economist, developed his gainsharing plan about the same time as did Joe Scanlon. The Rucker design was based on the economist's concept of value added by manufacturing. At its simplest, value added means that if the Acme Widget Company purchased $1 million of steel and other materials and manufactured $2 million of widgets, Acme had added $1 million in value to the original steel and other materials. As widgets, the original materials are more valuable, just as a chair is more valuable than the wood it contains.

Rucker's research determined that labor costs in many manufacturing companies tend to remain a constant percent of value added despite variations in costs and selling prices. With the Rucker value-added model, a company determines the percent of labor costs to value added. This calculated percent becomes the productivity base for the Rucker share of production plans.

As employees reduce costs or increase output by better methods or greater effort, actual labor costs are less than the Rucker standard. This difference between actual labor cost and the standard is the gain in a Rucker plan. This gain is the bonus pool that is distributed to all participating employees. Employee shares are usually paid monthly as a percent of the employee's pay for the period.

Here, too, there is also a reserve for deficits, called a balancing account, where 30% of the gains are held in reserve to balance those months when losses occur. As with the Scanlon plan, the balancing account is closed out at the end of the year and started anew the following year.

Rucker plans are used in labor-intensive manufacturing companies, where a Rucker standard of labor costs to value added can be determined. In most Rucker plans it is necessary to restudy and recalculate the Rucker standard every five years.

Early Rucker plans consisted of an incentive formula alone. There was no special emphasis given to participative management practices, nor was there a formal process for employee involvement. Employees were encouraged to find ways to improve productivity but without a formal process. Later programs added formal employee involvement, borrowing from Scanlon experience and the general trend to participative management. A typical Rucker involvement process consists of a single plantwide suggestion committee made up of management and nonmanagement department representatives. Employee suggestions are encouraged through newsletters, bulletin boards, and department meetings. Suggestions are given to representatives, who take them to the Rucker committee for processing.

The Rucker plan was a registered product of the Eddy-Rucker-Nickels Company, which ceased operations in the mid-1980s. Although Rucker plans as such are no longer being installed, many continue, and other gainsharing plans continue to use the ratio of labor costs to value added.

Improshare

Improshare (*Im*proved *Pro*ductivity *Shar*ing) is a gainsharing program developed by Mitchell Fein in the mid-1970s. Fein is a well-known consulting industrial engineer, and the plan he invented draws heavily on industrial engineering principles. The unique feature of Improshare is the calculation of the base productivity factor, which is based on the standard hours, direct and indirect, needed to produce a unit of product. As improvements are made, the actual time to produce a unit of product declines. The savings are calculated as hours saved. These saved hours are the gain which is shared 50–50 between the employees and the company. Each employee is awarded a share of the hours proportional to the actual hours he or she worked. The bonus hours are paid at the employee's regular rate of pay.

Improshare plans include several unique features for ongoing program maintenance. Bonuses are paid weekly based on a running four- or six-week average, a technique that makes it unnecessary to maintain a deficit reserve. Each weekly bonus represents only one-quarter or one-sixth of the accumulated savings, leaving three-quarters or five-sixths in reserve. Except in prolonged periods of loss or a major one-time loss, this method provides an adequate reserve to cover negative periods.

Improshare has two other unique features. When significant productivity improvements have been made and sustained, there is a provision for the company to buy back a permanent change in the Improshare standard. Employees are paid a substantial bonus, up to the equivalent of a year's worth of the savings, and production standards are raised accordingly. When major capital investments are made which eliminate production time, standards are adjusted, but only by 80% of the time saved by the new machine or process. This leaves 20% of the savings in the productivity base, which, when divided 50–50, gives 10% of the savings to the employees. This is done as an extra incentive to encourage acceptance of the new process and new equipment.

Elements of Early Gainsharing Plans

Until about 1980 all of these plans were referred to by their specific names: Scanlon, Rucker, Improshare, or Profit Sharing. As new interest expanded the popularity of these programs, the term "gainsharing" emerged. Gainsharing generally refers to an approach that draws on the experience of all the earlier plans to create a customized plan for a specific company or plant. As we explained in our 1983 book *Gainsharing and Productivity*, there are three principal elements in a gainsharing plan:

1. Management practices
2. Employee participation
3. Shared reward[8]

These elements vary from plan to plan, but all are necessary for a true gainsharing plan.

Management Practices

Management practices refers to leadership and the various actions of managers supporting the gainsharing plan. Scanlon plans have made the strongest statement about the need for active management support and program leadership. Joe Scanlon typically interviewed top managers to determine if they had the values and competence to lead and support his program. If he concluded that management was not qualified, he would decline to work with them. Scanlon did not have management-development or training programs at his disposal, and there is no record of any formal program to teach management practices in the early Scanlon plans.

Later, management and supervisory training became more available and managers were taught the practices necessary to support a successful program. At Donnelly Mirrors, for instance, a major management development program was undertaken in 1968 using Blake and Mouton's Managerial Grid Program.[9] Other companies used this excellent program, and other management-development programs popular during that period.

The first and most critical element for success is the way managers, and especially the first-line managers, explain, promote, and operate the gainsharing program. Employee participation can be no better than the leadership supporting it.

Employee Participation

Employee participation is the second element of a gainsharing program. It consists of a formal process for encouraging, soliciting, and processing employee ideas and suggestions. The gainsharing concept begins with the conviction that employees have more to contribute to the achievement of the company's goals than their sweat. Gainsharing includes McGregor's Theory Y belief that all employees possess the ability to think creatively and to solve problems. The original Scanlon design and subsequent gainsharing experience have shown that some type of a formal process is needed to fully use this employee capability. As a result gainsharing programs usually include formal processes for employee involvement such as suggestion boxes, suggestion committees, or employee problem-solving groups.

In addition to these formal structures there is typically a variety of supporting communications efforts. Bulletin boards, newsletters, and promotional literature have been used to encourage participation by reminding employees of the need for ideas and suggestions. Special efforts to recognize employees for their ideas are also common and beneficial. Most gainsharing companies find that communications must be frequent in order to maintain employee interest.

Shared Reward

With good leadership and more participative management practices employees do participate and do find ways to improve productivity. This improved productivity results in financial gains which are shared with the employees. This third element, the shared reward, completes the gainsharing program. The two principal issues about the shared reward are the base productivity measurement and the ratio for sharing gains between the employees and the company.

The base productivity measure is the most important factor in the shared reward. Scanlon, Rucker, and Improshare programs all use labor cost only in calculating the productivity base. Scanlon plans use labor cost as a percentage of the sales value of production. Rucker plans calculate labor costs as a percent of value added by manufacture. Improshare plans use the sum of the direct and indirect labor hours to produce a unit of production.

Rucker and Improshare plans have seldom been modified beyond their original design but quite a few companies have tinkered with the original Scanlon formula. The principal change to the original Scanlon design has been to add costs other than labor to the productivity base as was done at Donnelly Corporation in 1954.

The second major reward issue is the ratio of sharing between the employees and the company. The early Scanlon plans paid 75% of the labor savings to employees as their bonus. This practice is still common in many Scanlon plans. The company receives as its share 25% of all labor savings and 100% of any other productivity improvements that happen as labor productivity improves.

In Rucker plans employees also get a large share of the labor savings. The bonus is the difference between actual labor cost and the Rucker standard labor cost. This is, in effect, a 100% payout of labor cost savings. The company's share is the savings in materials, supplies, and from greater output. Improshare plans divide the saved standard hours 50–50 between the company and the employees. The hours included in the Improshare base are only factory-direct and factory-indirect labor hours. Hours saved in supervision or staff labor are not included in the savings to be shared. Nor are savings in material, tools, utilities, or other costs shared.

Multicost plans, which include labor, materials, and other cost factors in the base, pay smaller shares of the calculated savings to employees and larger shares to the company.

The principle that has been followed in determining shares is that of fairness, namely, What is a fair distribution of the increased productivity between the company and the employees? We know that to sustain a gainsharing program this sharing of savings must both benefit the employees and strengthen the company. Beyond this principle of fairness there are no rules or formulas to help determine what an appropriate sharing ratio should be. Despite the lack of formal guidelines the sharing methods described above for Scanlon, Rucker, Improshare, and other gainsharing programs have been satisfactory to employees and to the companies. This experience provides a pragmatic, if not theoretically grounded, basis for sharing.

If a rule could be derived from past experience, it would be that most companies try to share the dollar savings equitably, that is, in equal dollar amounts to the company and the employees. In *Gainsharing and Productivity* we presented a mathematical formula developed by Bob Keeler of Honeywell that would allow a company to calculate a precise sharing ratio once it determines a basic definition of equity. In most companies sharing ratios are determined unilaterally by management, and in a few they are negotiated with the union.

In addition to the two major issues described above there are several other shared reward issues. Most gainsharing plans pay bonuses monthly, but quarterly payouts are fairly common. Improshare plans pay the bonus weekly. Semiannual and annual payouts have not been as successful in maintaining a high level of employee interest. The primary advantage to a more frequent payout is not financial, it is in the feedback of information. The size of the bonus tells employees whether and to what extent they were successful in increasing productivity. The more frequently people receive this feedback, the more they are able to problem solve and find new ways to improve.

Almost all gainsharing plans distribute employee shares as a percentage of the employee's actual pay in the month or quarter in which the gain is made. This provides larger rewards for more senior and more highly skilled, higher-paid employees. The logic supporting this has always been that higher-paid employees, with their superior skills and responsible positions, are able to make greater contributions to improving productivity. There are two other distribution methods. One is to give each employee an equal dollar share of the bonus pool. The second is to divide the pool by the number of hours worked and give each employee a share based on the number of hours worked in the month or quarter.

To have weekly, monthly, or quarterly payouts there needs to be some method to recover losses as productivity fluctuates from period to period. This is most commonly handled by withholding a portion of gains in positive months and accruing a reserve fund. This fund is used to make up losses when costs exceed the base. Other methods for handling fluctuations are averaging, as in Improshare plans, and accruing deficits that must be recovered before further bonuses are paid.

Gainsharing, 1975–1990

When concern with productivity and competitiveness heated up in the late 1970s, interest in gainsharing picked up considerable momentum. Major corporations had ignored gainsharing, thinking it appropriate only to small manufacturers, but began to reconsider. Traditional management methods weren't working, and a search was on for new ideas to improve motivation and reduce labor costs. The popular and professional press reported the success of a number of new programs, including quality circles and gainsharing.

In 1975 there were no titles in business literature using the term *gainsharing* and only two books in existence about the Scanlon plan. But interest picked up quickly after that. Following is a sample, in chronological order, of articles, books, and activities about gainsharing from 1975 to 1990.

1978   Brian E. Moore and Timothy L. Ross, *The Scanlon Way to Improved Productivity*, was published by John Wiley.

1979   The American Productivity Center began a series of gainsharing workshops. These seminars, which focused on solving productivity problems, were conducted throughout the U.S. and were attended by hundreds of line and staff managers.

1981   The U.S. General Accounting Office published the first-ever gainsharing research report, "Productivity Sharing Programs," AFMD-81-22, March 3, 1981. The study covered 54 firms that had or were planning to install productivity-sharing programs. In the concluding chapter the report states: "Because of the serious problems caused by the decline in national productivity and a high rate of inflation, we believe that firms should examine productivity sharing and other incentive plans more closely to determine whether they can contribute to their own productivity improvement."

1981   "Unproven but promising sums up the situation with regard to gainsharing plans and their role in improving organizational effectiveness," wrote Edward Lawler in *Pay and Organization Development* (Addison-Wesley), page 154.

1982   Jack Drexler, in a concluding essay to a volume of the *Journal of Contemporary Business*, predicted that gainsharing programs would soon become popular, based on a poll of his professional colleagues.

1982   The bestseller *In Search of Excellence*, by Tom Peters and Robert Waterman, published by Warner Books, included one reference to Scanlon plans at Dana Corporation, page 252.

1983   *Gainsharing and Productivity: A Guide to Planning, Implementation and Development*, by Robert J. Doyle, was published by AMACOM; first book with *gainsharing* in its title.

1983   Amitai Etzioni, sociologist and founder/director of the Center for Policy Research, listed in *An Immodest Agenda*, published by McGraw-Hill, the steps that must be taken to rebuild America before the 21st century. In discussing the need for rebuilding human capital, he states: "Three ideas illustrate the kind of thinking and experimentation that is needed, Scanlon plans, ESOP, and quality of work life" (page 329).

1984   The bestseller *The 100 Best Companies to Work for in America*, by Robert Levering, Milton Moskowitz, and Michael Katz, was published by NAL Penguin. Three companies, Dana, Donnelly, and Herman Miller, were on the list of the 100 best, to a great extent because of their Scanlon plans.

1986   *High-Involvement Management*, by Edward Lawler, was published by Jossey-Bass. His chapter on gainsharing included the following comments: "The term gainsharing is relatively new, the idea . . . is an old and well established one. . . . There is enough experience with gainsharing plans to clearly establish that they can improve organizational effectiveness through increasing employee involvement. . . . In conclusion, the best way to view such traditional gainsharing plans as the Scanlon plan is as a possible first step toward high-involvement management."

1987   Rosabeth Moss Kanter in *Personnel* magazine (January) reported that while estimates of the number of gainsharing programs were hard to come by, "interest is clearly going up as employers attempt to substitute variable bonuses and pay geared to profits for fixed wage bills."

1987   *Thriving on Chaos*, by Tom Peters and published by Alfred Knopf offered several prescriptions for proactive management performance including: "Partnership—the wholesale participation of and gain sharing with all people connected with the organization" (page 36).

1988   *Fortune* magazine, December 19, reported on new incentive plans suddenly sweeping through U.S. industry. Gainsharing was included among a list of new incentive plans that reward workers for increased productivity and let compensation costs rise and fall with the company's fortunes.

1988   Hay Management Consultants reported on what they termed alternative compensation programs in their annual wage survey. Gainsharing was listed as one of nine popular programs. They reported that 14% of surveyed companies had gainsharing programs and that 16% of the companies were considering them. At 16% gainsharing tied for first place with lump-sum payments as to intended future use.

1988   *Labor Relations Today* (December), a newsletter published by the U.S. Department of Labor, stated: "Gainsharing is one of the fastest growing alternative pay plans in industry today."

1989   *USA Today* (November 7) listed profit sharing and gainsharing among several new variable-pay programs that were growing more popular. The article reported that 32% of companies offered profit-sharing plans and 15% had gainsharing plans. According to the article the principal purpose of these plans was to control labor cost by having it flex with variations in productivity or profit.

1990   The American Compensation Association introduced a new gainsharing seminar as part of the association's series of alternative rewards seminars.

New interest emerged during this period as several Fortune 500 companies began to look seriously at gainsharing. Some quickly embraced the concept and began to implement it. Others conducted studies (from brief to very extensive) and set up pilot programs to experiment with the idea.

Some company-specific hybrids emerged during this time as companies devised their own special programs. Two that have attracted a great deal of interest are those of Du Pont and Motorola.

The Du Pont achievement sharing program has attracted a good deal of attention because of the company's size and stature in industrial circles. *The Wall Street Journal* referred to it as the most extensive and innovative program ever tried at a major U.S. corporation.[10] A Du Pont company brochure describes the program as follows: "Achievement sharing is a very simple concept: the better the department does in achieving its earning objective, the more its employees will benefit. Achievement sharing is a variable pay system; and once it is in place all participating employees will share in the rewards . . . as well as some of the risk."

The program was quite innovative in the area of vriable compensation, or, as it is sometimes called, pay at risk. Under the plan 20,000 employees of the fiber department would forgo 2% of three future pay raises to a maximum of 6%. This pay at risk would then be returned as a bonus based on how well the department met its annual profit goals. When the planned profit goal was met, the full 6% would be paid as a bonus. When the profit goal was not met, the employees would lose some or all of the 6%. When actual profits were 80% of target or less, there would be no bonuses. On the upside, employees could receive bonuses as high as 18% of the reduced pay, or 12% above normal pay levels, if profits were above goal.

Originally the plan was mandatory for the fiber department's 13,000 management and nonunion employees. Five of seven unions representing 7,000 union employees voted to participate. In the first year employees were allowed to take a 2% pay cut to accelerate their eligibility for the achievement sharing. In 1989, its first year, the department exceeded its profit goal by 2.31%, and participating employees received bonuses of 9% of their at-risk pay. An employee earning $30,000, with 2% ($600) at risk, received a bonus of $654 ($600 + 9%).

Unfortunately, the plan ran into the recession of 1990. When it became clear that the 1990 profit goals would not be met, employees in focus groups raised the issue that the program did not allow employees any choice about pay at risk. When the company looked into the idea of individual options, they were advised by legal counsel that the program would have to be treated as an investment and subject to government regulations requiring public disclosure. This was not a satisfactory alternative. The program was canceled effective December 31, 1990, and all wages and salaries were restored to their original levels.

Despite what now appears to have been a case of unfortunate timing, this was a bold experiment. Considering the serious problems with productivity and competitiveness, companies must continue to search for solutions that work. Some failures must be expected if learning is to occur.

In a letter announcing the cancellation of the plan, Executive Vice-President James F. Kearns had this to say:

> The achievement sharing program was a leading-edge effort to link pay with business success. Linking pay to business success exemplifies the culture we are trying to

adopt . . . a culture of innovation, prudent risk taking and leading-edge approaches to making us more competitive.

We have learned a great deal and are proud of the effort, which apparently was ahead of its time. All those who were involved in developing and executing the program are to be commended.

Du Pont should be proud of this innovative effort, and with this support from top management they will undoubtedly absorb their learning and eventually find a workable solution.

Motorola has also adapted gainsharing to the needs and special circumstances of the large corporation. Motorola calls their program PMP, participative management program, and describes it as "an innovative strategy for managing an organization. It is innovative in philosophy—participative. It is innovative in structure—formal committees to involve all employees in the decision-making process. It is innovative in compensation—a productivity sharing bonus."

The Motorola plan divides the employees into three groups for gainsharing: operating employees, staff support employees, and executives. These groups each have performance measurements appropriate to their work. For instance, operating employees earn monthly bonuses for such things as reducing current costs, improving quality, improving on-time deliveries, reducing inventory stocks, and safety. Each of the performance factors has a calculated base. Performance relative to the base adds to or subtracts from a total bonus pool that is divided among the participating employees as a percent of pay. In the Motorola plan the other two groups, staff support employees and executives, receive bonuses based on profit. Unlike the Du Pont plan, which included all 20,000 fiber department employees in a single program, the Motorola plan is decentralized to individual business centers. Motorola places heavy emphasis on employee participation. The participation structure is a hybrid of Scanlon committees and quality circles; each department has a representative working committee that processes employee suggestions and regularly solves operating problems. The company also places heavy emphasis on leadership and participative management practices. Local plans cannot be implemented until first-level and middle managers have been adequately trained.

These two examples represent a growing trend in major corporations to use the gainsharing concept to improve performance and productivity. Other larger companies such as the big-three automobile makers are using profit sharing for the same reason. Profit sharing was introduced in Detroit in the 1984 United Auto Workers national agreement. Studies show that the program has been quite successful at Ford but much less so at Chrysler and General Motors. Although some of the improvement at Ford has been due to product changes, increased sales, and new manufacturing methods, some of the credit goes to a highly participative quality improvement program.

This new interest in profit sharing has also attracted the interest of economists and politicians. Martin Weitzman, an economist at M.I.T., has proposed a national profit-sharing policy.[11] Weitzman's proposal is to lower wages to about 80% of their present level and institute a substantial profit-sharing program that would pay high bonuses in good times and lower costs in bad times. This, he feels, would help control inflation and unemployment. Companies would not have to lay off employees in bad times because their labor costs would automatically be reduced when they did not pay profit shares. This would hold down unemployment, he says. At the same time companies could reduce prices based on these lower labor costs, and this would hold down inflation. This is similar to the situation in Japan: low base pay and big semiannual bonuses when the company is profitable. Weitzman also points out that this plan, in principle, was proposed to General Motors by the United Auto Workers in 1982. The union said it would lower its wage demand if General Motors would lower prices.

This idea was picked up by politicians in both the U.S. and England. Senator Dale Bumpers of Arkansas, chairman of the Small Business Administration Committee, introduced legislation in 1987 proposing a tax incentive to encourage profit-sharing plans. Under this proposal employee profit-sharing dollars would be taxed at a lower rate than regular earnings. Such a bill was proposed and adopted by Margaret Thatcher's Conservative government in England in 1987, but so far the idea has not caught on in the United States.

A New Incentive Plan

As gainsharing programs became more popular through the 1980s, they began to change in character. There has been a distinct move to view gainsharing as the incentive plan of choice to replace failed piece-rate, day work, and other individual and group incentive plans.

The Hay Group of business consultants refers to gainsharing as an "alternative compensation plan." A Hay survey reported an increasing interest in and use of profit sharing, group incentives, and gainsharing among other alternative compensation programs. Newspaper and magazine articles consistently refer to gainsharing plans as incentives and incentive compensation. Very few of the current writers use the terms "a way of industrial life" or "a philosophy of management," which Douglas McGregor used in describing the early Scanlon plans. There are no articles being written with titles like "Every Man a Capitalist" or "The Greatest Opportunity on Earth."

Managerial thinking seems to be so addicted to the idea of incentives that it blocks out messages that say we must change our way of industrial life, our philosophy of management. Traditional incentive thinking is what McGregor described as Theory X. He said traditional management is based on the assumption that people dislike work and must be coerced and controlled to get them to work. He said, "Within the framework of Theory X, the ability to provide or withhold economic rewards is the prime means by which management exercises authority in industry."[12] It is Theory X thinking that has led to the increasing use of gainsharing as a financial incentive.

There is no logic in making people's pay contingent on their performance and then denying them the opportunity to change their performance. The use of gainsharing as an incentive plan has no greater prospects for success than the countless incentive plans that have been tried and discarded over the past 80 years. Incentive plans have a history of working for a few years and then going stale. If gainsharing has any promise, the basis for the promise must be something more substantial than the incentives that characterize System 2 management.

Summary

More than 50 years of experience with gainsharing forms the foundation for GainManagement. This experience is a rich source of information for helping to understand the basic principles involved. In some cases gainsharing programs were frozen, and in time they ceased to be effective. In others, notably at Donnelly Mirrors, gainsharing was a living system that evolved with the changing times and as lessons were learned.

Beginning in the 1980s, as its popularity grew, gainsharing

evolution took a turn for the worse. It changed from a "philosophy of management" to no more than a group incentive. As an incentive, gainsharing lacks its most powerful component: worker participation in making gains.

Notes

1. John Chamberlain, "Every Man a Capitalist," *Life* (December 23, 1946), p. 93.
2. Russell Davenport, "The Greatest Opportunity on Earth," *Fortune* (October 1949); "Enterprise for Everyman," *Fortune* (January 1950).
3. Douglas McGregor, *The Human Side of Enterprise* (New York: McGraw-Hill, 1960).
4. Max De Pree, *Leadership Is an Art* (New York: Doubleday, 1989).
5. John F. Donnelly, "Participative Management at Work" (interview), *Harvard Business Review* (January–February 1977), pp. 117–127.
6. Editorial, *Life* (December 22, 1952), p. 14.
7. John Chamberlain, "Every Man a Capitalist," *Life* (December 23, 1946), p. 93.
8. Robert J. Doyle, *Gainsharing and Productivity* (New York: AMACOM, 1983).
9. Robert Blake and Jane Mouton, *The Managerial Grid* (Austin, Tex.: Gulf Publishing, 1964).
10. Laurie Hays, "All Eyes on Du Pont's Incentive Pay Plan," *The Wall Street Journal* (November 5, 1988).
11. Martin L. Weitzman, *The Share Economy, Conquering Stagflation* (Boston: Harvard University Press, 1984).
12. Douglas McGregor, *The Human Side of Enterprise* (New York: McGraw-Hill, 1960).

Chapter 4

From Gainsharing to GainManagement

Throughout its short history gainsharing has demonstrated some spectacular successes such as Adamson Steel, LaPointe, Parker Pen, Atwood Industries, Donnelly, Herman Miller, and Lincoln Electric.[1] Of all the many gainsharing programs started, only a handful have been highly successful. Many programs had short-term successes but have since been abandoned. Others continue operating with only moderate results. All of the experiences—the good, the bad, and the spectacular—are useful for understanding the overall gainsharing process.

Many reasons are offered to explain why gainsharing programs succeed and fail. Success is often attributed to such elements as:

- A serious threat to the business and to the jobs of the workers
- Strong leadership
- Exceptionally high bonuses

A serious threat, such as in the early Scanlon plans, causes everyone to focus on critical survival factors and to risk new ideas. Strong leadership, such as at Donnelly and Herman Miller, taps some of the unlimited potential of active employee participation. Exceptionally high bonuses, such as at Lincoln Electric, are strong incentives. The reasons for the failures are not so clear, but they tend to be the opposite of the success factors:

- The business threat disappears, so people lose focus and lose sight of the critical elements and return to the safe ideas.

▲ Leadership fails to fully use the human organization as a resource.

▲ A lack of bonuses or low bonuses result in a failure to meet workers' expectations.

Despite the absence of a great number of success stories the gainsharing idea continues to intrigue everyone searching for organizational excellence. There is a deep-seated feeling that if people must work as employees in organizations all of their lives, they want more from those organizations. The day before yesterday people wanted more basic (Maslow's Level 1) satisfactions. Yesterday they wanted more security (Maslow's Level 2). Today and tomorrow they want personal satisfaction and fulfillment (Maslow's Levels 3, 4, and 5).

In this chapter we will review the strengths and weaknesses of gainsharing as they can be determined from its successes and failures, demonstrating that gainsharing was an excellent program for its time but it offers only a partial solution to current human and organizational needs. It is now time to move on to a more active, more participative, and more equitable process—GainManagement.

The analysis to be presented here will examine each of the principal elements of gainsharing from the perspective we offered in our 1983 book, *Gainsharing and Productivity*. There we showed how gainsharing has three main elements: management practices, employee participation, and shared reward. Taken separately, there are successes and failures, strengths and weaknesses, for each of the elements from past gainsharing experiences.

Management Practices

Managers provide the leadership, the organization structure, and the systems needed to support the gainsharing effort. The role and work of managers in gainsharing programs come first. While good management practices will not guarantee the success of the gainsharing program, the lack of good management practices will guarantee its failure. Gainsharing programs can only be as good as the management practices that lead and support them.

Strengths

When managers decide to install a gainsharing program, they send a leadership message that improvements are necessary and that all employees are invited to join in the effort to change the organization. Some managers do an excellent job of using the gainsharing program as a way to encourage the organization to strive for excellence. Just by starting a gainsharing program management sends a message that productivity improvements are needed. The more this message is clearly articulated, the better.

Establishing structures and processes for employee participation encourages employee involvement and participation. More active processes encourage greater employee participation, but even the suggestion box can be a start in the right direction. The better these programs are administered, the more the workers will participate. The key to effective administration is to process employee suggestions to a speedy resolution, implementing the good ideas and explaining why the others cannot be used.

Gainsharing programs are very effective in improving labor/management cooperation. In fact, in some of the early literature about programs in union settings, gainsharing was often hailed as a labor/management cooperation program. In a 1981 study by the U.S. General Accounting Office 80.6% of the programs in the study reported improved labor/management relations and 47.2% of the companies reported fewer grievances.[2]

Gainsharing programs are also successful in improving organizational communications. One of the first things that happens in a gainsharing program is the establishment of a productivity base for the shared reward. The base and how it works to produce bonuses is communicated to all employees. This provides information employees have never before had about the business. For many employees this is a new experience and a very good one. Even when the message is not perfectly understood, just instilling a beginning awareness of productivity and its importance to the business is healthy. With the monthly or quarterly gainshare checks and the accompanying explanatory statement, this productivity message is repeated over and over, leading the workers to a better understanding of the business and the factors in its success.

Another strength of communicating the gainsharing productivity base and bonus information is the message that there is a goal common to all employees. It shows that everyone shares in the results of the business; whether success or failure. From this the understanding grows that to win at the gainsharing game requires a common effort. These are valuable lessons that are routinely reinforced in a well-managed gainsharing program.

A big stumbling block for many managers, especially in small, closely held companies, is the need to release heretofore confidential profit information. With some prodding managers accept that employees must have more information for problem solving and to know where productivity needs to be improved. Faced with this decision, many managers conclude that it is better to give the information, and they find creative ways to provide it without disclosing critical confidential company data to competitors or customers.

Gainsharing programs help managers to do a better job of providing measurements of productivity, quality, and profit. Measurements and feedback are a chronic problem in most organizations and the gainsharing measurements are a good step in the right direction. Good news about gains or bad news about losses is valuable because everyone knows how the business is doing—what is working, what needs fixing. Regular feedback taps into the employees' need to achieve, which is a strong motivator.

Most gainsharing programs include some manager and employee development activities. Training programs about how to lead meetings, group problem solving, and how to develop effective teams are common. Developing people, teams, and organizational effectiveness are important management practices that accompany gainsharing programs.

All gainsharing programs include a specific structure for soliciting and processing employee ideas. As suggestions come from employees, the traditional authoritarian top-down communications flow begins to turn into a two-way or circular process. These are small but critical steps in a trend. Little by little there is positive movement to more openness. When management listens to their ideas, employees are encouraged, and some of their attitudes of mistrust and cynicism begin to thaw. As good ideas are used, the process improves with each cycle.

Weaknesses

Although the gainsharing experience has produced some encouraging changes in management practices, the process is by no means complete. Too often the target of gainsharing plans has been limited to labor-cost containment. Plans designed only to control labor costs function on the edge of the real business. Bonus formulas that focus on a limited range of cost-reduction ideas fail to encourage employees to consider broader business issues such as new products or services, new technology, and conservation of capital resources. When the focus of gainsharing is limited, the results of the program are limited as well.

Even in successful gainsharing programs it is quite common to find that only a handful of managers are skillfully practicing participative management. Many others just go along, and a few openly resist the move to greater employee involvement. In the growing number of companies using gainsharing only as a financial incentive there is practically no change in management practices.

Organizations need strong, competent leadership to give the employees a compelling vision and the challenge to excel. Too often managers just administer, failing to provide dynamic leadership. As companies and other institutions grow in size, senior managers, in particular, lose touch with the people in their organizations. Preoccupied with growth and tied to their computers, many managers have become number crunchers. By concentrating on the quantitative aspects of management, they overlook the qualitative and human side of their organizations.

Very few managers have made the complete transition to Systems 4 and 5; many are stuck at System 3. They consult with their employees but seem unwilling or unable to take the next step to real participation. Some managers, resisting any change in their management practices, oppose the trend to more employee participation. Their opposition can be open but more often is less obvious. Resistance occurs in many ways. Meetings are missed for many plausible reasons such as a conflicting meeting, the need to ship a critical order, a machine breakdown. Suggestions are written up incompletely, leading to misunderstanding and disapproval, or suggestions are somehow lost in the paper-processing maze. Employees are given insufficient information to solve a problem properly. And, finally, there is the long list of discouraging words to thwart the most eager problem solvers: We tried that before. They will never let us do that. We can't afford that. It won't work. Is anyone else doing it? It needs more study. Let's get up a committee.

There are two factors that cause managers to hold on to authoritarian power and to resist employee participation. First, authoritarian management practices are firmly grounded in our culture and our experience. For generations people have lived in societies where only a few had the education and experience to lead and make decisions. For centuries the educated nobility and clergy were the authorities, and people had no choice but to listen to them. In addition to their authority by virtue of their knowledge they had civil and ecclesiastical power to punish anyone who challenged their authority. We are well beyond this type of absolute authoritarianism, but it is in our history and our culture and continues to influence all of us. New leaders and managers learn their trade from those who manage and lead them. In this way traditional beliefs and practices are passed on. New values and new practices enter the system as experience, and education demonstrates better methods and systems, but this is a slow process.

The second factor causing the persistence of authoritarian management is that in many of life's experiences authoritarian leadership is not only valid but essential. Parents of infants and preadolescents and teachers in the elementary grades are necessary authorities for their immature charges. Doctors and others with specialized knowledge are necessary authorities. In crisis situations competent authorities, such as police and firefighters, are needed to preserve life and property and to restore order. Authoritarian management is good and proper in its place. We are surrounded by appropriate authoritarian models, a situation that, unfortunately, tends to reinforce System 1 and 2 practices where they are not appropriate.

Only a hundred years ago authoritarian management was not only proper in business management, it was the only known system. It is no surprise that it persists, but as we explained in Chapter 1, the workforce is changing and new practices of management are vital. New, more participatory systems are emerging, but authoritarian management practices are still abundant.

System 1 (pure authoritarian) and System 2 (paternalistic authoritarian) seem to be on the decline. They are regularly criticized as inappropriate for today's workforce by the popular media and most current management books. All the talk these days is about employee participation and participative management. Surveys report that 80% to 90% of today's managers consider participative management a promising new approach. Only a handful see it as a fad that will not last. Despite this growing awareness few of today's managers use participative management practices effectively. As we said before, many managers are stuck at System 3. For the manager to go beyond System 3 is a risk. It places the manager's authority at risk and it runs the risk of employees making mistakes. So far the majority of managers have been unable, or unwilling, to take these risks even though the reward can be huge: a responsible, committed, high-performing workforce. However, the reward is not certain, and so the risk remains a stumbling block.

In addition to being unwilling to risk participative management many managers seem to lack a full appreciation for the extent of the changes required to meet the needs of today's workforce. Surveys show that at least 60% of today's workers want to be more involved in meaningful work improvements. When participation programs are installed and workers start making suggestions, they expect to be heard. Often managers are not sensitive to the strength of this employee energy and fail to respond quickly and seriously.

Another weakness in management practices is the reluctance to share information about profit, performance, and future plans. Of course there are some cases where information must be protected from competitors or even customers. Knowledge about new processes, new product plans, and some cost data could be used to hurt the company. Smaller companies supplying major customers need to keep their profit information confidential. Larger companies have a nasty habit of demanding price reductions of smaller suppliers when they feel the supplier can afford it. On the other hand, keeping secrets becomes a problem when too much information is classified as confidential and is withheld from employees. Problem solving and productivity improvement in organizations requires full and accurate information to be on target. When employees are not aware of a problem, there is little likelihood they will offer a solution to it. When they know only part of a problem, they can only suggest part of a solution.

An excuse sometimes used for not giving information to employees is that they don't fully understand things like profit. This is quite true, but it is management's job to educate employees to the point where they do understand important business information and concepts.

Finally, most gainsharing programs fail to include an active development plan. To achieve excellence every aspect of the business must be growing and developing: people, products, leadership, systems, processes, and so on. Too often gainsharing programs are installed with meetings and memos and are then expected to run by themselves. But the programs at Donnelly and Herman Miller bear little resemblance to the programs of 40 years ago. They have gone through many major and minor changes over the years. Successful companies constantly learn, grow, and develop from their successes and their shortcomings. Even so, most companies fail to include a formal aggressive development step as part of their planning. Gain-sharing programs that fail to develop eventually wither and die. Organizations that fail to develop inevitably succumb to the competition.

There is a serious need today, and therefore a real opportunity, for organizations to significantly increase productivity, competitiveness, and quality of work life. To capitalize on this opportunity fully managers must take the bold step past System 3 consultative management and make a genuine commitment to the more participative Systems 4 and 5.

Lessons Learned About Management Practices

What has been learned about management practices from past gain-sharing experience can be summarized as follows:

- ▲ Organizations need strong, competent leadership.
- ▲ Organizations need more participative management practices.
- ▲ Participation must be extended to include the total business or work of the organization.
- ▲ Employees are ready for more active participation.
- ▲ All employees need more information and education.
- ▲ There is a need for continuous organizational development.

These lessons are substantial, and applying them will take us beyond gainsharing as we have known it.

Employee Participation

Employee participation is a tool or a system and, like all other systems, must be organized and used effectively. Gainsharing programs are intended to include a formal process for soliciting, processing, and using employee ideas and suggestions. There are many methods that have been used with varying degrees of success. All of the experiences, good and bad, are useful in helping us to understand how to organize and use participation effectively.

Strengths

Gainsharing programs have created some very good opportunities for employees to participate in problem solving and innovation. Suggestion systems, suggestion committees, Scanlon and Rucker committees, quality circles, and work teams have opened the door to employee participation. Good ideas have come from employees who are in a position to see waste, error, and opportunities not visible to others.

The popular press and professional journals regularly report cases of small and large savings resulting from employee suggestions. Most programs begin with a few nickel-and-dime fix-it suggestions but, with experience, expand to big-dollar process changes and methods improvements. The 1981 General Accounting Office study of productivity-sharing plans reported an average improvement of 8.5% in workforce cost among companies with less than five years of gainsharing experience and a 29% average improvement for companies with more than five years' experience. Improvement among the latter group of experienced gainsharing companies ranged from 13% to 71%.[3]

As companies move from passive (suggestion box) participation systems to more active committees, quality circles, and work teams, there occurs a dramatic increase in the quality of ideas from employees. Geniuses aren't very common, so the suggestion boxes seldom produce breakthrough ideas. Group problem solving in committees, quality circles, and work teams, on the other hand, frequently produces creative breakthrough solutions.

In addition to the good ideas coming from active employee participation the problem-solving experience has a buoyant effect on employee work habits. As workers begin to take a greater interest in the success of the business, they begin to pay more attention to the task at hand. There are hundreds of opportunities in the course of their daily work to save time, materials, and energy, to ensure good quality, to help each other, to prevent accidents and damage, and so on. As employees develop more positive attitudes toward the success of the business, they act on those opportunities. Parts that can be salvaged or recycled are put into the salvage bin rather than the trash. Inventory is stocked more carefully to avoid breakage. Material is placed on conveyors more carefully to avoid jam-ups. Retail clerks respond more quickly and eagerly when asked for help by customers.

An operator will check a questionable instruction to prevent an error rather than blindly following an instruction with an "it's not my job" attitude. One manager expressed genuine delight when employees turned off the lights after they finished work in a warehouse.

Taken individually, incidents like this are almost insignificant, but they add up. And over time these small bits of performance are the margin of difference between average companies and excellent ones. Opening the door to greater employee involvement and influence produces cost savings and better-quality products and services. It also contributes to a better quality of work life for employees, who experience achievement and trust and feel challenged and more secure. The participation process also allows employees to become better informed. As each suggestion receives its response, and as each improvement shows up in the gainsharing bonus, everyone learns just a little bit more about what makes the company go and how excellence is achieved.

These are the strengths of employee participation—some obvious and visible, others quite subtle, but all valuable.

Weaknesses

The major criticism of employee participation systems today is that they seldom deliver what they promise. When a company launches an employee-participation program, whether it be a suggestion box system or quality circles, there are letters from the president, posters, meetings, and training sessions to encourage employee ideas. Too often, however, what management says in its memos and meetings and what it does are not the same. "They talk the talk but don't walk the walk."

In company after company this story is repeated:

January: The new employee suggestion program is kicked off with a great deal of fanfare.

February: The suggestion boxes are installed in the lunchroom and near the time clocks. Suggestion forms are distributed to all employees. A suggestion coordinator or the personnel manager holds meetings with each department to explain the new program and urge everyone to participate. Employees are appointed or elected to suggestion committees.

March:	Committees begin to meet and suggestions start to come in.
April:	There are 25 to 100 suggestions in the works, and employees are feeling good about the new program.
May:	A few suggestions have been approved, and some have been implemented, but the backlog of suggestions is starting to grow. A few minor complaints are heard. Some employees made suggestions that, to them, seemed to be simple and obvious solutions to nagging problems. It is puzzling that their ideas weren't implemented three weeks ago.
June:	An undercurrent of dissatisfaction with the suggestion system is apparent. More and more employees are wondering when the idea they submitted last month will be approved and implemented. Some are wondering if their ideas will be used at all. The grapevine talk is about the suggestions that are stuck in engineering, at the bottom of the production manager's in-basket—or worse, lost. One wag in the employee lunchroom introduces the notion that the employee suggestions have disappeared into an administrative black hole. The sarcasm finds a ready audience among others who have not heard anything about their suggestions either. The new program is in trouble.
July:	The dissatifaction with the suggestion program is growing rapidly. Genuine complaints are voiced, and the sarcasm turns to impatience and frustration. Employees are openly voicing their dissatisfaction to each other and to their managers. The first-line managers don't know how to speed up the process, so they do nothing.
August:	Most employees have stopped submitting suggestions. When asked about it, they say they will put in another when the first one is acted upon.
September:	Employees are putting candy wrappers and nasty suggestions in the boxes.

The new program that had such promise in January is comatose. Employees expected management to be serious about their request for suggestions. Suggestions were made in good faith and with the confidence that ideas would be welcomed and used. Many employees were excited by the prospect of seeing their ideas in action—achievement is a strong motivator. Before participation programs start, employees are moderately dissatisfied that no one ever asks for their ideas. People sense they are not respected as competent and feel that the managers and professionals don't think them capable of solving problems or having good ideas. When a suggestion program is installed and fails, the dissatisfaction is much worse. Now management knows employees have good ideas and is refusing to act on them. What before was partially excused as an oversight is now seen as rejection, and it feels much worse.

Many employees feel they were deliberately misled, but it is wrong to assume that management conspired to draw them into a program just to put them down. The reason why most programs fail is that management fails to completely structure the suggestion program and plan for an adequate response. In the beginning it seems like a good idea to ask employees for suggestions, so programs are designed to get suggestions. What doesn't get designed is a way to communicate priorities to the employees and a process for responding quickly to suggestions when they start coming in.

Without clear priorities many suggestions are made on a myriad of topics. One hundred employees will have 99 priorities. When suggestions about assembly and accounting problems are received by a manager who is preoccupied with a sales problem, the outcome is predictable. The manager continues to work on the sales problem and all other issues are put on hold to be resolved when time permits. The assembly and accounting department suggestions are put aside until the sales crisis is resolved. The manager's action is understandable and probably a sound management decision considering the immediate needs of the business. But that reality doesn't help the assembler or the accountant, neither of whom know those other priorities. The employees' dissatisfaction is made worse when no one takes the trouble to explain to them why their suggestions have been held up.

Without a process for resolving suggestions quickly, backlogs develop. In manufacturing companies many suggestions must be reviewed, approved, and implemented by engineering, quality control, or maintenance. But the people in these departments usually have full work schedules, so working on employee suggestions is an extra load. When this extra work is mismanaged, it becomes the source of trouble.

An engineer who has been assigned to design a product upgrade for the Model 200 widget knows that the Model 200 will be the primary topic on his or her next performance review—the performance review that will determine a pay raise, a bonus, or a promotion. When a suggestion from a machinist to eliminate an unnecessary operation on the Model 100 widget is referred to that engineer, it is unlikely to receive much attention. Often no provisions are made for the engineer to stop work on one design and attend to the suggestion—it is an unwanted distraction. To the suggester who continues to perform the unnecessary operation on the Model 100 widget, any delay is seen as a waste of time and tools. As the machinist is likely to say, "This is sheer stupidity!" Such situations can quickly escalate into serious interdepartmental conflicts. To keep these problems from happening, management must establish a process for resolving employee suggestions expeditiously.

Another problem that stems from management's failure to communicate priorities for the employee participation system is that suggestions remain peripheral to the business. For a suggestion program to produce optimum results suggestions need to be aimed at critical business problems. Too often suggestion programs and other forms of participative management are not integrated into the mainstream of the business. There are examples of employee participation, quality circles being one, where management does identify priorities. Where circles are asked to problem-solve special projects, employees have produced excellent solutions and action plans. Problem solving and performance improvement can not, however, be limited to occasional special projects. These processes must become continuous, a regular part of every team's work, if major improvements in productivity are to be achieved and sustained.

Lessons Learned About Employee Participation

What has been learned from successful and unsuccessful gainsharing experiences can be summarized as follows:

▲ Employee participation must be carefully and thoroughly planned. The process must be complete.

⏷ Employee participation must be focused on important factors of organizational performance.

⏷ The use of employee ideas must be given as high a priority as soliciting their suggestions.

⏷ The participation process must be a closed-loop system with feedback to the suggesters.

These lessons, properly applied, will bring participation into the mainstream of the business and significantly increase employee participation.

Shared Reward

The third element of a gainsharing program is the shared reward. When productivity exceeds the gainsharing productivity base, the savings or additional earnings are divided between the company and the employees. The employee portion of the savings is then divided among the employees as their share of the improved productivity.

Strengths

Gainsharing plans pay a monthly or quarterly bonus to employees. In good times bonuses of 5% to 15% of base pay are fairly common. These bonuses act as incentives especially in the early stages of a gainsharing plan. The prospect of a bonus check keeps people interested in finding ways to save money and increase productivity. The gainsharing productivity base provides a simple way to show the value of a cost-saving idea and how an idea will impact bonuses. Used effectively, the base is a way to educate employees and encourage more and better employee suggestions.

Gainsharing plans have been an effective way to control labor costs. Scanlon plan and Rucker plan formulas both freeze labor costs at the level used for the productivity base. Employees look for ways to save labor expense because the savings go into their bonus pool. When wage rates are increased, Scanlon and Rucker bases are not adjusted. Productivity must be improved to offset the increase in wages, or bonuses will decline by the amount of the wage increase. Thus labor-cost control is built into these programs. In long-running gainsharing plans it has been common for bonuses to drop for a month or two following a wage increase and then quickly recover to their previous levels. Once employees have grown accustomed to bonuses of, say, 10%, they tend to work to keep them at that level. John Donnelly observed this phenomenon and commented wryly, "I believe the people could double productivity if they had a reason to. For three years our bonuses have hovered around 12%. Every year within a month or two after our May 1 wage increase the people find ways to improve productivity enough to cover the wage increase and restore bonuses to 12%. Why do they stop at 12%?"

The monthly or quarterly bonuses are useful scorecards letting employees know how well productivity improvement efforts have succeeded. This feedback is especially useful to employees, who need to know if their ideas and extra effort are doing any good. The quick feedback provided by a monthly bonus (or even a notice that no bonus was earned) tells everyone how well or poorly they did last month. When they do well and get a bonus check, they are encouraged to do well again.

Bonuses also act as a celebration of good ideas and extra effort. Some companies announce monthly bonuses over the public address system as soon as the numbers are known. When the bonuses are good, it is not uncommon to hear cheers throughout the factory and offices. Failure to earn a bonus coupled with good diagnostic information is also helpful because it tells where effort and attention should be directed. Entirely independent of its function as a reward, the gainsharing bonus is an excellent communication tool.

Another important benefit of the shared-reward feature of the gainsharing program is that it requires management to determine an appropriate productivity base. Very few companies have accurate, useful measures of productivity. There are plenty of cost records and an abundance of partial productivity measures. Most companies know how much they pay for labor, materials, energy, and capital equipment. But these measures are seldom related to output as a productivity measure to guide the company's efforts. Most use only partial measures of labor productivity such as labor cost per unit or output per work hour. Traditional productivity measurements don't even include all labor costs. The common practice is to measure only direct factory labor, excluding the labor cost for supervision, engineering, and other support functions. Some go so far as to include only base wages, excluding so-called fringe benefits (which are no longer just fringe expenses).

> The chairman of a large West Coast manufacturing company
> was bragging about how his company had increased produc-
> tivity steadily for ten years. When asked how the company
> measured productivity, he pulled out the graphs that showed
> a steady ten-year growth in dollar sales per employee. He
> explained that by reducing staff they had been able to show a
> steady increase in the ratio of sales dollars per employee.
>
> It was suggested that the numbers in the graph be recal-
> culated to eliminate the effects of inflation and to use total
> labor costs rather than the number of employees. When recal-
> culated, the graph was virtually flat, reflecting no gain at all in
> productivity over the ten-year period.
>
> By adjusting the sales figures for inflation, the increased
> dollars that had nothing to do with internal productivity were
> removed, showing slightly lower sales figures. When labor
> costs were used in the ratio rather than head count, the chair-
> man discovered that their downsizing had eliminated about
> 10% of the employees but only about 3% of the labor costs.
> The jobs eliminated during downsizing were the lower-paid
> jobs, which had only a minor impact on total labor costs.
>
> The chairman immediately asked for better productivity
> measures.

Most of the traditional so-called productivity measures are at
best gross approximations of how well or how hard the employees
are working. Few are true productivity measures. A company that
adopts a gainsharing plan often discovers these weaknesses in its
historical productivity measures. The search for the productivity base
is in fact an eye-opener for management. It often leads to better
productivity measurements for the company and better performance
measurements for individual departments—a very useful, unexpected benefit.

Weaknesses

Some weaknesses can also be identified from past experience with
the shared reward. There are many plans that base gains on labor
cost alone. Many plans are blue-collar-only plans or exclude senior
management or field sales personnel. There are also imperfections in

productivity measurements and in the ratio of sharing between the company and the employees.

Gainsharing plans based on labor savings alone direct employee attention to that one factor of productivity. By so doing, these plans tend to concentrate employee participation on something less than the total success of the business. Labor-only gainsharing has its roots in Scanlon and Rucker plans. For their day and in the kinds of businesses in which they were used, labor-only plans appear to have been adequate. Although this was a good starting place for gainsharing, it is clearly insufficient for today's problems of productivity and competitiveness.

When John Donnelly started his Scanlon plan in 1952, he installed the program as it was explained to him and used the traditional labor-only Scanlon formula. Within two years he discovered that the labor-only formula was causing a conflict of interest between the workers and the company. On the one hand, workers resisted management's efforts to buy less expensive materials that required more labor-hours. On the other hand, workers found ways to increase labor efficiency but at a cost of greater tool wear. Donnelly made a change in the gainsharing base to include the costs of all direct, indirect, and overhead labor and of all direct and indirect materials. This expanded the productivity base from 33% of sales value of production to about 75% of sales value of production.

With this broader base employees were challenged to find productivity-improvement ideas to increase labor efficiency without increasing other costs such as tool wear. The scope of their participation was expanded to include the success of the total business, not just the efficiency of the operation in their direct line of sight. They were being challenged to manage productivity more completely. For the Donnelly Corporation this revision to the basic formula was useful for the next 25 years. Then in 1980, using the same logic of removing restrictions to employee participation, Donnelly instituted a third change to the calculation of productivity. The company began using return on investment (ROI), the broadest possible gainsharing base.

This was a major departure. With the ROI formula every employee in the company was invited to participate in managing total productivity. To the base, which already included all labor and materials accounts, were added all other costs, including interest expense, taxes, and depreciation. Then it all was related to the value of the capital investment. The most innovative aspect of this development is that for the first time the productivity of capital was

included with the productivity of labor, materials, and other resources. As technology forces companies to make larger capital
investments, Donnelly's innovation will prove to be a harbinger of
things to come.

Today there is too much talk about limiting the gainshare to the
things employees directly control, or, as some refer to it, the employees' line of sight. In reality, employees control everything that happens in the business except for tax rates. What is needed is to expand
the employees' line of sight with more and better information and
broader measures of productivity.

Another practice limiting the potential of gainsharing plans is
that of excluding some employees from the gainsharing bonus. A
principal goal in gainsharing is to maximize teamwork in the company. This goal is jeopardized when some members are not included
in the gainsharing. The worst case is when the gainsharing program
includes factory or nonexempt employees only. No organization
today can achieve maximum productivity without good leadership
and without a great deal of support from staff and professional
departments. Omitting engineering, production control, data processing, accounting, personnel, and the first-line managers seriously
limits the potential of gainsharing to pull all employees together in
one common effort to improve total productivity.

Less serious but still a problem is the more common practice of
excluding senior managers and field sales personnel from gainshares.
The argument goes that senior management is already on a profit-
based bonus system, so it would not be fair for them to take a
gainshare, too, a practice sometimes referred to as "double dipping."
No satisfactory method has been found to extend gainsharing to
salespeople who are paid on a commission basis. Salaried salespeople
pose no such problem and are usually included. These difficulties
have prevented gainsharing programs from creating a single productive team with a common purpose.

There is another weakness in the productivity base that goes
beyond the problem of limited labor-only measurements. Even with
broader measures such as multicost and ROI, there are no true
standards for productivity. There are massive statistics about what
businesses achieved in the past, but these are only history; they are
not standards. We know in painful detail how productive or profitable
paper mills, machine shops, or hospitals have been, but these statistics do not tell how productive or profitable these organizations
should have been. Lacking absolute measures, most companies have

settled for doing better each year. Making productivity or profitability a little bit better, say 4% each year, is fine until a competitor comes along and improves productivity more than a little bit, say 10% or 25%.

This happened to the U.S. automobile companies. Japan caught them napping and raced past Detroit in the early 1980s. But the productivity battle in automobiles was not lost in 1980. It was lost around 1960, when the Japanese perfected the design of a fuel-efficient small car that appealed to the American market. Around this same time the Japanese started the push for superior quality, robotics, and more efficient manufacturing processes. Back in 1960 Detroit lacked productivity measures that would have predicted trouble to come. The U.S. automakers lacked a definition of productivity that would have enabled them to include their basic design concept in measuring productivity. Without adequate warning they allowed their unit labor cost to get too high and their plant and equipment to get too tired.

Many analysts have pointed to high wage rates as the major problem in the auto industry. This is more evidence of limited understanding of true productivity. Although the autoworkers are among the highest paid in American industry, the problem is not just their high rates. The problem is also that it takes more hours of labor to produce an auto in Detroit than it does in Japan. These extra hours, more than the labor rates, are what make Detroit—and businesses, hospitals, and government agencies—nonproductive. Productivity of labor is unit labor cost, not labor rates. Labor costs could double as long as productivity offsets the increase.

Most gainsharing programs use a historical average as their productivity base point on the assumption that improvements over the past are true gains and can be shared. In many cases this assumption is true enough to produce satisfactory results. But the assumption is not always true. Without ways to tell how productive a business should be, the historical base may be too high, it may be just right, or it may be too low. Better ways are needed to determine the correct measurement for the productivity base.

Peter Drucker pointed out this problem years ago and offers some general guidance.[4] He says that when doing strategic planning, managers must set productivity objectives for all key resources: labor, materials, and capital. He also says there must be a single overall productivity measure. Drucker defines productivity as obtaining the maximum output from the least amount of input. He advises that the company must calculate a minimum profitability: the amount of profit the company needs to fund itself into a healthy future. Productivity goals and minimum profitability planning would be a major improvement over the present practice of improving productivity a little bit over last year and maximizing profit.

The weakness in productivity measurements also makes it difficult to determine how to share productivity gains fairly between the company and the employees. Without absolute measures of profit and productivity there is only historical practice to serve as a guide. In our 1983 book we described how shares are determined in Scanlon and Rucker plans. We also included a formula for calculating a sharing ratio devised by Bob Keeler of Honeywell, Inc.[5] History more or less implies that the amount of the gainshare money retained by the company should be approximately equal to the money paid out in employee bonuses. This rule never has been clearly stated in gainsharing literature, but it has been common practice. Unfortunately, there is no way to know whether equal dollar amounts is either equitable or reasonable. A 50–50 split sounds good, but without a solid productivity base there is no way to test its reasonableness.

Is it fair to employees to pay large bonuses and have the company go under five years later for lack of modernization? Is it fair to take the ideas and extra effort of the employees and pay higher dividends to the shareholders and bigger bonuses to managers? Traditional gainsharing measurements do not provide good answers to these questions.

Lacking sound profit and productivity measures, companies are tempted to be overly conservative when deciding how to share gains with the employees. When a company does not know how profitable it should be or how much is enough, there is the temptation to keep just a little bit more. And one way to keep a little bit more is to give the employees a 25% share when 35% would be more equitable. Too often the popular press and antimanagement rhetoric attribute such decisions to motives of greed and exploitation. More often the motive is the fear that comes from inadequate planning and not knowing how much profit is enough.

This problem cuts both ways. Just as some companies hold back fair shares due to a lack of proper measures, others pay out too much of the gains and deny the company the reinvestment it needs for growth, development, and expansion. In 1990 the CEO of a company long famous for paying very large employee bonuses had just concluded a presentation about his company's successful program. He was asked if there were any difficulties with his program. He stated that his only concern was that the company was not retaining enough earnings to allow it to expand and take advantage of the new markets opening in Eastern Europe.

Just as the farmer must allocate each harvest to this year's consumption and seed for next year's crop, businesses must allocate their gains to wages and to reinvested capital. There is a definite balance that should be struck between wages and profit for reinvestment. But current strategic planning does not identify this proper balance, and so the shares in most gainsharing programs are under a cloud of suspicion. We just do not know if the sharing ratios are fair to the company and to the employees.

Finally, there is the issue of gainshares as incentives. During the 1980s, when average annual pay increases dropped from 10% to 4%, gainsharing bonuses became an attractive way to soften the blow. There were quite a few instances during labor contract negotiations when companies offered gainsharing or profit-sharing opportunities in lieu of wage increases. Many nonunion companies also turned to gainsharing as a way to take some pressure off wage demands. This was the origin of the idea of pay at risk, or so-called alternative pay. It was also at this point that gainsharing began the shift to primarily an incentive plan.

There is very little evidence to support the idea that the shared reward alone in the gainsharing programs is any more than a weak incentive for better work. History tells us that incentives were successful when workers were motivated by Maslow Level 1 needs and when incentives amounted to 50–150% of their very low pay. It is doubtful that today's employees who are reaching for higher levels on the Maslow scale will make major productivity, quality, and performance improvements for a 5%, 10%, or even a 20% bonus. Workers want to do better work, but it is more likely they will do it for achievement than for a few dollars more.

Lessons Learned About Shared Reward

What we have learned from past experiences with the shared reward can be summarized as follows:

▲ There is a need for broader, more inclusive measures of productivity.

▲ Productivity measurements must be anchored in the organiza-
tion's strategic objectives.
▲ All employees must be included in gainsharing to encourage
maximum teamwork.
▲ The gainshare is important for communications.
▲ Gainsharing is not important as an incentive.

These lessons point to the need for solutions well beyond traditional gainsharing experience.

Conclusions

Gainsharing plans are viewed by many experts as the wave of the
future. The American Compensation Association and the U.S. Department of Labor list gainsharing as one of the most promising and
fastest growing of the new alternative pay plans. Surveys by the
American Center for Productivity and Quality and leading compensation consulting firms indicate a growing interest among companies
in the use of gainsharing. If gainsharing did not reach full-blown fad
status in the 1980s, it will be sure to do so in the 1990s.

As the popularity of gainsharing grows, one serious weakness is
developing. Gainsharing, as popularized, is moving away from an
active employee-involvement process and becoming primarily an
incentive plan. Among the newer gainsharing plans there is entirely
too much emphasis on the bonus, and not enough emphasis on
participative management practices and employee involvement.

The newly popular gainsharing plans had some success in the
1980s while the economy was expanding. Increases in sales volume
alone will generate bonuses in any dollar-based gainsharing formula.
And so, as volume went up and prices increased, bonuses were paid
and gainsharing programs seemed to be successful. Employees didn't
complain as long as they received bonuses. Management was satisfied as long as the bonuses were paid out of additional profits. But
such programs are only fair-weather programs. They are not successful when market conditions change. If the economy slows down or
competition heats up, volume and sales income decline and the
bonuses disappear. Employees become dissatisfied and blame the
lack of bonuses on management. Without active participation employees feel helpless when bonuses are not paid.

There is a logic flaw in the idea of a gainsharing program without

Frank Sullivan, vice-president of human resources for a high-tech firm of about 800 employees, called in consultants to help design a gainsharing program. He explained his problem as follows: "We are getting close to the time of year when we give our employees an annual increase. Things are tight this year, and we must do something to hold down our labor costs. I'd like to offer the employees a gainsharing plan in lieu of an increase. If we give an increase, it could not be more than 3% or 4%, and I understand gainsharing programs typically pay out in the 5% to 10% range.

"I'd like your help designing a gainsharing formula for our company. If you are interested, please give me your proposal to help us develop our gainsharing formula. I don't want any participative management garbage in the proposal. We did quality circles last year and it bombed, so I don't want any more of that. Just give us a formula, and we will take it from there."

employee participation. Management cannot tell employees that their bonus depends on how well the company performs and then withhold the opportunity for employees to change that performance. There must be active employee participation in any plan of pay for performance. Managers who complain that employees want to get something for nothing should not deny employees the opportunity to get something for something.

If we are to make major improvements in productivity and the competitiveness of our businesses, if we are to see major improvements in the performance of other institutions, we need a much more powerful remedy than a new incentive. We need an entirely new process to manage gains in performance and to tap the human will to work—the need to achieve. We need a process that goes well beyond the popular definition of gainsharing.

In our 1983 book we identified the three major elements of a gainsharing program as management practices, employee participation, and a shared reward. These three elements are still critical to success if we want a process that will significantly improve productivity, competitiveness, and quality of work life. For today's realities—the knowledge workers and the demands for much improved performance—we must go beyond traditional notions about gainsharing.

The term itself now appears to be misleading because it places too much emphasis on the financial reward, thus leading to the erroneous incentive idea. Gainsharing no longer adequately describes the total process needed for today's situation. We need new terms to avoid past misunderstanding and to describe a total, continuous process for improvement of performance, quality, productivity, and quality of work life. The new terms are GainManagement, GainPlanning, GainMaking, and GainSharing. The relationship among these factors is shown in Figure 4-1.

GainManagement A total management process to involve all departments and every employee in a common effort to excel and achieve the organization's purpose

GainPlanning The management practices and structure necessary to lead the organization to excellent performance

GainMaking A formal process that involves every employee working in teams in a focused effort to improve productivity, quality, profitability, and quality of work life

GainSharing An equitable sharing of performance gains among all

Figure 4-1.   GainManagement triangle.

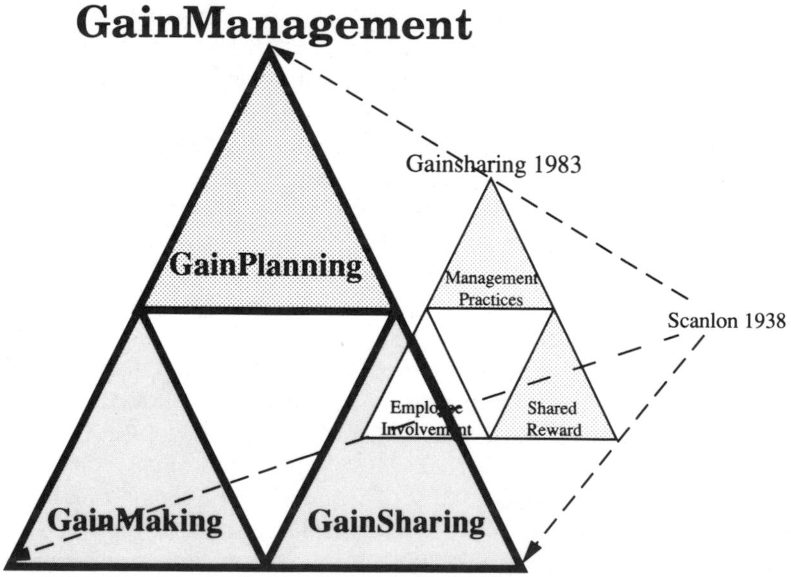

GainManagement

the organization's constituents and a sharing between the company and the employees of financial gains over a required base level of profitability.

This is the direction in which we must go: beyond gainsharing to GainManagement.

Summary

The three basic elements of gainsharing were management practices, employee participation, and shared reward. In practice, gainsharing programs have demonstrated strengths and weaknesses in each of the three elements, providing valuable lessons for the new Gain-Management process.

The term "gainsharing" has lost its original meaning as gainsharing plans have become incentive plans, with little or no emphasis on management practices and employee participation. New terms are now needed to more accurately reflect a total process for managing continuous performance gains and to give proper emphasis to GainMaking, which is the heart of the process, and GainPlanning, which drives the process.

Notes

1. Fred G. Lesieur and Eldridge S. Puckett, "The Scanlon Plan Has Proved Itself," *Harvard Business Review* (September-October 1969), pp. 109–118.
2. U.S. General Accounting Office. Productivity Sharing Programs AFMD 81-82 (March 3, 1981), Washington, D.C.
3. Ibid.
4. Peter Drucker, *Management: Tasks, Responsibilities, Practices* (New York: Harper & Row, 1973).
5. Robert J. Doyle, *Gainsharing and Productivity* (New York: AMA-COM, 1983).

II

GainManagement in Practice

There are three principle elements in the GainManagement process: GainPlanning, GainMaking, and GainSharing. All are equally important to the total process, but all are not equal in their impact on performance results. GainMaking is the direct cause of improved performance. GainPlanning enables GainMaking to occur and determines how effective GainMaking will be. GainSharing does not cause performance to improve; it functions within the process to maintain trust, commitment, and focus.

Chapter 5

GainPlanning

GainManagement begins with GainPlanning—the management principles and practices it takes to lead an organization in the continuous pursuit of excellence. Planning and the way plans are communicated are the first and most important tasks of management in highly participative systems. Management must change from ordering workers to do this and that to enabling workers to achieve this and that. To make the change from authoritarian to participative management, there are new management principles and new management practices to be learned and applied.

Management principles that foster higher levels of employee participation do not diminish the role of managers. Managers need not give up their responsibilities to lead and to provide expert guidance to their organizations. On the contrary, to meet the challenges of the future, managers must become stronger leaders and more competent. Authority and power are all that is needed to manage using Systems 1 or 2, but Systems 4 and 5 require real leadership skills and very high levels of competence. It takes leaders who are strong and competent to open their decisions to genuine participation. Errors and omissions will be the first things to catch the attention of a participating workforce. Managers with big egos and weak leadership skills will find this a very troublesome prospect. Managers with the self-confidence that comes from honesty, integrity, and competence will be able to implement these new management principles and practices.

GainPlanning Principles

The new principles required for GainManagement have been written about with increasing frequency over the past several years. Current authors, such as Tom Peters and Max De Pree, are quite compelling and deserve their great popularity. In fairness, though, it must be acknowledged that the first calls for new management principles were put out by Drucker, McGregor, Likert, and others over 30 years ago. Typical of prophets, scant notice was paid to their early warning messages. Their books were displayed on executives' shelves but had little impact on the daily practice of management.

In the 1960s there was no great pressure to change. The world knew that American management was bulletproof. The U.S. economy was healthy and expanding worldwide. Jean-Jacques Servan-Schreiber, a leading French journalist, wrote *The American Challenge*, in which he described American management as invincible and destined for world domination. U.S. managers were lulled into a complacency from which they are only now beginning to recover.

In 1980, when Japan Inc. hit Detroit with a two-by-four, managers started to pay attention. NBC produced an excellent documentary in that year, "If Japan Can Do It, Why Can't We?" With increasing frequency government and business leaders were asking, What can we do to make our companies perform better? The correct answer was and is better management. The only correct answer to that question is better management. Management is the function that causes an organization to perform. A lack of management or inappropriate management prevents an organizaton from performing. Good management causes good performance. Excellent management causes excellent performance.

Better management means that there must be changes. Not everything about management must change, but changes are needed in those management principles and practices that have been made obsolete by the changing workforce and a changing world economy.

In this chapter we describe four fundamental principles and seven key practices of management necessary for a successful GainManagement program.

The four management principles that provide the foundation for GainPlanning are:

1. Commitment to excellence
2. Openness to new ideas
3. Equity for all partners
4. Teamwork

Commitment to Excellence

GainPlanning must embrace the principle of commitment to excellence for two reasons. First, in a highly competitive environment only excellence survives. Second, the pursuit of excellence is the only goal that truly dignifies human work. This commitment to excellence must permeate every action and aspect of the organization.

In a noncompetitive situation any level of performance is sufficient. As a market becomes more competitive, the level of performance that is sufficient rises steadily. Inevitably, only excellence is sufficient. This principle has been dramatically demonstrated in the Olympic games. In 1952 Bob Mathias set the Olympic and world record in the decathlon with a score of 7,468. In 1991, with that score, he would not have qualified for the U.S. national collegiate finals. In 1991 a college athlete had to score 7,550 points just to be admitted to the national (NCAA Division 1) finals.

In 1960 General Motors, Ford, and Chrysler produced automobiles that were the standard of excellence against which all others were compared. In 1990 Buick bragged that at fifth place it was the only U.S. car rated in the top ten of the world's automobiles. Ironically, the 1990 Buick is a far superior machine than its 1960 counterpart. In 1960 the term "Cadillac" was synonymous with excellence, as in "This is the Cadillac of vacuum sweepers." Today that expression is in danger of going the way of "Remember the Alamo." No company can stand still in a competitive environment. Excellence is constantly being redefined, and effective leadership embraces the principle of constantly striving for excellence. This principle of excellence does not refer to product qualities alone. The Packard was an excellent automobile right up to the day the company stopped making it. But the Packard Motor Car Company failed to maintain organizational excellence. There must be excellence in every aspect of the organization, including products, services, structure, leadership, employment, facilities, tools, and systems.

In *Up From Slavery* Booker T. Washington wrote, "No race can prosper until it learns that there is as much dignity in tilling a field as in writing a poem." What dignifies work are the opportunities it provides to learn, to grow, and to serve. The more a worker strives to excel, the more these opportunities can be realized, and the more the work is dignified. A poorly made refrigerator is no more dignifying than a poorly written poem. The excellence of work must apply to both the product and the process by which it is made.

The commitment to excellence as a GainPlanning principle must permeate every person, every department, every product, and every action of the organization: It must become part of the organization's very spirit, and it must be put there by management.

Openness to New Ideas

The second principle of GainPlanning is openness to new ideas. Managers must understand and convince the rest of the organization that everything they are doing will be done better by someone sooner or later. New ideas are constantly occurring in and around the organization, and everyone must be alert and open to the ones that will enable the organization to excel.

Ideas will come not only from employees but also from customers, suppliers, competitors, and others outside the organization. Ideas from every available source must be eagerly sought, carefully screened, and promptly used. Most important of all there must be a new openness to ideas coming from employees. There has been a lot of talk about listening to employee ideas, but not nearly enough action. Experience with employee suggestion programs shows that, although there are suggestion boxes and quality circles, genuine openness to employee ideas seldom lives up to the advance publicity.

The evolution of management systems helps to explain why this principle of openness to new ideas is essential to GainPlanning. Systems 1 and 2 are appropriate in organizations where leaders and managers have all of the expertise, as they do in organizations with unskilled workforces. In those situations leaders are not expected to be open to employee ideas because employees seldom have useful ideas.

In developed economies such as the United States, Japan, Europe, and others with workforces that are skilled, literate, and knowledgeable, openness to employee ideas isn't just a good idea, it is an absolute necessity. These employees have ideas, and they must be used if managers are to truly lead workers. Managers who are not open to legitimate employee ideas lose credibility with their employees. This is one major cause for the lack of trust in management that is frequently detected on employee surveys. When a person's ideas are denied or rejected, to some extent that person is denied and rejected. It is difficult for people to follow the lead of someone who denies or rejects them.

Max De Pree has very artfully shown that employees, especially in U.S. companies, are volunteers.[1] Because they can leave and go to work elsewhere, they are voluntarily working in their present company. That employees don't always leave and go elsewhere when dissatisfied does not take away from the fact that they could do so. Thus, the burden of being responsive to employees and their ideas rests primarily with management because of the voluntary nature of the employees' relationship to the organization.

On the positive side managers who are open to employees' ideas create a culture where everyone is more open to each other's ideas. Good things happen. The most obvious and measurable results are that people's ideas are used, problems are solved or avoided, innovation occurs, and the company performs better. When employees experience having their ideas used, they are stimulated to generate more and better ideas. Trust in the credibility and integrity of management improves, and the whole spirit of the company grows positive. A company's physical resources (machines, technology, etc.) can only be conserved. Machines are not capable of increasing their efficiency or becoming more effective on their own. Only the company's human resources can grow and become more effective. People can increase their skills, effort, cooperation, creativity, and commitment—and they will, too, in response to management's openness.

Management must demonstrate and advocate openness to new ideas. Everyone must be encouraged to seek out new ideas from every possible source, both internal and external. Employees must be encouraged to be open to new ideas from outside the organization. Staff departments must be open to ideas from line departments and vice versa. Labor and management must be open to each other's ideas. This openness must include every person, function, and department and apply to everything the organization does.

Equity for All Partners

The popular definition of equity in business refers to shares of stock in the company or owners' equity. The concept of owners' equity is easy to understand and easy to measure, as shown clearly on company balance sheets. The dictionary has several definitions of equity. One is the financial idea just described—the residual value of a business beyond any mortgage and other liabilities. But the first definition in the dictionary is the idea of justice or fairness. As a GainPlanning principle equity must include both definitions: fairness and ownership.

Without in any way diminishing the legal and traditional concept of owners' equity, the idea of equity needs to be expanded to include all of the partners of the business—owners, employees, customers, suppliers, the community. Owners' equity is well defined and protected by many laws, regulations, and professional accounting standards. But the traditional concept of owners' equity reflects only part of the value of a business, the physical or tangible assets such as buildings, equipment, tools, fixtures, inventory, and accounts receivable. This is only the financial value of the business. Businesses and other organizations have social value, too. They have value to customers as sources of goods and services to satisfy wants and needs. They have value to employees as sources of work and wages. They have value to communities as sources of employment and taxes to help pay for education and government services. They have value to suppliers as customers for their goods and services.

It is the job of management to bring owners, employees, customers, suppliers, and the community into a mutually beneficial partnership. To accomplish this managers must acknowledge each partner's equity in the enterprise. This GainPlanning principle of equity for all partners is a feature of GainManagement. Real partners have a real stake in an organization, and having a stake in something means having equity.

This new principle of equity for all partners finds specific expression in GainSharing, Chapter 7, and in the GainManagement council to be explained in Chapter 11.

Teamwork

GainPlanning also includes the principle that a true spirit of teamwork is essential for excellent performance and for a satisfactory quality of work life. As organizations have grown in size and complexity over the past 50 years, frictions have developed. The causes of this friction are turf professionalism, reward systems, the hierarchy, and a lack of common goals. Authoritarian management Systems 1 and 2 tend to encourage managers to stake out territories and be authorities on their own turf. This occurs between line and staff, home office and field, between functional departments, and between shifts.

Professionalism and jargon make it difficult for functional departments to communicate with each other, thus creating horizontal we/they differences. Engineers don't understand budgets, and accountants don't understand the performance data that operating departments want. Sales doesn't understand why R&D can't do something a customer wants. This lack of ability to communicate between functions prevents teamwork and is a source of inefficiency and management scrap. In its 1990 annual report General Electric referred to "boundary-busting" to remove roadblocks between functions to achieve greater teamwork.[2] The hierarchical structure of organizations creates vertical distance and additional we/they differences that hamper teamwork. Each level seems to have its own emphasis, information, and understanding. While the different emphasis and information are the primary causes of the lack of teamwork between levels, the problem is further aggravated by the differences in status, pay, and perquisites.

Reward systems tend to be divisive in many organizations. Money for wages, salaries, and bonus plans is always a scarce resource. Pay and status differentials between departments and levels can create resentments that are expressed as a lack of cooperation and teamwork. Also, because pay systems are exclusively oriented to individuals, individual performance is stressed to the detriment of teamwork and cooperation.

An organization, by its very nature, has a common goal, but all too often that common goal is not clear to everyone. This weakness begins in the planning process and is complicated by the lack of effective communications. Lacking a clear common goal, departments and functions define their own goals. These independent goals, expressed in the jargon of the function, are usually shortsighted and are, or at least appear to be, in conflict. Whether the conflict is in appearance or in fact, the cost to teamwork is severe.

Conflicts and frictions, unaddressed, become a part of the culture of organizations. It is sad that no one is surprised at the lack of coordination and cooperation between the sales and operations departments or between the first and second shifts. It has come to be expected. But such frictions are intolerable in an organization that must excel in order to survive a serious competitive threat. Gain-Planning leadership must reduce these frictions and establish teamwork in principle and spirit throughout the organization.

From "Them" to "Us"*
by John Ricketts, Green End Supervisor,
Columbia Plywood

For years I was taught about "them." Learning about "them" did not have much to do with me until Columbia Plywood began speaking with me about "us"; and that has everything to do with me.

Recently swing shift green end has awakened to the reality of "us." We pooled our ideas in a problem-solving meeting, and after much cooperation those ideas turned into actions. In just two short weeks swing shift turned their 228,000-ft. combined daily average into a 241,000-ft. average! That is comparable to batting a thousand in the last 13 games of a 26-game baseball season!

Did we do this alone? Not on your life! We thank Maintenance for great-running machinery; part-timers for relief through breaks; Barker Crews for working 13-hour shifts; Log Dump, Boiler House, and Vats for quality; well-conditioned logs; green end day shift, supervisors, and office for direction and support; and Hardwood, Drying, Gluing, Finishing, and Shipping for helping to produce the finished product. We on the green end believe it took Columbia Plywood as a whole to turn "us" around.

When faced with the challenge of maintaining our present 288,000-ft. shift average, I wondered how much we could ask of our employees. Couldn't we just bask in the glory of our success for awhile? Pondering, I found that the answer lies in our ideals and our behavior. We have succeeded for a brief moment, should we stop now? Preposterous!

Last month's 8.7% bonus was a measurable credit to our financial well-being, and I know now what part we played in making it a reality. Working in teams was and continues to be the key to our success, cooperation, the mortar that holds everything together. We all have a responsibility to contribute to the team effort, to accept the challenge with faith in Columbia's potential to be even better.

We all need to challenge ourselves to overcome our negative attitudes and strive to see eye-to-eye. By removing the

*Reproduced with permission from the *Hardwood Herald*, newsletter of Columbia Forest Products, Inc. (vol. 2, 1991).

barriers that distance us from each other, we must work to build bridges of trust. We are truly many striving to meet a common goal.

From "me" to "we," from "them" to "us." One part of one system of people and a key to gainmaking success.

GainPlanning Practices

The four principles described in the preceding section—commitment to excellence, openness to new ideas, equity for all partners, and teamwork—are the foundation for GainPlanning. The new Gain-Planning principles are only good thoughts until they are put into practice. Management is not just good thoughts, it is action and practices. Management is work, hard work that must be done skillfully. It is through the practices of management that the Gain-Planning principles are brought to life and create a new organization culture committed to the achievement of excellence.

The GainPlanning management practices are grouped into seven key areas:

1. Leading
2. Directing
3. Organizing
4. Communicating
5. Motivating
6. Measuring
7. Developing

These titles are common to all management literature, but in the GainManagement process these practices of management take on new meaning in light of the four leadership principles.

1. Leading

Every organization exists for a purpose—has a goal it wants to achieve—and every organization is made up of individuals. Whether few or many, these individuals must work together in such a way that the organization achieves its purpose. The management practices that bring individuals together in the pursuit of a common purpose is leadership. Although leadership will be discussed in detail in Chapter 6, in this section we will introduce and highlight it. Leadership has four main responsibilities:

1. To continually develop people
2. To build teams
3. To guide the work of individuals and teams
4. To promote goals—individual, team, and organizational

1. *Develop people.* People are the organization, and every person is important to the success of the whole. Leadership requires that people be carefully selected, assigned, and trained, and then rewarded for their contributions to the organization. It is a common complaint among people in organizations today that they are treated just like numbers. An organization of such people will never achieve excellence. An organization made up of people striving for personal excellence is more likely to become an excellent organization. The first leadership responsibility is to develop people.

2. *Build teams.* Work has become so complex that it must be performed by groups of individuals working in teams. Leadership builds work teams and develops teamwork within and among the teams. Building teams for efficiency and for a better quality of work life requires the personal involvement of the leader with individual employees and with the teams. Working effectively in teams satisfies workers' needs for belonging and for membership (Maslow's Level 3). Building teams is the second responsibility of leadership.

3. *Guide work.* For an organization to do excellent work leaders must guide the work of individuals and teams to excellence. Plans must be made, explained, and followed. Resources must be provided. Problems must be solved to keep work on track. Results must be analyzed and the analysis used to make improvements. Guiding work is the third responsibility of leadership, and it must be done in a way that develops people and builds teams.

4. *Promote goals.* Good leaders develop enthusiastic commitments to the goals of the organization, the team, and individuals. The GainPlanning principles of commitment to excellence must be turned into action as the organization pursues its mission and goals. The leaders, in all they do, must demonstrate an enthusiastic commitment to the excellent achievement of goals.

Leaders must be visible to people, which sometimes means being "out on the floor"—the current slogan calls it management by walking about. This commitment is also expressed in memos, newsletters, employee meetings; in promoting quality, customer service, employee safety; in hiring, firing, promotions, and merit pay. It means that leaders really know what contributes to organizational success and openly, actively, and consistently support every contribution, large and small. It also means that leaders hold people accountable and do not support or tolerate anything that does not contribute. Sad but true, in many organizations today leaders have institutionalized mediocre performance simply by tolerating it. Mediocrity is the enemy of excellence and must be actively opposed. Promoting goals is the fourth responsibility of leadership.

GainPlanning leadership means that managers continuously develop people, build teams, guide work, and encourage the excellent achievement of the organization's mission and goals.

2. Directing

The second GainPlanning practice is directing the organization. This involves:

- ▲ Establishing the organization's mission
- ▲ Strategic planning
- ▲ **Focus** and **Charges**

Mission

Organizations are formed by people to do something: make products, provide service, cure sick people, educate students, keep the peace, and so on. An excellent *Harvard Business Review* article refers to organizations as having a strategic intent.[3] This is the mission that describes in broad terms the overall purpose of the organization. The function of this mission is similar to that of a destination for the pilot of an airplane. Every action in the cockpit is done with the one crucial goal in mind: to land safely, on time, at the distant airport. The destination, the distant airport, does not do anything, it is just there. But the existence of the destination causes a great deal of action and provides direction, purpose, and harmony to all of the actions in the cockpit. What is easily understood in the case of a pilot is no less true for an organization. For the many separate actions of an organization to have direction, purpose, and harmony there must be a mission—a destination. Without the mission there may still be action but not harmony. In a working organization harmony is efficiency.

In May 1961, a year before the first manned space flight, President John F. Kennedy expressed the mission of sending astronauts to the moon and bringing them back safely to earth. Eight years later it was done. That mission directed and harmonized millions of actions of thousands of people in hundreds of organizations. A characteristic of successful leaders is that they have a clear vision of their destination and are able to communicate and rally people to that mission.

In businesses and other organizations missions have tended to be limited to the products or work of the company. Henry Ford's mission was a Model T in every garage. It failed to include an outstanding Ford organization of committed people making the new American dream. His failure to include the human organization as a part of his company mission led to some very acrimonious labor conflict in 1938.

Leaders must extend their vision beyond products, services, market share, and profit to include a human organization of people dedicated to the work of the company, the hospital, the school, or other organization. Too often this purpose or mission of the organization is assumed and never clearly defined. In the absence of a clearly defined mission organizations sometimes define themselves in terms of their activity. Armies fight wars, but this is their activity, not their purpose, which is to prevent wars. In the early days of AT&T Theodore Vail defined the mission of the telephone company as *service*. Their activities were installing and operating telephones. Concentrating on the simple, clear, and powerful mission of service, AT&T became the greatest telephone company in the world.

Celestial Seasonings, Inc., is the world's largest maker of herbal teas. While making teas is their activity, the mission set by Founder Mo Siegel was to promote healthy living. Missions like promoting healthy living, service, and preventing war are missions that motivate organizations, dignify work, and make it possible for people to experience worthwhile achievement.

It is the job of management not only to define the organization's purpose or mission for all to see and be guided by, but also to redefine it when and as necessary to keep up with changing times.

Strategic Planning

By its nature the mission is broad and not easily quantified, so there needs to be several more specific strategic objectives to direct the work of the organization. Setting these objectives is particularly important for the organization serious about achieving excellence. Excellence in today's complex organizations means high performance in several areas critical to the achievement of the organization's mission.

It is not enough to produce in volume. Products and services must also meet higher and higher quality standards. On-time deliveries are important in many industries, especially among companies using just-in-time techniques. Growing competition limits price increases, so operations must be made more efficient and productive. Resources must be obtained, conserved, and used productively. In a rapidly changing environment higher profits are needed to fund future growth and ensure the long-term security of the enterprise. An excellent organization in today's global village needs many strategic objectives to guide it toward the fulfillment of its purpose.

Drucker provides a good list of eight categories in which strategic objectives must be set (see Figure 5-1, step 2):[4]

1. *Marketing**
   - For current customers
   - For new markets
   - For current products and/or services
   - For new products and/or services
2. *Innovation*
   - In products and services to meet the needs of the market
   - To use new technology for products and processes
   - In management systems such as GainManagement
3. *Financial Resources*—supply and use
4. *Physical Resources*—supply and use
5. *Human Resources*—supply, use, and development
6. *Social Responsibilities*—to and for the communities where the organization operates
7. *Productivity*—for capital, materials, labor, other key resources, and an overall productivity objective

*Until recently marketing has been the one function that differentiated a business from other institutions, such as hospitals, schools, churches, government. More and more, however, nonbusiness organizations are setting strategic marketing objectives and using marketing techniques to improve their performance.

Figure 5-1.   The strategic planning process.

Step 1:   Define the Business Mission.

What is our business and what should it be?

As the purpose of a business is to create customers or clients, the above questions must be answered in terms of marketing and innovation:

- Who are our customers now, and who will they be?
- What do they want, need, and value, now and in the future?
- Is the definition focused, simple, and clear?

Step 2:   Set Strategic Objectives for

1. Marketing
2. Innovation
3. Human resources
4. Physical resources
5. Financial resources
6. Productivity
7. Social responsibilities
8. Profit requirements

Do these objectives make sense . . .
- considering where we are and where we want to be?
- compared to each other?
- considering the needs of our customers?
- considering our competition?
- considering the general economic environment?
- based on our assumptions about the future?

Step 3:   Prepare Strategic Plans to Achieve Strategic Objectives.

- What work must we do now and over the next several years to ensure our future?

Step 4:   Prepare Annual Operating Objectives and Plans.

Assign resources to ensure achievement of operating objectives:

- People
- Budget
- Time

Are these allocations consistent with the priorities of Steps 1 and 2?

Step 5: Work.

- The planning process must result in action . . . clear, focused action.

---

8. *Profit Requirements*—to meet current obligations and future needs for growth and development

The direction of the organization is made more specific and clear by establishing strategic objectives in each of these key areas. In setting strategic objectives the GainPlanning principles of commitment to excellence, openness to new ideas, equity for all partners, and teamwork must guide both the content of the objectives and the process by which they are set.

Once the strategic objectives have been determined, plans are made to achieve them. Objectives are commitments, not wishes, and they are not validated until the commitment is expressed in action.

Strategic objectives often take years to reach, and progress proceeds at a varied pace. Marketing, innovation, and resource-development plans move at different rates and are accomplished sometimes sequentially, sometimes concurrently. Work is therefore organized into one-year segments. The annual operating plan coordinates the work of many functions—sales, manufacturing, engineering, R&D, finance, and human resources—toward the accomplishment of the several strategic objectives. Manufacturing and sales will be busy making and marketing current products at the same time R&D is busy developing future products. Engineering will be looking for ways to improve designs, productivity, and quality while human resources is concentrating on organizational development and training for future operations.

The process is one of setting specific annual operating objectives for sales, production, inventory, product development, productivity, profit, financing, advertising, hiring, training, employee compensation, and other areas. Plans to accomplish annual goals are usually expressed in the form of department operating plans, budgets, and individual work plans. Objectives are measured in terms of their impact on or contribution to the annual profit plan. Year-end variance analysis is done to see where the plan was met and missed and how the year's results contributed to the achievement of the strategic objectives. This analysis is also used as a learning process to improve future operations.

Strategic planning is serious work, hard work. The future is not easily predictable, but with careful analysis strategic opportunities can be anticipated and plans can be made to take advantage of opportunities as they occur. By doing the hard work of analysis and planning management will generate the information employees need to do effective and efficient work. Second in importance to creating strategic and operating plans is communicating the plans to those who will make them happen.

In most organizations there is not a sufficient follow-through to the annual planning process. Plans and budgets are made by top management without much involvement with or communication to the first- and second-level managers and employees who must execute the plans. Planning and budgeting are often done under pressure in the six to eight weeks before the beginning of the fiscal year. Then, once the plans and budgets have been approved, everyone breathes a sigh of relief, puts the planning books on the shelf, and goes back to the "real work." When the budgets are complete and approved, they are said to have been "put to bed," where everyone hopes they will sleep peacefully for the rest of the year.

Throughout the year monthly budget variance reports are prepared and occasionally reviewed. Sales and production figures are checked regularly, but no actions are taken unless there is a severe negative variance. Sometimes there is a flurry of activity in the fourth quarter to make the year's results come out close to plan. For the most part planning is a once-a-year activity without a sufficient direct impact on daily events.

Focus *and* Charges

GainPlanning includes a management practice designed to extend the planning process to the daily work of the organization, to ensure that everyone is informed of and stays focused on the company's direction and objectives.

Each month top management selects the productivity improvement **Focus** for the whole company, which is derived from the annual operating plan. (*Note:* The word *company* is used here and throughout to mean the GainManagement unit, be it a single company or a plant, division, office, region, or other part of a larger corporation or organization.) The monthly **Focus** is further divided into **Charges** for each work team. Throughout the month, employees are expected to find ways to solve the problem or meet the goal expressed by their team's **Charge.**

In this way the planning process is kept alive and meaningful throughout the year. At the same time the employee-participation process is integrated with and made relevant to the company's business plan and purpose. Employee participation will be haphazard or focused, poor or excellent, to the extent that it is planned and coordinated with the larger and longer-range goals and efforts of the company. The **Focus** and **Charge** will be explained in more detail in Chapter 6. Here we want to emphasize that in GainPlanning the management practice of directing is extended in a way that encourages all employees to participate actively in the achievement of the company's operating plan. In GainManagement employee participation is not an extra added attraction, it is the main feature.

3. Organizing

The third GainPlanning practice is to organize resources to do the work of the company. Efficiency especially requires organization, and in situations where there are several competitors seeking to serve one market, the major share will go to the company best organized to serve the market. Organization makes it possible to be the low-cost, high-quality producer. Organization enabled Ford to assemble a Model T in 93 minutes and sell it profitably for $400.

The organizing issues to consider in GainPlanning are:

- ⌃ Providing good tools, technology, and systems
- ⌃ Establishing a structure for participation and teamwork
- ⌃ Decision making at the proper level

Tools, Technology, and Systems

As pieces of the Berlin Wall were carted away and Eastern Europe emerged from the dark night of communism, it became obvious that geopolitics was not the only residual problem. The productive capability of these countries was in shambles. They simply did not have the plants, equipment, tools, technology, or systems to compete in world markets. In fact, they were unable to meet their own basic needs. It would be difficult to find more dramatic proof that for an organization to succeed management must provide the tools people need to do good work. In stark and ironic contrast was the East German athletic enterprise. The East Germans dominated the Olympic Games from 1976 to 1988 because at Leipzig they had an athletic institute with more tools, technology, and systems than the world of athletics has ever seen. The political leaders of East Germany decided they wanted excellence in athletics to bolster the country's international image. To achieve this goal they provided modern electronic tools, state-of-the-art chemical and medical technology, and systems for careful selection and superior training. Few organizations have the ability to divert resources from other essentials to a single goal as East Germany did, but the lesson is clear. When management provides the tools, organizations can excel.

Management must see to it that the organization has excellent tools, technology, and systems, but in GainManagement all employees participate in this process. Production machine operators are included in the selection of new equipment and challenged to think of ways to make it better. Secretaries and typists select word processing software, and truck drivers help select new trucks and tires. This is the principle of openness to new ideas in action.

In Oregon the truck drivers in one of the large forest-products companies wanted Michelin tires for their logging trucks. The drivers knew that Michelin tires were more expensive but were convinced that they were safer, more durable, and overall more cost-effective. The purchasing department ignored their request and continued to buy another less expensive brand.

It was a common joke among these drivers that the less expensive tires seemed to hit rocks more often, causing blowouts. With a wink and a nudge the drivers complained that when the cheap tires blew out, they took almost three hours to change. The drivers claimed that Michelin tires were safer, did not blow out as often, and when they did blow out could be changed in about thirty minutes.

This not so subtle resistance on the part of the truck drivers was not only about tires, it was also about management's responsibility to provide excellent tools and about employee participation in this management process. It was about the principle of openness to new ideas, about making the "best" decisions, and about decisions being accepted by those who must execute them.

Structure for Participation and Teamwork

Another aspect of organizing is structuring the organization for participation. All organizations must be structured for work, for communications, and for reciprocal influence. The most common organization structures are functional, decentralized, or matrix. Management must structure and staff using whatever form is best suited to the work and communications needs of the company.

In GainPlanning special attention must be given to structures that allow every employee to participate actively. The basic structural unit for work and participation is the work team. Today, in organizations, large and small, no one works isolated from other workers. All work is done by workers in teams. In many cases this team structure is already in place. There are sales teams, toolroom teams, accounting teams, quality-assurance teams, management teams, lab teams, purchasing teams, store teams, and so on. Most teams are made up of workers doing similar tasks, such as customer-service teams, or around a specific work function, such as the maintenance team. Certain structural patterns have become traditional and are repeated in company after company. GainPlanning must provide structures that facilitate maximum participation. Some conventional structures or those set up for administrative convenience may have to be altered to facilitate worker participation.

The basic work team structure for GainManagement is the overlapping work team form of organization. It is pictured in Chapter 6 (Figure 6-4). In this model there are functional work teams overlapped by management work teams. Many work teams will be the same as those in traditional departmental structures. Larger departments such as production or assembly may have to be subdivided into smaller work teams to improve participation.

Almost every organization has its "orphans," workers who are not on a team. The most common of these are secretaries, receptionists, clerks, staff specialists, and some factory indirect workers such as janitors. All these employees must be assigned to teams and given full membership. For instance, the secretary to the CEO works with top management and is, therefore, a member of the top management team. This is also true for the engineering, sales, or manufacturing secretary or file clerk. That secretaries are not vice presidents, engineers, or production managers must not exclude them from full team membership. Receptionists are usually members of the purchasing, human resources, or other administrative team. Solitary staff specialists can be included with a related team: Janitors can be added to the maintenance team and so forth. It is not difficult to identify the orphans, and a bit of analysis and thought will find an appropriate team for them.

Structures must expedite the free flow of communications and influence throughout the organization. The growth in size and complexity of businesses and other institutions has led to more organizational levels and greater specialization. Multiple organizational levels create more vertical distance between people in companies. Vertical

When work teams were first set up at a specialty food processing company, there was a question about how to structure the
material handlers. This was a department of seven forklift
drivers, each of whom supported one specific manufacturing
line. The seven drivers worked in four different buildings and
seldom moved from their department or building.

The planning committee began to consider how problem
solving might proceed among these seven materials handlers
and in the manufacturing lines each serviced. The committee
discovered that, aside from some routine maintenance issues,
the seven material handlers had little in common and knew
very little about each other's daily work. On the other hand, it
was anticipated that problem solving in the manufacturing
teams would often include material handling solutions. The
decision was made to disband the material handling department and assign the workers to the production teams they
served, not only for problem solving but for all of their work
assignments. The material handling manager was reassigned
to an open position in shipping. This resulted in an annual cost
savings of more than $25,000 and was implemented before
the company's first problem-solving meeting.

distance, with its status, pay, and perquisite differentials, is a major
obstacle to open communication.

Experts claim that communications flowing downward in a hierarchical organization lose 20% of their content, meaning, understanding, and acceptance as they pass through each level. At this rate in a
small machine shop with three levels—an owner-president, production superintendent, and toolroom foreman—the toolmaker gets
51.2% of the communications that originate with the president. At
huge companies such as the auto and electronic giants the president
and toolmaker aren't even aware of each other's existence, let alone
able to communicate effectively. The impact of this is to limit how
open workers are to one another's communications and influence.
Limited openness is a cause of misunderstanding and misdirection,
which shows up in inefficiency, wasted time and effort, poor quality,
late deliveries, and poor service.

There is a healthy trend to eliminate unnecessary layers in
organizations. However, it will be impossible to remove all vertical

distance, so organizations must develop structures that are more open to communications and influence—up, down, and sideways.

The structure of the organization, in addition to facilitating communications and participation, must create vertical and horizontal teamwork and cooperation. The we/they adversarial relationship that has characterized so many organizations in the past is an impediment to productivity and quality of work life. Managers must take the initiative to reduce the psychological distance between levels in the organization. Some of the trappings of rank and status are obstacles to communications and a healthy spirit of teamwork. These status symbols and perquisites need to be reexamined and, where they obstruct teamwork, modified or eliminated. The real issue, however, is not office furnishings or parking spaces, it is the we/they attitude that must be rooted out and replaced with a spirit of partnership. Everyone and every team should be accountable for cooperation and coordination. The responsibility to cooperate should be written into job descriptions for individuals and teams.

There is also a problem of a lack of teamwork and coordination between functions in organizations. The cause of this problem is the growth of professionalism and specialization in complex organizations. Engineering, marketing, sales, manufacturing, finance, and other disciplines are becoming so specialized that it is difficult for them to communicate with each other. Each department tends to concentrate on its own goals and standards which, combined with a lack of understanding of the other functions, leads to a lack of cooperation. What begins as a lack of understanding and cooperation can easily escalate to serious and often hostile competition. No organization can afford the inefficiency and waste of internal competition. There needs to be a high level of internal teamwork for a company to be an excellent competitor in the market or for any organization to be an excellent performer. GainPlanning must provide structures that encourage teamwork and communications to and from all parts of the organization.

Decision Making at the Proper Level

Considering all of the talk in management training courses about delegation there is very little of it actually taking place. One reason for this is that most management training does not correctly explain delegation. It is frequently presented to managers as delegating their own work and decisions to lower-level managers and workers. Managers should not delegate their own work to others; rather they should delegate work that properly belongs to others.

If the maintenance manager is responsible for repair and maintenance of machines and equipment, he or she should have the authority to carry out that responsibility. Too often decisions of the first-line managers must be reviewed by two or three more levels of management before they can be implemented. This not only wastes time, it also wastes talent. When managers are allowed to make most of their own decisions, those decisions are implemented more effectively and efficiently. In addition, the manager learns responsibility and develops experience and self-confidence for making decisions.

The GainManagement process encourages senior managers to push decision making to its proper level.

The third time the motor burned out on the surface grinder, the electrician told the maintenance manager that the machine was too heavy for a five-horsepower motor. He recommended they install a seven-horsepower motor to prevent future breakdowns. If the manager and the electrician had been given the proper authority, the problem would have been solved immediately with no further loss of production. But the decision had to go up the line for review and approval.

While the decision was being approved two levels up, another five-horsepower motor burned out and more hours of production were lost. In addition, the manager and the electrician had the experience that their expertise was not respected and that they were not trusted. The irony of this is that in the approval chain were line and staff managers who did not know one horsepower from another. The net effect of this failure to put decision making where it belongs was lost productivity, unnecessary expense, and a negative experience for two employees.

---

4. Communicating

The fourth GainPlanning practice is communications. In the words of Tommy Badley, "Communication is creating understanding. It's not communications until understanding exists on both ends of the megaphone." It is not enough to write a memo, hold a meeting, put a notice on a bulletin board, or complete a report. The memo, the meeting, the notice, or the report must be understood. There are three building blocks to effective GainPlanning communications. Structure, the first block, was discussed above under organization. The other two, the communication processes and their content, will be covered in this section.

Communications Processes

There are many components to the communications processes of an organization. Much has been written and said about the processes of communications including techniques such as memos, reports, and meetings. Training is readily available on the subjects of effective writing and meeting leadership, techniques that must be done well in GainManagement. However, two other aspects of the communications process, often overlooked, must receive special attention as a GainPlanning management practice. They are basic education and responsiveness.

First, all employees must be educated to the point where they understand the information in newsletters, memos, and meetings. In the 1960s there was a major effort spearheaded by U.S. Steel and the Council for Economic Education to explain the American business system to employees. Training programs were conducted that explained such basic business concepts as capital formation, how to read profit and loss statements and balance sheets, how the stock markets work, and the fundamentals of the free market system. Today the need for this kind of education is greater than ever. It must be included in GainPlanning.

In addition, new ways must be found to explain business information so that it can be understood. Many companies hold monthly or quarterly business information meetings where sales, cost, and profit data are presented to employee groups. Too often this information is presented in a technical format that only the professionals can fully understand. This frustrates employees because they want to know but can't understand the information in the way it is presented—and they don't often feel comfortable asking questions. Managers are also frustrated when they get blank stares and continuing complaints about the lack of information. Employees must know what the business is all about and how things are going for them to be an effective resource for improving performance. It is good

GainPlanning practice for management to explain organizational information in ways that are easily understandable, clear, and concise.

The second process element is responsiveness. When teams are charged to solve a problem or to raise a standard of performance, they respond with suggestions and action plans. Management must then respond by acting upon those suggestions and action plans, and quickly. Managers respond to suggestions and action plans in several ways. To suggestions requiring decisions their response is approval or disapproval—again, quickly and thoroughly. Approvals should be accompanied by recognition and celebration. Disapprovals should be accompanied by education and explanation. Unacceptable action plans are as useful to the company as acceptable ones. They indicate a lack of understanding that, properly corrected, will lead to future acceptable suggestions and action plans. When management invites workers to participate, they must respond to that participation.

Content

To make real gains in productivity everyone must know and understand where the company is going and how it intends to get there. The employees must also have up-to-date information about the successes and failures along the way. These three things, which can be summed up as goals, plan, and progress, are the essential content of communications. Knowledge and understanding in all three areas will determine the level of performance and quality of problem solving.

Management must communicate its vision and the mission or purpose for which the organization exists to all the constituents of the business, but especially to the employees. In high-performing organizations workers know, understand, and are committed to the purpose of the organization. In mediocre companies workers may know the company's mission through posters or brochures, but they neither understand it nor are they committed to accomplishing it.

Next, management must communicate the strategic objectives, which are a source of ideas and energy for GainMaking. An understanding of and commitment to strategic objectives will cause work teams to reach for the best solutions rather than be content with good-enough solutions. Communicating strategic objectives is not a simple matter of making an announcement or printing a brochure. These communications require thorough explanations as well as the basic education to help workers understand the business and its strategies.

The ideal in GainPlanning is for managers to open the process and enable workers to influence the organization's strategy. Those employees who create the strategy know it, understand it, and are committed to it. They own it. The more that employees participate in these processes, the greater will be their understanding and commitment. This does not mean that every employee must attend all of the strategic planning meetings. It does mean that when an employee has an idea or suggestion about the organization's strategic planning, it must be heard with respect and there must be an appropriate response. Most employees will not try to influence strategy early in the program, but as their understanding and commitment grow and the organization becomes more open, they will certainly do so.

The annual operating plan with its objectives, budgets, and schedules must also be communicated to employees so that they understand it in detail. For most companies this is a formidable undertaking because so few people today understand operating plans and budgets. A start must be made because this lack of knowledge is a major cause of low performance, loss of market share, and internal company ailments such as lack of trust and cooperation. There is no special technique for communicating annual operating plans and budgets. By analyzing the current level of awareness and understanding, however, the needs of different groups of employees can be determined. The first step is to remove the veil of secrecy that has covered so much of this information. This will allow teams and individual employees to act on their own to satisfy their need for information. Beyond this first step we would advise a slow but steady program to educate and inform all employees.

GainPlanning includes monthly goal setting. Each month top management reviews operations and selects a problem area or an opportunity area as the **Focus** for the monthly work team problem-solving meetings. From the **Focus** comes the individual team **Charges**. As teams struggle to solve their assigned **Charges** and develop action plans, their understanding of budgets, operating plans, and strategic objectives will gradually increase. This will not be instantaneous but will come little by little. As workers understand each monthly **Charge**, they will begin to understand the larger goals and plans from which they were derived. Some specialized training and education will accelerate this process.

Another valuable understanding that occurs as a result of the monthly **Focus** and **Charge** is that of common effort. Management can preach endlessly about common fate, teamwork, and interunit cooperation with little impact. But the experience of the whole organization attacking a common problem, and succeeding, is a lesson with impact.

Finally, there must be good communications about how things are going. There is a very good reason why there are big elaborate scoreboards at athletic contests: Both players and spectators want to know how things are going. If one team is behind by one run or one basket, its players will try just a little bit harder and its fans will cheer just a little bit louder on the next at-bat or possession.

Imagine a basketball game where only the scorekeeper knows the score until the game is over. The spectators would lose interest very quickly. The players might continue to pass, dribble, and shoot

---

One of the major goals for the GainManagement program in a West Coast machinery manufacturing company was to improve teamwork between the office and the factory. In the first month the office folks were surprised when management set as the monthly *Focus*: To improve factory margin by 10% . Work teams in accounting, engineering, sales, and data processing were sure that they had little to do with factory margin. This perception changed with a simple explanation that factory margin could be improved by either of two actions: higher prices or lower manufacturing costs. Factory margin is just one of many measures of profit. The accounting team took as their **Charge** the task of increasing the accuracy of quotes to increase revenue, and the sales team selected as their **Charge** to increase selling prices. The data processing team chose the **Charge** of getting more timely cost information to the factory, and the engineering team agreed to the **Charge** of redesigning two products. With these **Charges** the office teams acknowledged that they indeed have a stake and a significant impact on the profit margin that can be earned in manufacturing. Workers in both office and factory were surprised and pleased at the number and variety of action plans to improve factory margin that came from the office work team problem-solving meetings. For many this was a first experience of office-factory cooperation and a big step toward the elimination of one of the company's major obstacles to improved productivity.

because they enjoy working on their individual skills. However, they would lose intensity and teamwork as the experience would be more like a practice session than the game we know.

People have the same need to know the score at work in the office or factory. Progress and results should be reported back to the employees who are working to achieve those results, and the reports should be quick. As the whole communications process increases workers' understanding and commitment to results, good progress reports become a cause for celebration and continued effort, while bad progress reports are a stimulus for extra effort and creative problem solving.

There should be progress reports for the total organization and for each work team. Organization progress reports should include monthly sales, production, productivity, quality, and safety reports. For each team there should be reports of output, errors, efficiency, and so on. GainShare statements, in addition to telling employees whether or not they earned a bonus, are very valuable as an organizational scorecard. (This is explained in Chapter 7.)

Efforts to improve communication have benefits well beyond the knowledge and information that are exchanged. Better communication builds trust. It provides the raw material for better problem solving. It unifies an organization as more employees feel that they are part of the inner circle, those "in the know." Hiding and hoarding information leads to mistrust and mistakes that no organization can afford.

5. Motivating

The fifth GainPlanning practice is to motivate. Leaders must create a spirit of excellence in their organizations. The most publicized examples of excellent spirit come from military units and team sports. We often refer to the esprit de corps of elite military units such as the West Point Corps of Cadets, the U.S. Marine Corps, or the Green Berets. Even more frequently we note team spirit of excellent athletic teams such as Notre Dame football teams or the 1980 U.S. Olympic hockey team. Although team spirit is not as common in business, there have been examples of companies with a spirit of excellence. In 1983 7,000 employees of Delta Airlines turned out to christen a new airplane named "The Spirit of Delta." The $30 million plane was purchased by voluntary employee contributions and presented to the company as an expression of employee satisfaction.

Spirit in an organization is not easily defined, but it is easily observable whether it is a good spirit or a mean one. It is possible to observe the spirit of an organization as customers, employees, suppliers, or neighbors. Customers observe the spirit of an organization at the checkout stand or when they open the box and use the product. Seattle-based Nordstrom department stores and Federal Express have become famous for the spirit of customer service that characterizes their operations. Employees see the spirit of their organization in the attitude and performance of managers and coworkers. Suppliers see it in fair treatment or on-time payments. The community sees the spirit of the organization in its buildings, its willingness to maintain a healthy environment, and in the socially responsible actions of the company and its employees.

The people in the organization manifest the spirit of excellence, but it is the work of management to create that spirit. This is done by openly espousing the principle of commitment to excellence. Managers must constantly remind the organization to strive for excellence. They must talk it, recognize it, and reward it in all they do.

The second step is to make achievement the primary motivation for individuals, for teams, and for the entire organization. In Chapter 1 we presented lists of today's satisfiers and motivators (see Figure 1-2). The list of motivators has one dominant theme: *achievement.* When workers are motivated by higher-order needs, as they are in the United States and other developed countries, managers must manage in a way that enables workers to achieve. Managers must accept that they cannot buy excellent performance. Wages and benefits alone will only buy average performance. Workers today, especially the growing numbers of knowledge workers, will put forward basic effort for wages, but achievement alone motivates excellence.

GainManagement provides a process that enables workers to achieve. It involves workers in planning, goal setting, problem solving, innovation, and policy. This involvement enables all workers, not just a few managers, to contribute to the success of the organization. It enables everyone in the organization to say with conviction; "Look what we did." This is the new motivation: achievement. To motivate, management must make it possible for the worker to achieve.

6. Measuring

Measuring is the sixth GainPlanning practice essential to high levels of performance. Without a stopwatch Roger Bannister would never have broken the four-minute mile barrier. First, it is doubtful that anyone would run a mile that fast unless he could prove it. Second, without a stopwatch who would know that it had been done in three minutes and fifty-nine seconds? Measuring and maintaining records is one of the primary reasons why the Olympic Games are so exciting and produce efforts of Homeric proportions.

Businesses, governments, hospitals, schools, and other organizations record, count, and analyze a great many things. Computers on almost every desk create a virtually unlimited capacity to process data. Despite this remarkable capability most organizations do a poor

---

The president of a foundry in the Northwest had just concluded his quarterly profit-sharing status report to the employees. He had given them the bad news that there would be no profit sharing for the quarter and most likely for the entire year. The primary cause, he explained using color graphics, was excessive scrap. Scrap had increased 28% during the quarter to a monthly cost of $317,000—more than enough to wipe out profit sharing.

In the lunchroom after the meeting two melt shop employees were overhead discussing the meeting and the president's report.

Andrew | You know, that was a bogus report he just gave us about the cost of scrap. The $317,000 is the sales price of the parts that were rejected at final inspection. Most of those parts are repaired and sold at full price. The only lost profit is the extra cost of repair. And there is some salvage value even to the parts that cannot be repaired. They are remelted and recast. Scrap may be up but not to the tune of $317,000. I wonder what really happened to profits last quarter?

Brendon | I really believe scrap is a problem, though. I'd do something about it, but I don't know if my operation is causing any of the scrap. The only time I hear there is a problem is at these quarterly meetings. If scrap is coming from my furnace, why doesn't somebody tell me? If I knew what was wrong, I'll bet I could fix some of it.

job of measuring the performance and productivity of work. Some-times the wrong things are measured. Sometimes the measurements are improperly applied. One thing is clear: the measurements of work and of people at work do not produce effort reminiscent of Olympic performance.

Organizations need to have measures for profit, productivity, quality, and delivery that are accurate and that are meaningful to those who use the information to improve performance.

Multiple measures of profit are needed because none of the common measures is completely satisfactory. Profit margin and per-cent to sales are good measures for setting selling prices and to indicate when costs are excessive. Return on investment is a good measure of how well assets are being used. Dollar profit goals in a budget are useful as targets and as limits on spending. Another profit measurement that goes with strategic planning is minimum profit— the profit needed to cover current obligations (dividends) and future growth (to fund strategic plans). Several profit measures should be used, and all must be explained to increase employees' understand-ing of the business and to give them an accurate perspective for their problem solving.

A footnote on the measurement of profit is the time frame for measuring profit. Many businesses measure profit monthly, quar-terly, and annually. These are useful checkpoints, but the only meaningful profit measurement is over a period of three to five years. Excessive concern about short-term profits causes poor management decisions and is responsible for much of the current negative em-ployee feelings about profit. Organizations must spend money to develop, and such spending lowers profits in the short run. Periods of low profitability may alternate with periods of high profitability. Only the cumulative average of several years tells the true story of profit.

Productivity is another very important measurement, the single most important measurement for improving performance. Unfortu-nately, productivity is poorly understood. Managers either equate productivity with profit or apply it only to labor cost and, what is worse, only to direct labor cost. Employees tend to misunderstand productivity as output per hour or just more volume. They often equate higher productivity with working harder or speedups.

This limited definition of productivity as output per labor-hour comes from economists who develop national productivity statistics. These economists divide the gross national product by the total number of hours employees worked to create a national productivity index of output per hour of work. These statistics are somewhat useful to track annual changes and trends in a nation's economy, to compare sectors of the economy, and to compare one country's economy with that of others. However, this output per labor-hour definition of productivity not only is of very little value to a company, it is actually harmful because it is misleading.

Labor is only one factor in the operation of a business. What businesses and other organizations need are productivity measures for every key resource they use in making their products or service. They need productivity measures for capital, raw materials, labor (both physical and mental), utilities, office space, and even for other resources such as credit, advertising, and R&D.

Productivity measures are ratios of inputs to outputs. Productivity means the amount of output obtained for any given amount of input. GainPlanning should provide each work team with one overall measure of their productivity and separate measures for the productivity of the major resources they use in their work. At the individual or work team level productivity is measured as dollars, hours, or materials used per unit of output; i.e., unit labor cost, unit material cost, and total cost per unit. At the company level productivity is the ratio of all inputs (total costs) to the sales value of the output. The sales value must be included because the customer decides what the company's output is worth. The best overall measures of productivity are return on investment or one of several similar other measures such as return on equity and return on assets. These measurements combine the productivity of labor, materials, and all other expenses with the productivity of the company's capital investment and compare both to revenue in a single, comprehensive ratio of total productivity.

Quality is another important measure and a major preoccupation of businesses aspiring to be serious competitors in world markets. Customers can now buy automobiles, electronic equipment, clothing, food, and gift items from all over the world. For some products price alone will determine what the customer will buy, but for many products, especially "big-ticket" items, quality is the decisive factor. Quality must be measured and steadily improved not only to please the customers and keep production costs down but also to satisfy the internal need for excellence. The organization and the work teams require meaningful quality measurements and timely feedback. Current programs of total quality management and statistical process control provide very good quality measurements.

The use of these excellent techniques should be expanded. Sophisticated measurement programs, however, are not sufficient in and of themselves. To be effective these techniques must be applied using the principles and practices described throughout this chapter. While measurements are essential to improvement, the measurement alone is not the source of motivation. Achievement is the motivator, and it takes all of these principles and practices to motivate people to achieve.

There is also the need to measure the timeliness of work. This varies according to the mission of the organization, but it would be on-time deliveries for an express mail company or time to design and make a customized machine for a toolmaker. Critical internal times should also be measured to provide problem-solving information to help teams reduce operating times. Tools and techniques for time measurements have been available from industrial engineering for years. Unfortunately, these techniques have been used to control people rather than to control work. Time study, M-TM, work sampling, and other methods take on a whole new dimension when they are used to provide information for workers to do problem solving rather than to control workers.

The purpose of all of these measurements—profit, productivity, quality, and time—is to provide information for problem solving and performance improvement. Measurements make it possible to set goals, concentrate problem-solving efforts, and determine progress. Providing the measurements needed for excellence is a twofold management task. First, there is a need to invent simple and meaningful measurements for the organization, for work teams, and for individual workers. Second, there is a need to educate work teams and members to understand the more complex broad-scale measurements that show the work team's role and contribution to the work of the organization.

7. Developing

The final GainPlanning practice is the responsibility of management to develop. This is the last management practice to be discussed in this chapter and, in a sense, *develop* is the last word on the subject of management practices. This word *develop* occurs regularly in management literature. There is market development, product development, organization development, research and development, management development, and business development, to name a few. In fact, one of management's most consequential practices is to develop. The dictionary provides several definitions for the word *develop:*

- ▲ To grow
- ▲ To expand
- ▲ To make more effective

An organization can be grown, expanded, and made more effective: It is management's task and responsibility to do just that.

In the short run—a day, a week, a month—there is not much management can do to make the business perform. The salespeople are out in the field or in the stores talking to customers. Machinists are in the shop, and engineers are designing. The refinery is refining. The train is moving down the track. Everything happening today is the result of past management practices. Strategies were set, materials and machines were purchased, people were hired and trained last month or last year. What the organization does today is what management has developed it to do.

What management does today will determine the organization's performance next month and next year. Management's concern with today's performance is to measure it, analyze it, and decide what can and should be done to develop it. Management's attention should always be on improving future performance. Managers who spend time nagging people for better short-term performance have allowed their attention to stray from their true objective. System 4 or 5 managers have little time to police the work of employees. They are preoccupied with developing the organization for tomorrow. They use today's results for planning tomorrow's performance.

The company, hospital, school, or agency must be developed to produce better-quality products and services. Management devises measurements and systems to determine how well products and services meet the quality and value expectations of the customers, who define quality and value. When products and services are not meeting the needs of customers, action is initiated to correct the problem. When products and services are meeting the current expectations of customers, managers determine what the customers' future needs will be. They also determine why the organization's products and services are not meeting the expectations of those who are not customers. All of this information is used to develop the quality of the company's output and expand its markets and sales.

Productivity is the efficient use of all the company's resources. It is management's job to develop productivity. Managers personally account for only a small fraction of the company's total work time, and they hardly ever touch the company's raw materials or capital equipment. Managers develop the company's productivity by ensuring that workers are informed, trained, and motivated, that work is organized for productivity, and that the necessary capital equipment and raw materials are available. Then management measures and analyzes today's productivity and plans how to develop it for even better productivity tomorrow. Managers provide more information and training, organize the work better, and provide better resources for tomorrow's improved productivity.

The organization's most important resource and the one most responsive to development is people. Things begin to wear out the moment they are made. All we can do with things—machines, tools, buildings, trucks—is slow down their rate of deterioration by careful use and maintenance. With people the opposite is true. The day a person is hired he or she is almost useless to the company. In fact, new people have a negative effect on performance because they require the attention of other workers, who must stop productive work to train the newcomers. But with experience new people grow and become more valuable resources. Best of all they have an unlimited capacity to grow throughout their working career.

Under authoritarian management Systems 1 and 2 management was content to develop new people to an acceptable level and leave it at that. In GainManagement there is no upper limit on the development of people. Strategic objectives are set for human resources development, and management sees to it that adequate resources are committed to the task.

The purpose of most human resource development programs, especially the popular manager development programs, is to prepare people for promotions to higher levels of responsibility. Organizations are pyramidal, so only a few people from each level will ever be promoted. Today's development programs apply only to that small proportion of the organization's human resources who will be promoted.

In GainPlanning every person must be developed to do a better job of the work at hand. Human resource development must be expanded to give more attention to the horizontal dimension. Salespeople must learn more about how the products they sell are designed and manufactured. Production people must learn more about what goes on in engineering. Engineers must learn more about sales, and everyone must learn more about finance, human resources management, and marketing. Excellence is the goal not just for products but for people . . . all of the people. Excellent people will make excellent products and an excellent organization.

Finally, management must develop teams. The idea of the individual contributor in today's complex organizations is as obsolete as the Model T. There is very little of consequence one person can do working alone in a modern organization. Individual workers depend on other workers for information, materials, maintenance, authorizations, recommendations, reports, designs, drawings, and expertise. As the size and complexity of organizations has grown, the basic working unit has become the team.

Teamwork is necessary to operate big crew-served machinery, to produce engineering designs, to sell a computer, to complete complex reports. This is not to say that individuals don't accomplish things. They do. But what the individual does only takes on meaning when it combines with the work of others to become a complete product or service that has value for a customer. Today at work, more than ever before, no one is an island; everyone is a piece of the whole.

It is fairly simple to design a basic work team structure and assign people to their proper teams. It is much more difficult to develop effective teamwork. There is very little experience to draw upon, and the American culture still worships at the altar of rugged individualism. Team sports are used as primary examples, but they are not perfect examples of work teams in business or other organizations. A football team, for instance, only really functions as a team for about three hours a week. Athletic team experience is more comparable to project teamwork such as quality circles. We must develop teams to work harmoniously and effectively eight hours a day, 40 hours a week, for years.

This is the big development task facing today's manager. How to develop teams . . . make them grow and be more effective. Team development must include efforts to improve the quality of work life. It is not enough that teams produce more and better widgets, designs, or sales. They must also produce a better quality of work life for themselves and their members. Fortunately, all the experimentation of the past 30 years has produced many useful ideas to help the

Figure 5-2. Job description for GainManagement production manager.

Δ DELTA MANAGEMENT GROUP   *JOB DESCRIPTION*

Title Assembly Manager   *Name*   John Davidich   *Date* Jan 1992

Department   Production   *Reports to*   Manufacturing Manager
==

BASIC PURPOSE:

To develop and lead an excellent Production Department capable of assembling high-quality products efficiently and on time.

PRINCIPAL RESPONSIBILITIES:

1. Carefully and thoroughly selects, assigns, and trains assembly personnel for safe, effective work.
2. Coaches employees to high levels of performance, achievement, and personal growth. Responds well to employee needs and concerns.
3. Plans and organizes personnel, materials, systems, schedules, and tools for productivity. Helps to resolve problems and handle exceptions as they occur.
4. Provides direction to work team. Sets high standards and leads by example. Communicates Focus, Charge, goals, and priorities. Provides useful performance feedback to teams and individuals.
5. Leads work teams in effective goal setting, problem solving, and innovation. Encourages constant thinking and creativity. Holds effective team problem-solving meetings to analyze work and develop action plans. Follows through on all action plans.
6. Communicates regularly and accurately to superiors, peers, subordinates. Listens well and communicates effectively, both orally and in writing.
7. Ensures the effective and consistent administration of all company policies and programs within the department (wages, benefits, safety, EEO, OSHA, performance coaching, recognition, and the collective bargaining contract).

DIMENSIONS:

Sales: $ N/A   *Operating Budget FY92:* $ 495,200
People: Direct reports 19   *Total* 19
Other: Two work teams: subassembly, final assembly

KEY RESULTS EXPECTED: *(annual or permanent)*

1. Meet all assembly schedules with high-quality products.
2. Achieve annual department productivity goals. FY92—8% improvement
3. Steadily increase employee involvement and commitment. FY92—20% increase in suggestions and Action Plans.
4. Continually improve the climate of trust between management and employees. FY92—survey score 4.00
5. Coordinate the work of the department with other production and staff departments.

SCOPE OF AUTHORITY:

The assembly manager has authority to carry out the responsibilities of this job within the constraints of the law, company policy, and the labor contract.
Signing authority for up to $500 for work team Action Plans.

SIGNATURES: /s/ John Davidich   /s/ Rose Ann Ashcraft
                     Incumbent   *Manager*

managers develop their teams. Team problem-solving meetings, which will be described in Chapter 6, provide a good starting place for team development. Management must set themselves the task of defining team excellence, measuring it, and little by little developing more team effectiveness.

Summary

GainPlanning is the first step in the GainManagement process. It consists of four principles: (1) commitment to excellence, (2) openness to new ideas, (3) equity for all partners, and (4) teamwork. These principles are the basis for the seven GainPlanning practices of management: (1) leading, (2) directing, (3) organizing, (4) communicating, (5) motivating, (6) measuring, and (7) developing. The bulk of this work and the final responsibility rests with the managers of the company: CEO, vice-presidents, department managers, and first-line managers. However, consistent with the need for greater participation by all employees, GainPlanning is not exclusively a task for managers. All employees should be encouraged and developed to participate with managers in the management processes of the company. This is the ideal and a central concept of GainManagement. How to bring all employees into the process of management will be further explained in the next chapter.

The material in this chapter should be used to create new job descriptions that incorporate GainPlanning management practices. Figure 5-2 is an example of one GainManagement company's job description for a first-line manager, which incorporates many of the preceding GainPlanning practices. These management practices must become the center of performance appraisals for managers and the basis for manager development programs. One key to developing an excellent organization is developing excellent managers.

Notes

1. Max De Pree, *Leadership Is an Art* (New York: Doubleday, 1989).
2. 1990 Annual Report, General Electric Company. Fairfield, Conn.
3. G. Hamel and C. K. Prahalad, "Strategic Intent," *Harvard Business Review* (May–June 1989).
4. Peter F. Drucker, *Management: Tasks, Responsibilities, Practices* (New York: Harper & Row, 1973).

Chapter 6

GainMaking

GainMaking is where things start to happen in the GainManagement process. As traditional gainsharing programs atrophy into incentive plans, they lose their ability to create real gains in productivity, performance, and quality of work life. Since there can be no Gain-Sharing without GainMaking, GainManagement goes well beyond the level of employees participation that was characteristic of the gainsharing programs of the 1980s.

In our 1983 book, *Gainsharing and Productivity*, we presented three possible levels of employee participation: (1) suggestion boxes, (2) suggestion committees, and (3) work teams.[1] In light of today's needs, both organizational and personal, the first two levels, which are passive systems with a less than total commitment to employee involvement, are no longer adequate. Past programs provided opportunities for employees to participate in problem solving and, to some extent, innovation. This was a good start, but the situation in the 1990s requires that employees participate even more in problem solving and innovation and that they begin to participate in the design of work processes, goals, strategy, and policy.

In the GainManagement process there are three key GainMaking thrusts:

- ▴ A formal team problem-solving structure
- ▴ System 5 team leadership
- ▴ The GainManagement council

These three activities are designed to facilitate high levels of employee participation in the five areas of work shown in the participation model described in Chapter 2. Team problem solving enables employees to participate in problem solving and innovation. System 5 team leadership encourages participation in the design of work processes and in goals and strategy. The GainManagement council allows for greater participation in policy making (see Figure 6-1).

The first part of this chapter describes an advanced work team participation program: a structured program for increasing participation in problem solving and innovation. The second part of the chapter explains team leadership as the essential skill for increasing participation, especially in the design of work processes and in goals and strategy. The ways to use the GainManagement council to involve employees in issues of policy are described in Chapter 11.

Team Problem Solving and Innovation

In *Leadership Is an Art* Max De Pree quotes Oliver Wendell Holmes's idea of simplicity: "I would not give a fig for simplicity this side of complexity, but I would give my life for simplicity the other side of complexity."[2] De Pree makes the case that leadership and management are not simple, but those who have wrestled with the complexity can make it look simple, just as Olympic divers make triple flips with two twists look simple. Simplicity is the result of a great deal of work to get past the complexity. GainMaking has the look and feel of simplicity. However, establishing GainMaking as the way an organization does business requires a lot of hard work—complexity. Devel-

Figure 6-1. Participation in management matrix.

STEP 1: Participation Opportunities

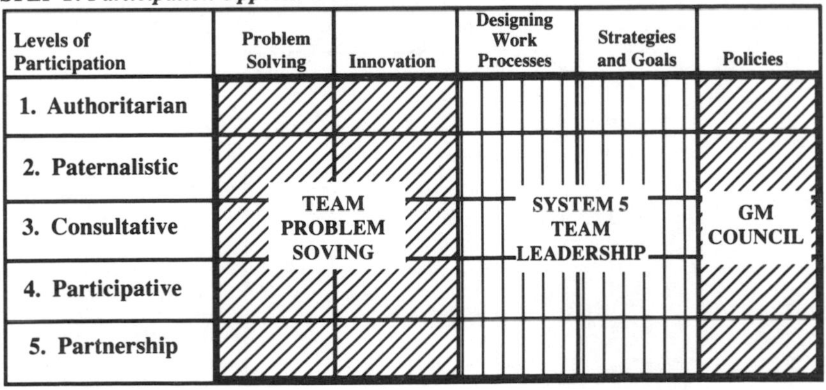

Levels of Participation	Problem Solving	Innovation	Designing Work Processes	Strategies and Goals	Policies
1. Authoritarian					
2. Paternalistic					
3. Consultative	TEAM PROBLEM SOVING		SYSTEM 5 TEAM LEADERSHIP		GM COUNCIL
4. Participative					
5. Partnership					

oping team problem solving into a highly successful management process takes a lot more than a batch of forms and suggestion boxes in lunchrooms. Managers must provide direction, structure, and information. Employees must be informed and skilled and must know how to use the structure. The GainMaking team problem-solving model in Figure 6-2 presents an overview of the GainMaking process that will produce useful employee ideas.

Team problem solving produces a variety of gains in productivity and quality of work life. This is a high-intensity process that must be mastered. The details of team problem solving will be presented under four main headings, as follows:

1. *Work Teams.* In the modern organization work is accomplished through a structure of overlapping work teams. GainMaking requires effective work teams, each with a clear purpose and measurable results.
2. *Meetings.* Team problem solving occurs in a series of meetings: management and team leader meetings, where problems are identified and coordinated; informational meetings, where problems and opportunities are communicated; and team

Figure 6-2.   GainMaking—team problem solving.

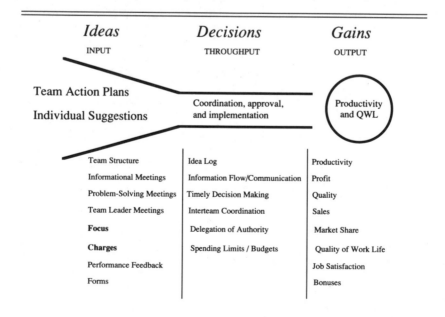

problem-solving meetings, where problems are solved and innovations created.

3. *Team Problem-Solving Process.* Once each month work teams meet to problem solve their team **Charge.** In one hour each team develops two action plans that will improve the performance of the work team and, therefore, the business.

4. *Processing and Resolving Ideas.* The action plans and suggestions developed by the teams will only benefit the organization when they are used. All these ideas must be resolved expeditiously. Procedures are needed to be sure ideas are tracked, implemented, and evaluated.

1. Work Teams

The work team is the basic organizational unit for working and for GainMaking. Every employee, from the CEO to the newest trainee, is a member of one or more work teams, and every work team has a defined role in the success of the organization. Teams have the potential for much greater accomplishment than groups of people working as individuals.

Work teams usually consist of 5 to 12 workers who share the responsibility for an important task. Teams are not teams simply because the members work in close physical proximity. Teams exist

Figure 6-3. Traditional departments vs. work teams.

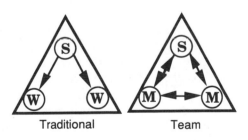

Traditional   Team

Department
workers
accountable to
the supervisor
for their own work

Members
accountable
to each other
for the team's
work

Figure 6-4.   Overlapping work teams.

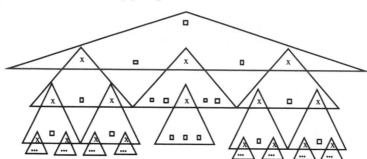

because they have a shared responsibility, which means that team members are accountable to each other for the work of the team. Figure 6-3 shows the relationship pattern between the team leaders and team members in traditional departments and in work teams.

Organizations are made up of a series of overlapping work teams. At the first level there are production teams and service teams. Traditional production departments usually consist of 15 to 30 workers. An analysis of tasks and relationships often shows that within a large production department there are two or three separate work teams. Above the production and service teams are first-level management work teams, staff work teams, and department management work teams. At the top of the organization is the executive work team. Figure 6-4 shows a model of overlapping teams.[3]

Each team has a specific function to perform, which is spelled out in a team job description (Figure 6-5). This job description defines the team's basic purpose, principal accountabilities, and relationship with other teams. A group of workers cannot begin to develop teamwork until they clearly understand what they are responsible for as a team. Teams within organizations are customers and suppliers of other teams. They receive work and information from some teams and provide the same to other teams. Most teams operate both inside and outside of the organization, although a few have exclusively internal relationships. All of these relationships must be spelled out so that employees better understand how unity of purpose and results is achieved in the organization. With this understanding coordination and cooperation grow.

In too many organizations today there is a serious lack of coordination and cooperation between functional departments. In this

Figure 6-5. Team job description.

Job Description

Region Management Team   Department: Southeast Region

Reports to: Vice President of Operations

Basic Purpose: To lead the region in accomplishing its mission of
managing assigned corporate assets to supply raw
materials to company manufacturing facilities and
sell surplus resources profitably.

Principal Accountabilities:
1. Develop and communicate strategic and operating goals and plans.
2. Organize the work of the region and provide support and resources.
3. Staff for the present and future with well-trained, highly motivated
   people.
4. Create a climate in which excellence is the standard according to
   corporate values and policies.
5. Measure and hold individuals and teams accountable for the
   continuous improvement of safety, productivity, profitability, quality
   of work life, and community relations.

- 1 -

Δ Delta Management Group

Figure 6-5 (*continued*).

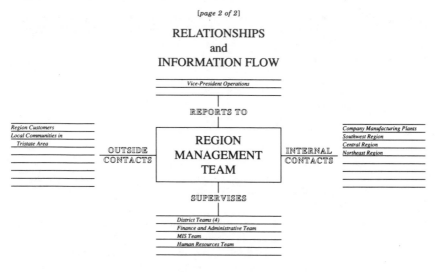

[page 2 of 2]

RELATIONSHIPS
and
INFORMATION FLOW

- 2 -

worst case there is overt hostility, which is very wasteful and a cause of lagging productivity. The work team organization in the Gain-Management process is intended to correct this problem by emphasizing the importance of teams and teamwork.

Performance measurements are essential for productivity improvement. The list of team accountabilities on the job description is used to establish standards of performance. In turn these are used to develop performance feedback information, which the team needs to review its operations and find ways to improve. There should be one overall team performance measurement and one or more micro measurements for each accountability.

It is important that the team determine or at least participate in establishing these performance standards and the information feedback process. A chronic complaint of employees under a traditional management system is their lack of control of their work. In these authoritarian systems management sets the standards and develops measurements to control the workers. The typical worker response to traditional controls is not so much to improve performance as to try to beat the system. GainMaking puts the measurement and the control in the hands of the workers, and they respond by improving performance.

An important role for the team leaders in this organization structure is that of the "linking pin" (shown by the Xs in Figure 6-4). First-level and middle managers are leaders of the teams they manage and also member of the next higher team. As a member of both teams they are the linking pins uniting the two work teams. The work of all the team leaders, as linking pins, unites the organization into a productive whole. This concept, pioneered by Likert[4] and employed in the GainManagement process, goes further than traditional notions about linkage. It includes the standard organization roles (chain of command and communication link), but it is also a unifying principle that enables a complex organization to coordinate its many separate tasks into a single output. Through these linking pins information, ideas, and suggestions flow up, down, and sideways to all parts of the organization. It is this coordination and free flow of information that enables the GainManagement organization to be highly productive. Information about goals, progress, and problems flows to where it is needed. Ideas and suggestions for innovation and problem solving flow to where they can be used.

2. Meetings

The GainMaking work of the teams is planned, coordinated, and executed through a series of meetings. There are three types of meetings in the GainMaking process, and while they serve several functions, each has a primary purpose in the GainMaking activity.

- ▲ Staff planning and coordination meetings are where the managers and team leaders decide the monthly productivity **Focus** and **Charges** and coordinate action plans and information.
- ▲ Team information meetings are where team members learn of plans, goals, problems, **Charges**, and issues of daily operations.
- ▲ Team problem-solving meetings are where teams develop action plans to solve problems of productivity according to their **Charge**.

All these meetings occur monthly as part of the company's standard meeting schedule. With the exception of the problem-solving meeting, most of the GainMaking meetings may be combined with staff meetings and information meetings that already exist. Figure 6-6 is an example of a monthly GainMaking meeting calendar.

Because meetings are a major commitment of time and resources, each meeting must be held to high standards of quality and productivity. GainMaking meetings are not downtime; they are work time and need to be productive. Meetings are evaluated on the results they produce, not the time they take. At one company where the annual budget for work team meetings was $14,000 the teams generated ideas that reduced costs by more than $500,000! The company was quite satisfied with their 35:1 return on the cost of the work team meetings. While this would be a difficult standard to maintain, it does represent the type of expectation that should be set for meeting effectiveness.

Planning and Coordination Meetings

There are several meetings to direct and coordinate the monthly GainMaking process. These meetings all involve team leaders and

Figure 6-6.   Monthly GainMaking calendar.

	MONDAY	TUESDAY	WEDNESDAY	THURSDAY	FRIDAY
Last week of the month	Team Leaders: Communications from teams to staff	Focus: Staff selects the Focus for the next month		Team Leaders: Team Charges are set	
WEEK 1	INFORMATION MEETINGS: Announce Charges			TEAM PROBLEM-SOLVING MEETINGS	TEAM PROBLEM-SOLVING MEETINGS
WEEK 2	INFORMATION MEETINGS: Progress Reports	Coordination Meeting: Team leaders meet to coordinate action plans			
WEEK 3	INFORMATION MEETINGS: GainShares Progress Reports				
WEEK 4	INFORMATION MEETINGS: Progress Reports Suggestions for Focus				

top management. Planning meetings decide the monthly productivity **Focus** and **Charges**. Coordination meetings coordinate action plans and information between teams and levels of the organization.

▲ *Planning Meetings.* At the end of each month the top management team meets to decide the productivity **Focus** for the following month. The team reviews the company's performance and decides where to direct the problem-solving resources of the company in the coming month. Focusing employee problem solving on important operating results keeps team problem solving relevant to the business. To make a decision about the monthly **Focus** top management reviews a variety of operating results, the annual operating plans, and suggestions for the **Focus** that have come from the work teams.

After the top management team selects the company **Focus** major department heads meet with their team leaders to decide **Charges** for each work team. The process of deciding **Charges** is usually a give-and-take discussion until the manager and team leader agree on what the **Charge** will be. It is best to do this in a meeting with all of the department's team leaders present so that each knows the others' **Charges** and can prepare to coordinate and assist each other's teams.

▲ *Coordination Meetings.* These meetings, two or three per month, are for team leaders to coordinate their teams for maximum Gain-Making impact. In these meetings action plans that require interteam coordination and joint problem solving are discussed and resolved. Other action plans are reported to the group for information. Meetings to review and coordinate action plans should occur shortly after all of the teams have held their problem-solving meetings.

Toward the end of the month the team leaders meet to discuss suggestions they have been given by their teams for next month's **Focus** and **Charges**. They formulate a consensus recommendation for the **Focus**, which the department manager takes to the top management team.

Planning and coordination meetings should be integrated into regularly scheduled department staff meetings. GainMaking activities, including setting **Focuses** and **Charges**, coordinating and approving action plans and suggestions, and sharing information must become the new routine. GainMaking will never reach its full potential if it is looked upon as a special project.

Team Informational Meetings

A critical feature of the GainMaking process is to keep all team members informed about the operations of the company, their department, and their team. Every week leaders meet with their teams for a brief (15-minute) informational meeting. Each meeting has a two-part agenda. First, there is information specific to GainMaking: the monthly GainMaking team **Charge**, progress on action plans and suggestions, and information about GainShares. Second, the team leader provides other information about the business, such as sales, profit, customer complaints, and so on. Information about events or activities of interest to the team is also included. In addition to giving information at the weekly information meetings the team leader listens to the team members' comments, reactions, questions, or concerns and decides which should be passed up the line. By listening, the team leader also determines how well the team members understand what has been communicated. When necessary, the team leader must take extra steps to ensure understanding. Knowledge is power, and powerful people produce better results.

Many organizations do not communicate regularly with employees, so these meetings will be new. At first team leaders may be uncertain about what information to present in the meetings. Conducting good information meetings requires some skill, but it is much more a matter of having information to communicate and a noise-free space in which to hold the meeting.

Following are some examples of agendas and information checklists for the weekly information meetings:

Information Meeting—Week 1

GainMaking Agenda
- ▲ The productivity **Focus** and **Charge** for the month
- ▲ Time and location of the monthly team problem-solving meeting
- ▲ Status of all open action plans and suggestions

Other company information
- ▲ See information checklists

Information Meeting—Week 2

GainMaking Agenda
- ▲ Review action plans from the last problem-solving meeting
- ▲ Status of all other open action plans and suggestions

Other company information

▲ See information checklists

Information Meeting—Week 3

GainMaking Agenda

▲ Distribute GainShare checks
▲ Distribute and explain GainShare statements
▲ Status of all open action plans and suggestions

Other company information

▲ See information checklists

Information Meeting—Week 4

GainMaking Agenda

▲ Status of all open action plans and suggestions
▲ Solicit ideas for next month's **Focus**

Other company information

▲ See information checklist

There is always other company information to communicate at the weekly information meetings. The team leader should search out this information for his or her team to keep them tuned in and up to date. Everyone likes to know the score. Certain managers, such as the controller, the sales manager, and personnel manager, create and maintain much of this general company information. It is their responsibility to send useful information to the team leaders in time for their weekly meetings and in a format that is easily understood. The following are checklists of topics to be considered for the weekly information meetings. Whenever this information is available, it should be communicated.

Business Information Checklist

▲ Strategic plans and progress toward them
▲ Business plans, e.g., shipping schedules, rush orders, special projects
▲ Sales forecasts
▲ Production plans and reports
▲ Market trends
▲ Customer information—good and bad

Safety Information Checklist

▲ Injuries and accidents
▲ Safety costs
▲ Plans for improving safety
▲ Safety training

Personnel Information Checklist

▲ Vacation schedules
▲ Retirements
▲ Shutdowns
▲ Layoffs
▲ Training plans
▲ Job openings within the company
▲ Parties and social events
▲ Activities: softball, bowling, blood drives, etc.

Team Problem-Solving Meetings

The core of GainMaking in the GainManagement process is the once-a-month team problem-solving meeting. This is the only truly special event in the GainMaking process. It is special in that it involves every team and every person in a focused effort to find faster, better, and smarter ways to do their work, accomplish their goals, interact with other teams, and demolish productivity roadblocks. There are activities that feed into the team problem-solving meetings, such as **Focuses, Charges**, and special training. Flowing out of the meetings are many actions to implement the ideas generated by the teams. While the activities leading up to and flowing out of the meetings must become routine (simplicity the other side of complexity), the team problem-solving meeting should always be a special event.

Individuals are capable of solving problems on their own, but experience shows that group problem solving consistently produces better results. With the exception of people like Thomas Edison and Albert Einstein, two heads are better than one, and the best solutions are most often developed by teams. Analysis and brainstorming in a work team that generates action plans is easily learned, fun to do, and very effective. There are many benefits to team problem solving:

▲ More worker involvement in investigating problems leads to more complete and accurate diagnosis of problems.

A small West Coast machine shop introduced monthly Gain-Making problem-solving meetings as part of the Gain-Management process. There were 14 teams producing about 30 ideas each month. A sudden sales increase prompted the general manager to reduce the frequency of problem-solving meetings to every other month so that more time could be spent in production. Contrary to his plan production did not go up as a result of the additional hour of production. In addition the rate of employee ideas per meeting dropped to a third of what they had been. The manager decided to return to monthly problem-solving meetings, but the flow of ideas did not immediately return to previous levels. From the Gain-Management Council representatives the manager learned that the employees interpreted his decision to reduce the meeting frequency as a lack of commitment to the Gain-Management process. It took this company several months to regain the confidence and support of the employees.

- The more workers there are looking for a solution, the more likely it is that the best solution will be found.
- When workers are involved in solving a problem, they are more committed to making *their* solution succeed.
- Working as a team builds accountability.
- Problem solving in teams builds teamwork, and teamwork leads to better problem solving.

When people solve problems in teams, a bond develops that holds the team together and builds responsibility and commitment in the individual members. The lack of loyalty and commitment that plagues today's organizations, and employees' feelings of isolation, of being just a number, can be reversed by building strong teams. It is quite easy for individuals to develop loyalty, responsibility, and commitment to the team. Then, as teams are more tightly linked throughout the organization, the team-centered commitment will expand to the larger organization.

Team meetings should be scheduled for 100% attendance. Meetings are held during normal work hours to reinforce the fact that problem solving is as much a part of everyone's job as making accounting entries, running a chain saw, responding to customer

Figure 6-7.   Monthly team meeting report.

Team _____ **Leader** _____ **Month** _____

WEEKLY INFORMATION MEETINGS

DATE   ATTENDANCE   SUMMARY OF INFORMATION

_____   _____ of _____ : _____%   _____

                                               _____

_____   _____ of _____ : _____%   _____

                                               _____

_____   _____ of _____ : _____%   _____

                                               _____

_____   _____ of _____ : _____%   _____

                                               _____

_____   _____ of _____ : _____%   _____

                                               _____

PROBLEM-SOLVING MEETING

DATE _____   ATTENDANCE _____ of _____ : _____%

FOCUS _____   CHARGE _____

       Causes: List on back or attach list.

ACTION PLAN # 1: Log # _____   What _____

                                               _____

       When _____   Who _____

ACTION PLAN # 2: Log # _____   What _____

                                               _____

       When _____   Who _____

OTHER ACTION PLANS or SUGGESTIONS submitted during the month:

Log # _____   _____

Log # _____   _____

Log # _____   _____

Continue on back if necessary.

orders, or planning an advertising strategy. Companies, such as those with continuous operations, must schedule meetings on overtime. This sometimes causes attendance problems because of child care and other personal commitments of the team members. With some effort and adequate planning, however, these problems can be resolved so that the team, when it meets, has the advantage of all of its resources, and all team members have the opportunity and advantage of being involved.

Once begun, problem-solving meetings should be held regularly. Consistency in holding the meetings sends a message to employees that their ideas are important and that they are expected to find better methods. When meetings are held intermittently or only when convenient, the message about importance is muted. Employee response will be muted as well.

Monthly Team Meeting Report

Each month the team leaders complete a summary report of their team meetings as shown in Figure 6-7. Records such as this have several uses. First, the team leaders benefit by having to review the past month and create the report. Meeting deficiencies show up and serve as a reminder to correct them next month. Team leaders, department managers, and/or the training manager review these reports and use the information to plan individual or group training. Finally, the reports provide basic data for longer-range trend analysis by the GainManagement council.

3. The Team Problem-Solving Process

Following is an overview of the team problem-solving process, showing the highlights of a typical month for Tom Michael's sanding department at the Great Northwest Plywood Company.

January 29: General Manager Mike MacDonell and his team hold their regular weekly staff meeting. From their various perspectives and information sources the team members identify six productivity issues and select excessive rejects as the most pressing problem. They then decide that the company's productivity **Focus** for February will be to reduce rejects from 12% to 8%.

January 31:   Major department managers meet with their team leaders to select team **Charges.** Production Manager Maureen Renezim meets with her first-line production managers and determines appropriate reject-reduction goals for each team. Tom Michael's team has been having particular problems with nicks and dents. Maureen and Tom agree to the following **Charge** for the sanding department: Reduce nicks and dents by 75% by April 1.

February 4:   At Tom's weekly tailgate (information) meeting he announces the **Charge** and encourages his team to begin thinking. Tom tells the team about the scope of the problem, including its anticipated impact on the productivity base and their GainShares.

February 6:   Tom and the sanding team hold their one-hour problem-solving meeting. The team lists seven causes for excessive nicks and dents, selects one, brainstorms, and develops two action plans. One of these plans is to install a pressure gauge on the patch line turner to allow the operators to monitor the pressure and thus prevent damage from the turner when the pressure gets too high. Tom writes up the action plans and sends them to be logged.

February 7:   Eric Smith from maintenance and the two team members who operate the patch line come in a half-hour early and install the pressure gauge. The action plan is completed, and notice is sent to the idea coordinator to update the log.

February 11:   Tom holds his second weekly tailgate meeting and asks the operators to report on the status of the gauge idea. They report that nicks and dents were reduced by over 50% for the two days after the gauge was installed. Tom also reviews all the other open action plans.

February 14:   Two team members present a suggestion to Tom on the floor. He quickly calls the rest of the team together and in five minutes they improve and

	approve the suggestion. It is written up and sent to be logged.
February 18:	Tom holds his third weekly tailgate meeting and distributes GainShare statements and checks for January. He again reports on the status of all the open action plans. The patch line operators report that the pressure gauge idea is working better than they expected and that rejects are down by 80%.
February 25:	Tom holds his fourth weekly tailgate meeting and presents his regular reports. He then asks the team for suggestions for the March **Focus.** The team tells him that there have been some near misses that could have been serious accidents. They would like to work on ways to improve safety.
February 25:	Tom and the other team leaders meet with Maureen, and Tom presents his team's suggestion for a **Focus** on safety. The other team leaders agree that safety needs some attention, and Maureen agrees to take it to staff as their recommendation. Then Mark Werle asks the team leaders to consider an action plan from his team that needs coordination. His team has suggested that production flow would be improved if the finished inventory was relocated. This action plan affects several other departments, so it was referred to the production management team. Mark explains the idea, and the team leaders approve it. Maureen asks each team leader to report briefly on their two action plans. She also asks if anyone had any special difficulties with this month's meetings. None were mentioned, and the meeting is adjourned.
February 26:	The general manager and his staff hold their regular staff meeting, which includes selecting the March **Focus.** The other department managers have also seen safety hazards and agree that the **Focus** for March will be to reduce safety hazards. Each department manager reports on the results of problem solving in their depart-

ments during the past month. No action plans
were referred to the staff for resolution, so they
move on to other business.

This was a typical scenario for the company's monthly Gain-
Making activities. With 12 work teams the company received 24 team
action plans and 20 individual suggestions directed at the reject
problem. Another six suggestions were made relating to other problems. The company reduced rejects to 7.4% by April 1. As each
percent of rejects represents $10,000 per year in lost revenue, the
company made a $46,000 annualized revenue gain during March. The
cost to implement the 44 action plans and suggestions was $8,694.

Focus *and* Charge

The **Focus** and **Charges** are the final steps in an organization's
planning sequence that begins with the company mission, strategic
objectives, and strategic plans (see Figure 6-8). In this way Gain-
Making is integrated into the ongoing planning process, and problem
solving and creative thinking efforts are focused on important organizational problems.

▲ **Focus.** Selecting the **Focus** is a top management responsibility.
A primary task of management is to give overall direction to the
organization, and selecting the monthly productivity **Focus** is an
important part of that task. Deciding the **Focus** involves gathering
information, analyzing, evaluating, choosing from alternatives, preparing good **Focus** statements, and ensuring the **Focus** is communicated, understood, and accepted. In making this selection management reviews a variety of information to determine which of several
options offers the best opportunity for the team problem-solving
process to improve the performance of the company. The process of
selection is one of presentation, discussion, and debate. All concerned parties have the responsibility for lobbying for what they
believe to be the best **Focus.** Finally, however, one selection must be
made, and everyone must support the decision. A good **Focus** is one
that:

  ▲ Will contribute directly to the achievement of the annual busi-
    ness or operating plan.
  ▲ Addresses a real problem or opportunity.

Figure 6-8.   The GainPlanning pyramid.

The Planning Pyramid

MISSION
The purpose for which the business exists

STRATEGIC OBJECTIVES
Goals for marketing, innovation, financial resources,
physical resources, human resources, productivity,
social responsibility, and profit

STRATEGIC PLANS
Work plans to achieve the strategic objectives

ANNUAL GOALS
Sales, production, profit, R&D, and other goals to be
accomplished during the current fiscal year

ANNUAL OPERATING PLANS
Work plans to achieve the annual operating goals

MONTHLY FOCUS
The companywide productivity improvement goal for the month

TEAM CHARGE
Each team's specific piece of the monthly **Focus**

▲ The teams can do something about.
▲ Will be interesting and challenging for the employees.
▲ Is measurable, at least qualitatively.
▲ Is clear.

Cost, quality, and delivery are the three most common areas of performance from which the **Focus** will come, but other subjects are common. The following are examples of monthly **Focuses**:

▲ Reduce annualized budgeted expenses by 1%.
▲ Increase factory margin from 48% to 52%.
▲ Reduce rejects from 11% to 7%.

▲ Increase on-time deliveries to 97%.
▲ Reduce field failures to zero.
▲ Increase inventory turns to 4.8.
▲ Improve interunit planning and coordination.
▲ Improve external relationships with local communities.

One GainManagement corporation uses the GainPlanning pyramid to facilitate selection of the monthly **Focus** in its divisions. The model in Figure 6-9 provides detailed information for each major planning level, from the mission through the annual operating plan. The model also shows an extensive list of possible topics for the monthly **Focus** for one division.

The purpose of the **Focus** is to concentrate all of the creative problem-solving efforts of the entire organization. All teams are expected to contribute to this common effort, and when they do, the experience has a very unifying effect on the organization. Occasionally it will happen that a **Focus** pertains to line operations to such an extent that it does not provide good **Charges** for other departments such as administration, accounting, or sales. The first step is to look again. Sometimes it seems that a **Focus** does not pertain to some departments, but on closer scrutiny the other teams are able to have some impact on the **Focus,** if only indirectly. This is particularly true of staff functions. Every effort should be made to discover a **Focus** that will provide **Charges** for every team. However, if none is found, an exception should be made that will enable all teams to have meaningful **Charges** for their problem-solving meetings.

Any teams that are allowed a **Charge** outside of the monthly **Focus** will not have a separate **Focus;** there is only one **Focus** for the month. In addition to its value as the source of thought for innovation and problem solving the **Focus** is a tool for communication and education. The **Focus** teaches everyone about what is important to the business. Despite occasional exceptions the **Focus** is the most pressing need for the month and should be recognized as such by everyone. It is still possible that individual suggestions from the excepted teams can be developed to help the **Focus.**

Some important problems, such as quality, may continue to be a problem for several months, so one **Focus** could be repeated for two or more months. There are two things to consider before continuing the same **Focus** from month to month. Some action plans may take two or three months before their impact can be assessed. Until the impact of one month's action plans is clear, it may be well not to ask

Figure 6-9. Corporate example of the GainMaking pyramid.

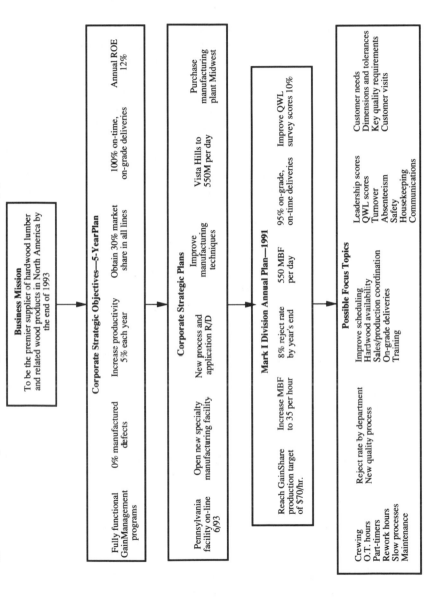

Business Mission

To be the premier supplier of hardwood lumber and related wood products in North America by the end of 1993

Corporate Strategic Objectives—5-Year Plan

| Fully functional GainManagement programs | 0% manufactured defects | Increase productivity 5% each year | Obtain 30% market share in all lines | 100% on-time, on-grade deliveries | Annual ROE 12% |

Corporate Strategic Plans

| Pennsylvania facility on-line 6/93 | Open new specialty manufacturing facility | Improve manufacturing techniques | New process and application R/D | Vista Hills to 550M per day | Purchase manufacturing plant Midwest |

Mark I Division Annual Plan—1991

| Reach GainShare production target of $70/hr. | Increase MBF to 35 per hour | 550 MBF per day | 8% reject rate by year's end | 95% on-grade, on-time deliveries | Improve QWL survey scores 10% |

Possible Focus Topics

| Crewing O.T. hours Part-timers Rework hours Slow processes Maintenance | Reject rate by department New quality process | Improve scheduling Hardwood availability Sales/production coordination On-grade deliveries Training | Leadership scores QWL scores Turnover Absenteeism Safety Housekeeping Communications | Customer needs Dimensions and tolerances Key quality requirements Customer visits |

for more ideas on the same **Focus.** Another value to changing the **Focus** is for variety and to give the teams an opportunity to generate new ideas.

The **Focus** must be measurable, at least qualitatively. This is very important for problem solving and feedback. "We need more" may be correct, but "how much more" will help teams develop the best solutions. **Focuses** that can be measured quantitatively are best, such as "reduce costs by 2%" or "increase production by 10%." There are **Focuses,** however, that cannot be easily quantified. In these cases a qualitative measurement should be found. **Focuses** such as "improve communications" will be more useful by specifying the type or nature of communications to be improved or the type of problem to be corrected with the improved communications. Sometimes just asking, "Why do we want this to be the **Focus**?" will lead to a useful measurement.

When the **Focus** that is selected can only be measured qualitatively, some extra effort is needed to make the **Charges** as specific as possible. Most often quantitative **Charges** are still possible with a qualitative **Focus.** In one instance "improving customer service" was selected as the **Focus** for a company making machine tools. With this as the **Focus** the following **Charges** were set:

Customer service team:	Reduce time to resolve customer complaints from an average of three to two working days.
Production teams:	Increase on-time shipments from 87% to 95%.

In another example a timberlands operation was receiving criticism from environmentalists. Top management selected as their **Focus,** "improve external relationships." For field operations teams the **Charge** was to improve relationships with specific local communities. For the home-office teams the **Charges** were to improve relationships with field offices and with corporate headquarters. These **Charges** produced excellent action plans because they included specific direction.

▲ **Charge.** Following the selection of the **Focus,** major department heads meet with their team leaders to develop **Charges** for each work team. The process for selecting the **Charge** is also one of discussion and debate but somewhat simpler than that for selecting the **Focus.**

Whereas top management reviews a broad range of information and goals in selecting the **Focus,** in selecting **Charges** it is only necessary to look at the **Focus** and ask what each team can or should contribute to its achievement. The department manager announces the monthly **Focus** and explains why it was selected by top management. The manager also mentions other options that were considered but not selected. This explanation of the deliberations of top management is important to the team leaders because it will help them explain the **Focus** to their teams with understanding and thoroughness. This explanation also helps to secure the team leaders' acceptance of and commitment to the **Focus.** They must understand why each **Focus** is important so that they, in turn, can convince their work teams to support the **Focus** and **Charge.** This is seldom a difficult process but is always an important one requiring careful, thorough, and open communications.

When the discussion about the **Focus** is complete, the meeting moves to selecting **Charges** for each team. Sometimes the **Charges** are quite simple and obvious, given the **Focus.** The department manager first asks each team leader what his or her team can or should contribute. Then the manager and each leader discuss alternatives until both are satisfied that the best **Charge** has been identified. The intent is to find the right **Charge,** not just a convenient or popular one. By having this discussion in an open meeting, team leaders can help each other identify proper **Charges.** And knowing each other's **Charges** will help coordination and cooperation when it comes time to implement the ensuing action plans.

A good **Charge** is one that:

- ▲ Will contribute directly to the **Focus.**
- ▲ Is something the team can do something about.
- ▲ Is of interest to the team members.
- ▲ Will challenge the team.
- ▲ Is measurable.
- ▲ Is clear.

Team Problem-Solving

Team problem solving begins with the team problem-solving meeting and continues with individual problem-solving suggestions following the team meeting. In one carefully structured hour the team develops two action plans. Team leaders are responsible for conducting the team problem-solving meeting. Coaches or facilitators cannot do the team leader's job. Team members can be assigned to write the flip charts and lead some of the discussions, but the team leader must lead the meeting. Team leaders are responsible for leading their teams to higher levels of performance and this is a key event in that process. This leadership responsibility cannot be delegated or assigned to others.

Most team leaders will need assistance and training as they begin holding problem-solving meetings. In a few hours of classroom training team leaders can be taught the basic five-step problem-solving sequence (see Figure 6-10). With coaching for the first few meetings, team leaders and teams can become proficient at this straightforward problem-solving process. After the first few meetings using this process teams are typically pleased with their achievement. Confidence builds quickly. Advanced skills and problem-solving techniques can be added to the teams' repertoire once they are comfortable with the basic process. (These techniques are explained in Chapter 10.)

Preparation: The team problem-solving meeting must be well planned and executed to have maximum GainMaking impact. The work teams are responsible for the quality and production of their monthly problem-solving meeting just as they are for all other duties on their job descriptions. Team leaders must plan for this meeting as carefully as they plan for other aspects of the team's work. The team

Figure 6-10.   The five-step problem-solving sequence.

Step 1: Clarify the Charge.	The team leader restates the **Charge** and makes certain that the team understands the problem they must solve.
Step 2: List causes of the problem.	Once the team members understand the problem, they list approximately 6–10 causes of the problem.
Step 3: Select one cause to solve.	The team selects the most significant cause to solve by brainstorming.
Step 4: Brainstorm solutions.	The team brainstorms solutions to the selected cause.
Step 5: Develop action plans.	The brainstorm list is discussed and debated, and the team develops two action plans. These plans state the solution, the action steps, who is responsible, and when action will start or be completed.

leader schedules a conference room and sees that flip charts and other equipment are available. The team leader thinks through the meeting to anticipate obstacles to the meeting's success. The team leader announces and explains the **Charge** at an information meeting two or three days in advance of the problem-solving meeting, thus giving the team members time to think and identify causes of the problem represented by the **Charge**. Team members must also prepare themselves to be responsible participants. They should know the **Charge** and have done some investigation and analysis. The members should come to the meeting prepared to work at finding good solutions.

The Team Problem-Solving Meeting: Following is a detailed description of the one-hour team problem-solving meeting:

Review the Last Meeting (5 minutes). The team leader opens the meeting with a brief review of the process and content of the team's last meeting. The content review covers not only the action plans developed in the last meeting but also suggestions received from members since the meeting. The team leader briefly reviews the status of these plans and suggestions. This review is motivational in that it allows the team to celebrate achievement or to make a new commitment if achievement fell short of expectations. It is also educational in that the analysis of successes and failures adds to the team's understanding. And the review is rewarding in that it provides recognition of excellence and effort.

The team leader also reviews the evaluation of the team's last meeting to help the team continually improve its meeting skills and process.

Clarify the **Charge** *(3 minutes).* The first step in solving a problem is the awareness that there is a problem. The problem must be understood by team members in a way that will allow them to take appropriate action. They must understand both the problem and the extent of the improvement needed. It is important that all members understand why they are present and what their task is. Otherwise, the meeting will ramble and fail.

List Causes of the Problem (15 minutes). Once the goal is clear and the extent of the improvement is understood, the team identifies all those things that are causing a deficiency or preventing them from being at the performance level identified by the **Charge**. Most problems have several causes. This problem-solving process is designed to solve the problem by eliminating or minimizing some of those causes. Typically a team will identify six to ten causes of a problem. The team should be encouraged to list all the known causes, even those they can't solve, such as the weather or market conditions. There will be some discussion throughout this step to clarify the cause statements, but the team should stick to listing causes and not discuss solutions prematurely.

Select One Cause to Solve (2 minutes). Once the team has generated a good list of causes, the team members select one cause for problem solving. Problems will be solved or reduced to the extent that causes are solved. Some causes cannot be solved or are beyond the scope of this process; they must be accepted and worked around. Others can be solved, and this is where the team should put its energies. Teams usually want to solve all of the causes, but they must develop the discipline to pick one cause and solve it. A simple majority vote and a brief discussion to resolve the different choices is usually sufficient to enable the team to pick one cause and move on.

Brainstorm Solutions (15 minutes). Brainstorming is at the heart of the problem-solving process; here is where creativity and ideas flow. The team uses standard brainstorming procedures and, with practice and training, becomes very proficient at developing ideas. As teamwork and experience grow, new breakthrough ideas emerge. The task in this step is to get the team to list a large volume of ideas for solving the selected cause. A typical brainstorming session proceeds through three distinct phases:

Phase 1:   Many ideas, usually the obvious ones
Phase 2:   Silence, as some members are out of ideas while others are thinking
Phase 3:   More ideas as a result of more thinking

A common mistake is to stop brainstorming after phase 2 on the assumption that the team is out of ideas. The best solutions often occur when brainstorming is allowed to run to phase 3. It is here that breakthrough ideas are often generated.

Develop Action Plans (15 minutes). The purpose of the meeting is to solve problems, not just talk about them, so the meeting concludes with action. The many ideas on the brainstorm list must be sifted, screened, and formulated into two coherent action plans. Some of the ideas will be incomplete; some will not be useful. The team discusses and debates the list, eliminating some ideas, clarifying or combining others, until workable action plans emerge.

The team develops complete action plans that include:

- ▲ What will be done—all the action steps
- ▲ Who is responsible for the action—this may involve different people for different steps
- ▲ When each step will be started and/or completed

This is a difficult part of the process, but it can be mastered in time. The most common problem is for a team to decide on a fairly complex solution and fail to think through all the steps necessary to complete the solution. One team decided to give company credit cards to truck drivers so they could take advantage of bargain-priced fuel as they traveled. This was an excellent solution because the contract fuel company was charging the company full retail price. What the team failed to do was detail the steps for obtaining company credit cards. As a result this excellent action plan and its savings were delayed several months.

The team leader must ask the team to think through the entire process of coordination, approvals, purchasing, and other steps necessary to complete the action plan. For each step someone must be assigned accountability. The date by which the action will be started and/or completed must also be set.

The team should use accountability for action plans or action plan steps as a way to increase employee participation. There is a tendency, especially at first, to assign all of the accountability for action plans to the team leader. This is to be expected in a new program and should not be regarded as a problem. However, both team and leader should be diligent in finding opportunities to involve team members in implementing action plans. Opportunities will abound for team members to do research, contact other teams and other employees for coordination, meet with purchasing to select a new tool or supplier, and so on. These experiences are both educational and motivating for team members. Delegating authority to work on action plan steps is desirable, but the team leader is still responsible for guiding the overall process.

In developing action plans teams should be encouraged to do as

In the 20th year of a very successful Scanlon plan the company mounted a major drive for cost-reduction suggestions. All work teams were asked for more and better suggestions than they had ever made before. Following the announcement of this big drive an electrician approached his manager almost timidly and said, "I've had this idea about the grinding machine controls for the past five years. I think it could save as much as $50,000 a year in labor costs and down time. I haven't turned it in before because it's such a big change. But now with this big push, maybe I should. What do you think?"

The manager not only encouraged the electrician to submit the suggestion, but he also helped him write it up. Then he expedited its approval and adoption. The new controls resulted in a $57,000 savings in the first year. Afterward the manager asked the electrician why he had hesitated to submit such a good idea. The electrician said he thought big ideas like that were supposed to come from engineering, thus would not be welcomed coming from someone in maintenance.

In 20 years this successful program had not broken through an unwritten class consciousness notion that somehow reserves thinking "big" thoughts to professional employees and limits blue-collar employees to manual work and minor improvements.

much of the action for themselves as they can. It is all too common for teams to pass the buck to others rather than take responsibility. A typical GainMaking goal is to have 60% of all action plans resolved in the work team where they originate. Another 30% go to the next level of management for coordination or approval, and only 10% are referred to top management for action.

Finally, the team must be realistic when deciding action plans. On the one hand, there are legitimate limitations on problem solving that must be respected and accepted. On the other hand, teams have a tendency to assume limitations where none exist. They must be willing to push on the boundaries to eliminate unnecessary limitations and create more freedom to act for themselves.

▲ *Review of the Meeting (5 minutes):* The final step is to review the meeting and the action plans. This serves to remind everyone of the steps they followed and why the team chose the action plans it did.

This review encourages the team members to critique their own performance and confirm that the two (or more) action plans are likely to achieve their **Charge**.

The team also conducts an evaluation of the meeting process. The employees must accept responsibility for conducting their meetings as productively as possible. As they analyze and evaluate their performance, the team meeting process will continue to grow and improve. This evaluation will be reviewed at the beginning of the next meeting to remind the team about what to do or what not to do to improve the quality of meetings.

▲ *Individual Suggestions*: In addition to problem solving in the team meeting employees are encouraged to submit suggestions throughout the month. This encouragement comes from several sources. First, the whole GainManagement process signals to people that their suggestions are welcome and expected. Team leaders constantly promote the idea of finding the better way. Job descriptions specify that continuous improvement is every employee's responsibility.

In the meeting the team members usually identify six to ten causes of the problem described by the **Charge**, but only have time to address one cause. Individual team members leave the meeting with ideas that were not deliberated by the team. Some of these ideas will be turned in as individual suggestions. One machine shop employee turned in 17 suggestions the day after the team meeting. In the same company one enterprising team leader posted the flip chart page with the cause list in his work area with a note that read: "Keep thinking." His team produced more suggestions per individual than any other team. In addition to the suggestions that come from the sources already mentioned, individual workers will produce suggestions from their own work experience. It is reasonable to expect two additional suggestions per month from each work team.

Team leaders help team members to develop their ideas and present them. If the idea only affects the individual's job, it can be resolved between the team leader and the team member. If the idea has a broader impact, it should be presented to the team to get their input as to the best manner to implement the change. Often this team review of an idea can be completed in a five-minute stand-up meeting in the work area. Others need more attention and may justify a special team meeting to discuss and resolve the suggestion.

▲ *The Idea Form*: Team action plans and individual suggestions are put in writing in order to facilitate communications, coordination, approvals, and implementation. In an active GainMaking effort there will be too many ideas requiring too much coordination to track them without forms and records. Such records should be minimal and streamlined, but some formality is unavoidable. A standard idea form, such as the one shown in Figure 6-11, is recommended.

This form is used to record and process team action plans or individual suggestions. Each action plan and suggestion is written on

Figure 6-11.   GainMaking idea form.

[*side 1*]

☒ Team Action Plan	☐ Individual Suggestion	**Log Number** 197
		Implemented 2-7
Date Submitted *Feb. 6, 1991*		**Withdrawn**
Team/Department *Sanding Team*		
Team Leader *Tom Michaels*		
Suggester *Team*		

Description of the Action Plan or Suggestion *Add a gauge to measure pneumatic pressure at the patch line turner. Operator to monitor pressure and adjust gauge to control the speed of the turner.*

Monthly Charge *Reduce veneer nicks and dents by 75% by April 1.*

Selected Cause *Patch line turn speed causes veneer to strike guide bar.*

Briefly summarize the idea in 5-10 words as you would like it to appear in the log.

Install patch line turner pressure gauge.

Action Plan

WHAT WILL BE DONE List steps	WHO IS RESPONSIBLE for each step	WHEN Planned / Done	
Contact maintenance to install stock pressure gauge in line.	*Tom Michaels*	*2-6*	*2-6*
Operators to assist maintenance to install gauge.	*Brad Faigle* *Emily Vehr*	*2-7*	*2-7*

THANK YOU FOR YOUR IDEA!!

[*side 2*]

Implementation / Approval Status

Date: __2-7____   This idea was immediately implemented by the work team.
Date: _____   This idea was referred for study, coordination, approval, or other action.

RECORD OF ACTION

Date	Name/Department	Action Required	Action Taken
N/A			

Cost / Benefit Analysis

Costs: Labor $ _42.00___   Material $ _89.75_____   Other $ _____

Benefit: Savings $ _7,500 (est)_____ (annualized)

Other _____

Discussion:
_Estimated savings based on improved yield (50%) and reduction in final inspection rejects (50%)._____

Δ *Delta Management Group*

a separate form. The form is prepared by the individual suggester or the team leader after the team problem-solving meeting. It is then logged, copied, and distributed to others who need the information for coordination, approval, or implementation. Forms not only facilitate the processing of ideas, they also allow for periodic analyses of the overall GainMaking effort.

4. Processing and Resolving Ideas

Getting ideas from employees is not difficult. In fact it is difficult not to get ideas. People are creative, and they will have ideas. The key to success is getting good ideas that can and will be used. The **Focus, Charge**, and team problem-solving meetings produce ideas that can be used. The next step is the process to ensure that the ideas will be used. Experience with all forms of employee suggestion programs shows that actually using employee ideas is the only way to ensure the continuous flow of good ideas. When a suggestion program is started with fanfare, employees will respond. But no program can be sustained with fanfare. Only when employee ideas are used will suggestion programs thrive. If employee ideas are ignored, the programs will die.

Goals and Guidelines for Processing and Resolving Ideas

Creating an effective process for resolving team action plans and individual suggestions begins with goals for what the process should do. The goals and guidelines necessary for an effective process to resolve employee GainMaking ideas are:

▲ All action plans and suggestions will be resolved.
▲ The average time to resolve ideas will not exceed two weeks.
▲ Ideas will be resolved at the lowest organization level possible within the following guidelines:
  —60% of the action plans and suggestions resolved at the work team level.
  —30% resolved at the department management level.
  —10% resolved at top management.

All Action Plans and Suggestions Will Be Resolved. Asking for employee ideas is important business. There must be a strong commitment to the principle that all ideas are welcome, will be treated with respect, and will be resolved. For participative management to work there must be a response when workers do participate. If managers expect workers to be responsible, then managers must be responsible. There are several ways to respond and resolve a new idea.

Some ideas are obviously useful, cost-effective, and easily implemented. These are resolved by approving and implementing them immediately. Other ideas may be marginally cost-effective or not so easily implemented. These ideas may require some coordination, additional study, or modification. It will take more time and effort

In a small high-tech division of a Midwest corporation, a painting team submitted a solution to a problem of noxious paint fumes. The team knew that the solution was not practical. The cost to install the suggested hoods and vacuum lines was out of proportion to the severity of the problem, which only occurred a half-dozen times each year when one special paint was being used. After three months and with no response from management, the team admitted their suggestion was a prank. They explained that they knew the idea could not be approved. They had submitted the idea to test the system and to see if management had enough courage and integrity to be honest with them.

before they can be implemented and approved. For these ideas an interim response to the team or the employee explaining the delay is required.

Some ideas cannot be used at all or are not cost-effective for a variety of reasons. These ideas should be resolved by explaining to the team or employee the reasons why the idea cannot be used at all or cannot be used immediately because of current conditions. This explanation has great value to the originating team and to the organization. If a suggestion was based on a lack of understanding by the work team or individual, the explanation educates and leads to better ideas. If a suggestion was premature, the explanation tells the team or individual when to resubmit the idea. If a suggestion was misunderstood by those who must approve it, the explanation provides the suggester a second opportunity to explain the idea and allow it to be reconsidered.

All of the resolutions described above carry the message that employees are respected and that their good ideas will be used. This message gives the whole GainMaking effort energy and integrity. The importance of this commitment and responsiveness cannot be exaggerated. Past experience has made employees skeptical and even cynical about management's willingness to listen to them and act on their ideas. Overcoming this skepticism will not be easy, but it can be done by the consistent application of the process described here. Sometimes the response is no, and even this should be done in a straightforward manner.

The Average Time to Resolve Ideas Will Not Exceed Two Weeks. When

A medium-size manufacturing corporation implemented GainManagement in eight different divisions. In a West Coast division ideas were ignored or took months to be resolved. In this division the idea flow dried up, and the company was forced to return to suggestion committees because people refused to attend team meetings.

In a small, 75-person Midwest division the plant manager and team leaders accepted the challenge to respond as quickly as possible to the ideas generated by the work teams. This division reduced the response time for almost every idea suggested to less than 24 hours. This speed of response encouraged more and more ideas from people. During the first year of the GainMaking process ideas from the plant floor increased the volume of production by 60%. The employees are pleased with the process, and the management team is proud of their record.

ideas are resolved quickly, employees receive a clear message that their ideas are wanted and will be used. The goal of maintaining a two-week overall average prompts the organization to give employees' ideas the priority needed to keep GainMaking vigorous. The few ideas that must be delayed for legitimate reasons are offset by many that are approved in much less than two weeks.

Ideas Will Be Resolved at the Lowest Organization Level. The goal for resolving ideas at the lowest possible organization level serves three useful purposes. First, when ideas are resolved by work teams and departments, they are resolved more quickly, which helps to achieve the previous goal of two-week resolution. Second, in order to resolve ideas at lower levels the organization must delegate more authority to team leaders and teams. Delegation is an essential ingredient in participative management. As teams and individual workers are given more authority and freedom to act, participation increases accordingly. Even when the work itself doesn't change, the additional responsibility changes the workers' relationship to their jobs. When workers have authority and control over their work, they can achieve. Without authority there is no responsibility, so the workers cannot achieve; they can only be busy.

Third, teams will be encouraged to devise action plans that are within their scope of authority. The authority a team needs to approve more action plans and suggestions is usually spending authority. When team leaders have such authority, they can approve ideas as soon as the idea is determined to be sound. They can authorize a purchase or work order or even overtime to implement an idea. The greater their spending authority the more ideas they can approve at the team level. Without this spending authority teams must send their ideas up the line to that level of management where the necessary authority resides. This not only takes time, but it also limits the amount of responsibility the team is willing to assume for its work.

There are a number of ways to delegate authority to approve ideas. Some companies simply increase the spending authority of each level of management. First-line managers may be given a $500 limit, with higher limits at each succeeding level of management. When this happens with the implementation of GainManagement, it is often the first time lower-level managers have had any spending authority whatsoever. This change is always welcomed by first-line managers.

Other companies add qualifiers to the spending authority of the team leaders. A common one is that all capital expenditures must go through a standard capital expenditure request process. Another is to give the team $500 authority for productivity-improvement ideas with a positive cost-benefit result and $100 authority for nonproductivity ideas. In one GainManagement installation the company decided to give each team leader an annual idea budget of $3,000. This had an interesting effect: Teams became very conservative and more creative, lest they blow all their budget the first few months and have nothing left for the remainder of the year.

60/30/10 Rule. When a team develops an action plan or a suggestion, there are three options for resolving it. First, the action required is within the authority of the team and does not require coordination or approval of any other team. Second, the action requires joint or coordinated effort with another team. Third, the action is beyond the authority of the team and must be sent forward as a recommendation. The goal in idea processing is to have 60% of the ideas in the first category, 30% in the second, and no more than 10% in the third.

In order for 60% of the action plans to be resolved within the team two things must be in place. First, the team must be given sufficient freedom to act and the authority to resolve ideas. If it develops that the teams are forwarding too many action plans for approval, the teams' authority and spending limits should be reviewed to see if they are too restrictive. A fairly common problem in manufacturing companies is that production operators are not permitted to make even minor repairs and adjustments to machines. Thus, rather than being able to carry out a simple action plan, the team must summon the maintenance department to take the action. When several work teams send requests for help to maintenance, it frequently causes a backlog that delays the implementation of all action plans. This can be remedied by having the maintenance department provide tools and training to production operators along with more freedom to get things done.

Second, teams must accept responsibility to choose action plans that are within their scope of authority. There is a tendency, especially in new programs, to pass the buck, to blame other departments for problems. This happens in organizations where turf battles and authoritarian practices have been the rule. Teams with this attitude often have many items on their brainstorm list of the "if-the-other-departments-would-just-do-this" variety. To move a team to the 60% rule the leader must constantly remind the team that the first priority in problem solving is to accept responsibility and to look for action plans where the team controls the action.

Teams will develop action plans beyond their authority limits, and well they should. Teams in organizations constantly interact in each other's work. Any one team is a customer of some teams and a supplier to others. These customer/supplier relationships are a rich source of productivity improvement ideas. Teams should be encouraged to examine their boundaries with other teams and look for ways to improve their own productivity and that of other related teams. It is not at all uncommon to hear of action plans where Team A spent an extra $100 that saved $1,000 in Team B.

These action plans require coordination and, in some cases, joint problem solving. Coordination means that the originating team implements its action plan but checks with, advises, or otherwise coordinates with the other teams affected by the change. For instance, say that the purchasing department decides to simplify and streamline a purchasing form and procedure. Every other team in the organization needs to be informed and trained in the new procedure before purchasing can implement the change. Ideas that change product features must be coordinated with and supported by quality assurance, engineering, sales, and any other related departments. The originating team is responsible for this coordination.

In other cases a team develops an action plan that seems a good idea to the members but requires action by another team. The originating team invites the other team to participate in joint problem solving. The originating team's action plan is the invitation to joint problem solving. In some cases the joint problem solving is as simple as the invited team agreeing to the action proposed by the originating team. In others the two teams may develop an entirely new and improved solution. Joint problem solving happens quite often between shifts in multiple-shift operations, as in manufacturing, process industries, and data processing. Roughly 30% of the action plans and suggestions should be in these categories of coordination and joint problem solving.

Finally, there will be ideas from the work team that have a companywide impact or require a major capital expenditure. These ideas go from team leader to department manager to top management for approval. The most common examples of this are major equipment purchases or a change in a plantwide procedure. Such action plans often require special budgeting or borrowing and may take some time to implement after approval. These ideas should make up about 10% of the total ideas.

In all of these cases the originating work team supplies the direction and energy to expedite the idea through the organization. Other teams that become involved in the action plan are required to respond with respect, cooperation, and promptness.

The team leader has the prime responsibility to see that the team's action plans and suggestions are processed expeditiously and either implemented or withdrawn. The leader helps the team map out the route for ideas that need coordination and approval (see Figure 6-12). As part of their linking role team leaders do much of the coordination and presentations for approvals. However, this work of processing ideas is a rich opportunity for participation by team members and should be used to its fullest. Often the team members who originated the idea are the ones best able to explain their solution to achieve the required coordination.

Idea Log

It is very easy for ideas to get lost in a busy organization. To minimize this problem organizations have idea forms and keep a log of each idea from inception to resolution (see Figure 6-13). All ideas, whether team action plans or individual suggestions, are processed in the same manner and entered in the idea log. The log has a twofold

Figure 6-12.   Idea processing map.

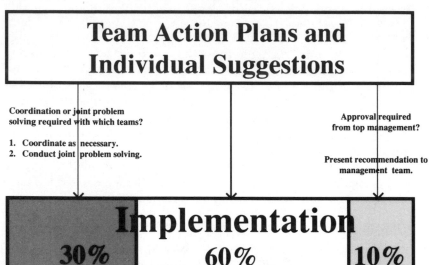

purpose: to keep track of individual ideas and to maintain a record of the entire GainMaking effort.

As soon as an action plan or suggestion is written up, it should be logged and assigned a number. The log records the originating team or individual, a brief statement of the idea, the date it was submitted, key events in processing, the date and type of final resolution, and the dollar value of the idea. The log can be easily maintained with the help of a desktop computer.

In most companies a coordinator is assigned to maintain and publish the log, but it is the originating work team's responsibility to process the idea and provide information for the log. The log should be posted on a bulletin board or published in a newsletter for all to see. It provides recognition to teams and individuals who submit ideas. It shows the whole organization what each team is accomplishing and stimulates more effort. It also identifies idea bottlenecks as they develop. The log stimulates idea processing, since no department will want to show up on the log as the bottleneck.

The log is a record of the overall GainMaking effort and is reviewed and analyzed by the GainManagement council. From this analysis the council decides development steps such as training, delegation, or the need for procedural changes. This analysis by the GainManagement council is discussed in Chapter 11.

Figure 6-13.   Idea log.

Number	Date	Originating team or person	Dept.	Idea Description	Processing Who	Planned	Actual	Resolution	Implemented Who	Planned	Actual	Annualized Savings
197	2-6	Sanding Team	Prod	Patch line turner pressure gauge.				Implemented	Team	2-7	2-7	$7,500
198	2-6	Green End Team	Prod	Modify automatic stacker.	Eric Smith	4-1	3-27	Implemented	Eng & Team	4-15	4-12	$14,000
199	2-7	Purchasing Team	Adm	Revise purchase order form.	Andy Ryan	3-1	3-15	Implemented	Team	4-1	4-1	Unknown
200	2-7	Ann Moy	Pers.	Use hospital satellite clinic for pre-employment physicals.	Purchas. A.Ryan	3-15	3-15	Implemented	Person-nel	4-1	4-1	$20 per
201	2-7	Drying Team	Prod	Mirror for 4 ft. stacker so operator can see malfunctions.	Purchas. A. Ryan	2-13	2-15	Implemented	Ed Bracke	2-15	2-15	Est. $1,000/yr
202	2-7	Finishing Team	Prod	Install dual controls from grace box to sander.				Withdrawn by team 2-10				
203	2-8	Green End Team	Prod	New employee training on green chain.	Brendon James	3-1	3-1	Implemented	Mike Stevens	3-1	3-1	Reduce accidents & turnover
204	2-8	Jeff Nelle	Prod	Build box to keep tape warm. Use light as heat source.	Bill Walter	3-1	2-25	Implemented	Ken Laib	3-1	2-26	Est. $1,000/yr
205	2-8	Maintenance Team	Engin.	Develop weekly PM schedule with production.	Pat Johns E. Smith	2-15	2-15	Implemented	Maint. & Prod. Teams	2-22	2-22	$3,120

Quality of Ideas

GainManagement experience, as well as experience with other employee idea programs, has shown that the quality of ideas increases with positive experience. In the first several months of the program, when the teams are learning the problem-solving sequence, there are good ideas but few creative ones. The ideas in the first few months typically come from a backlog of ideas that have been around for a while but not used. As ideas are used from the backlog, and as trust and confidence build, the new GainManagement program develops momentum. By the time the backlog is used up, the teams are experienced with team problem solving and their natural creativity is coming to the surface. In about the sixth month of a new program the teams should be introduced to more advanced problem-solving techniques.

System 5: Team Leadership

The second key GainMaking thrust is a skill rather than a structure: It is the skill of team leadership. Team leadership occurs in the hundreds of daily actions and interactions that enable people in teams to work, achieve their goals, and contribute to the successful performance of the organization. Team leadership includes not only actions that team leaders take with and on behalf of the team, but also actions by team members as they work with each other.

Team leadership facilitates and energizes all five areas of participation shown earlier in this chapter in the model (Figure 6-1). But as the idea program previously described primarily impacts problem solving and innovation, team leadership has its primary impact on work processes, goals, and strategy.

Team leadership involves employees both in the major decisions being made about the design of work processes and in the hundreds of small and large daily decisions about how to make the work safer and more productive and satisfying. Rather than telling employees how to work, as in obsolete authoritarian management systems, team leadership involves employees in these "how-to" decisions.

Team leadership involves employees in goals and strategy by first thoroughly explaining goals and strategy so they are understood and accepted. As employees' understanding grows, their natural desire to excel will draw them into more participation in the selection of goals and strategy. They will want to influence goals and strategy because they will be committed to organizational excellence.

Four Responsibilities of Leadership

Team leadership involves four responsibilities:

1. Developing people—skills, involvement, commitment
2. Building teams—for work and mutual support
3. Guiding work—for productivity, quality, safety
4. Promoting goals—for excellence

Team leaders and team members all have these four leadership responsibilities, although certain actions and practices are specific to leaders and/or to members. The first two responsibilities, developing people and building teams, concern quality of work life, while the last two, guiding work and promoting goals, concern the productivity of the team. An effective team has a balanced concern for people and work, for quality of work life and productivity. Emphasizing work concerns to the exclusion of people concerns causes the people to resent the work and the leadership. Excessive concern for people to the exclusion of concern for work may lead to contented people but also to poor work results. Neither extreme is a recipe for a successful, secure, high-performing organization. Balance is the key to success.

Teams where the leader takes on all of the leadership responsibility fail to use the strengths of team memebers. No matter how skillful team leaders are, an excellent organization cannot afford to waste the talent of team members. When member leadership skills are not used in behalf of the team, they are likely to emerge in opposition.

The four leadership responsibilities performed by the team leaders and by the team members must be understood and continuously developed for strong teams and productive GainMaking.

1. Develop People

Every person who joins a team has certain competencies and the ability to develop even more. People reaching for Maslow's Levels 3, 4, and 5 will bloom when they know that they are important to the team and respected by all others on the team. Leaders and members have the responsibility to help each other develop. They do this in many ways, direct and indirect, subtle and straightforward.

▲ *Selection.* The first step in developing people, the hiring decision, should be made by the team leader and members after a thorough analysis of the team's needs and the person's ability to fill those needs. The selection decision should reflect a consensus by the team that this person is the right one, an important addition to the team. When this consensus is communicated to the candidate, the new person experiences the support and commitment of the team. In turn, the new worker comes on the job with an attitude of loyalty to the team. Even before starting work, the new person begins to develop responsibility and commitment. The screening process prior to selection allows the team to select those whose competencies and motivations are compatible with the team and the larger organization—those who are most likely to develop in this situation. Two very successful organizations, the Jesuit Order of the Roman Catholic Church and the U.S. Marine Corps, use very stringent screening and selection processes as a first step to maintain the strength of their organizations. Making the cut in a tough selection process is a positive achievement experience for people . . . another step on the ladder of personal growth and development.

▲ *Education.* People in organizations need certain basic information and knowledge just to function in the organization. The effective team leader understands this and takes steps to provide members with a basic understanding of the organization's history, mission, strategic goals and plans, operating goals and plans, customer needs, financial structure, policies, and procedures. This enables team members to participate intelligently in every aspect of the organization's work.

▲ *Training.* All team members must be thoroughly trained in their own work and the work of the team. Performing one's job well is an achievement that is an important step to further achievement. Once a team member masters his or her assigned job, the door is open to adding to that job. In this way the worker participates in the design of work processes.

In GainMaking team members no longer view a job description as a ceiling; it is seen more as a floor or a minimum from which further gains can be made. Training occurs in the form of basic instruction, good coaching, constructive feedback, and regular performance reviews. This is primarily the work of the team leader but can involve other team members as well. The experience of cooperating adds to the personal development of individual members.

The potential for gains from the personal development of team members and better work processes is unlimited. There is a strong argument in favor of continuous learning discussed in Chapter 10, GainManagement Training.

▲ *Encouraging Responsibility and Participation.* Team leadership includes many actions that encourage members to participate and to be more responsible. GainManagement is not a permissive approach. All members are expected to participate and to be responsible for their own work and the work of the team. This involves encouragement rather than coercion. Team leaders and members encourage each other by involving each other in decisions about work processes and improvements and by giving each other freedom to act, by encouraging risk taking and initiative, and by trusting each other.

A study by Yankelovich and Immerwahr makes an excellent point about discretionary effort, which is defined as the difference between the maximum effort of which workers are capable and the minimum effort required to avoid being fired or penalized.[5] Discretionary effort is growing in importance as more educated workers join the workforce and work designs fail to keep pace. Team leaders that promote more participation and greater responsibility are encouraging workers to use more of this discretionary effort. This is the substance of GainMaking.

2. Build Teams

The second responsibility of team leadership is to build a strong work team. As previously described, work teams are the basic units of the modern organization. It is to the team that the individual makes his or her basic commitment. This commitment is personal and heartfelt: "These are my friends, and they are counting on me." From this base, commitment can be extended to the larger organization.

Building a team is like creating an orchestra from a group of individual musicians. The final product is much more than the simple sum of the individual performances. No one musician alone can play a symphony, and only with perfect teamwork can the orchestra do so. Well-developed teams can substantially outproduce the sum of their individual members working independently.

▲ *Clarify the team.* The team leader must clarify the purpose, membership, and measures of success for the team. Each team fulfills an important part of the work of the organization. When performed successfully and combined with the work of other teams, the team's work enables the organization to excel. The team job description presented at the beginning of this chapter is used for this purpose (Figure 6-5).

▲ *Promote teamwork.* The team leader and the members encourage teamwork among themselves. Friendly relationships are developed. Conflicts that occur are resolved quickly and completely. Members trust each other and share information and ideas openly and easily.

▲ *Hold team meetings.* The team leader and members understand and value effective meetings as the way they do some of their work. The team holds efficient information, problem-solving, planning, and other types of meetings. All members have good meeting skills and continually strive to increase meeting effectiveness. GainMaking occurs as the team develops strength and skills. The team participates in designing its own work processes and in improving interteam processes. The team also develops a commitment to achieving its goals. High-performing teams consistently set higher goals for themselves . . . and achieve them.

3. Guide Work

The purpose of the team is to work. The third team leadership responsibility is to guide the work of the members and of the team. This includes planning, training, designing work processes, providing resources, troubleshooting, and helping members solve work-related problems. The team leader sets the example and the pace and brings all members into the process. GainMaking occurs as members participate more in guiding the work of the team.

▲ *Directions.* The team leader sees that the team has complete plans, schedules, and instructions, and follows them. Members are encouraged to participate in planning and scheduling by providing feedback and analysis to improve planning.

▲ *Coordination.* All participate in coordinating the work of the team with that of other teams. The team leader and team members contact other teams and attend meetings of other teams to coordinate work and do joint planning.

▲ *Tools and Materials.* The team leader provides the necessary tools and materials. Members are involved in developing better tools and finding better ways to use materials, information, and other resources.

▲ *Helping.* The team leader and members offer each other suggestions for solving work-related problems. Suggestions are freely given and received. Members help and coach each other. New members are given special attention by the rest of the team. All members are challenged and encouraged to think and be creative in solving daily problems and looking for more efficient work processes.

4. Promote Goals

Attaining excellence begins with having goals for excellence. At the team level workers begin to participate in setting goals and strategy. Participation begins with an understanding of and a commitment to the team's goals, which contribute to the goals of the organization. As experience grows, participation expands until workers and teams are not only setting goals and strategies for their teams but also influencing the goals of the organization.

▲ *Excellence.* The team leader and members are committed to high standards of performance and excellent goals for the team and each other. The team leader sets an example by his or her personal commitment to excellence.

▲ *Goals.* The team leader and members set goals for themselves that will contribute to those of the larger organization. They concentrate on the contribution needed by the next higher level in the organization. The team leader explains the higher-level and longer-range goals of the organization. The members work at understanding and supporting those goals.

▲ *Standards.* The team leader and members develop their own standards of performance. They also design the feedback and controls they need to ensure the achievement of their goals.

▲ *Focus and Charge.* The team leader uses the monthly **Focus** and **Charge** to guide and educate team members as they do their monthly problem solving.

▲ *Achievement.* The team leader and members celebrate their achievements and foster the team's reputation for excellence within the organization. Teams develop and take pride in a "can-do" spirit of performance.

Summary

GainMaking will occur from three key thrusts. First, the formal idea processing structure enables employees to participate more in problem solving and innovation. This is the first step and the easiest to implement, so it is the place to start building momentum. Problem solving creates new experiences of achievement, involvement, influence, fairness, and trust that cause employees to feel more challenged, secure, and loyal. This causes creativity, productivity, responsibility, and commitment to grow and open the way to more and better GainMaking.

System 5 team leadership, the second GainMaking thrust, opens the door to participation in designing work processes and setting goals and strategies. In addition, team leadership enhances participation in problem solving and innovation. This comes about as a result of developing people and strong teams, by providing the help and resources people need to be productive and by encouraging commitment to excellence.

The third GainMaking thrust, participation in policy making, will be discussed in Chapter 11.

Notes

1. Robert J. Doyle, *Gainsharing and Productivity* (New York: AMACOM, 1983).
2. Max De Pree, *Leadership Is an Art* (New York: Doubleday, 1989).
3. Rensis Likert, *New Patterns of Management* (New York: McGraw-Hill, 1961).
4. Ibid.
5. Daniel Yankelovich and John Immerwahr, "Putting the Work Ethic to Work," Public Agenda Foundation, 1983.

Chapter 7

GainSharing

GainSharing, as the third element of GainManagement, is a great deal more, and a great deal more important, than simple financial incentives installed to get employees to work a little bit harder or smarter. GainShares, as we will show, are not incentives, they are dividends. Using the GainManagement principle of equity for all partners, all partners receive dividends—Gainshares.

GainSharing for All Constituents

Every organization has multiple constituents who contribute to the performance of the organization and share in the results of that performance. Constituents, depending on the type of organization, are shareholders, investors, owners, customers, employees, suppliers, taxpayers, contributors, volunteers, students, parents, citizens, parishioners, retirees, patients, and others. Whether an organization fails, plods, or excels, all constituents share in its results. More successful organizations are able to attract constituents because they provide results of greater value. The increased value resulting from GainManagement are to be shared with all of the organization's constituents. For instance, a publicly owned business has five principal constituents, each of whom contributes to the ability of the business to function:

- ▴ *Shareholders.* They provide the capital investment to start the business and to obtain the equipment, tools, buildings, raw materials, and working capital the business needs to operate.
- ▴ *Employees.* They provide the mental labor and manual labor for the business to function.

▲ *Customers*. They purchase goods and services from the business and provide the cash flow for continuing operations.
▲ *Suppliers*. They provide materials and services the business uses in its work.
▲ *Communities*. They provide workers, the political and social environment, and the public services the business needs to operate efficiently.

Each of these constituent groups contributes to and expects to share in the results of the business. Each has certain expectations they place on the business as a condition of their continued support—certain returns each expects from their investment in the business:

▲ *Shareholders*. They expect their investment to be protected and wisely used to return value in the form of dividends and equity growth.
▲ *Employees*. They expect wages, benefits, employment security, safety, and personal growth.
▲ *Customers*. They expect products and services of quality and value commensurate with the price they pay.
▲ *Suppliers*. They expect fair dealings, on-time payments, and a continuing relationship.
▲ *Communities*. They expect the business to abide by their laws, provide good employment opportunities, and pay taxes for the support of schools and other government services.

Nonbusiness organizations will have different constituencies, but the idea of constituent contributions and expectations is always the same. Each constituent contributes and expects a fair return. When the return is insufficient, constituents withdraw their support and the organization can no longer function. When the return is sufficient, constituents will maintain their contributions and the organization will continue to function. When returns are excellent, constituents will increase their support and contributions and the organization will grow and prosper. GainManagement intends to create this latter scenario of excellent results and increasing support by all constituent groups. To complete the process, therefore, there must be a GainShare for each constituent.

When a GainManagement organization achieves excellence, there are gains to be shared with all of its constituents. For some constituents—such as shareholders, customers, suppliers, and community—GainShares are an automatic result of excellent performance, as follows:

- ▲ *Shareholders.* Extra profits are reinvested, which causes a gain in stockholder equity.
- ▲ *Customers.* To attain excellence the organization first has to make its products and services of greater value to customers. Thus, customers receive their share of the gain in advance.
- ▲ *Suppliers.* Excellence causes organizations to grow and thus use more goods and services, creating increased business for suppliers.
- ▲ *Communities.* Profitable businesses pay a GainShare to their communities in the form of more taxes. They also use more services, provide new employment opportunities, and have the time and resources to support many cultural and social activities.

In the ongoing GainManagement process there is a formal review of all these GainShares to be sure they do occur as intended and that balance and equity are maintained.

In the case of employees some of their GainShares are automatic because they benefit directly from organizational excellence. The following are examples of automatic employee GainShares from the GainManagement process:

- ▲ Experiences of achievement, involvement, influence, fairness, and trust resulting from greater participation
- ▲ Personal growth that comes from more responsibility
- ▲ The opportunity to learn and grow by participating with others in teams
- ▲ More frequent promotional opportunities that occur in a growing organization
- ▲ Employment security in direct proportion to the level of excellence
- ▲ A share of the excellence achieved by the organization and the enjoyment of that success

The employee share of the financial gain is not automatic, so provision must be made to provide each contributing employee with a financial GainShare when it occurs. This is the financial GainShare that has taken on inordinate meaning in past gainsharing programs.

This minor, but important, element has become dominant to the point of overshadowing GainPlanning, GainMaking, and the other nonfinancial aspects of GainSharing.

There are three reasons why financial gainsharing has become so predominant. The first is the failure to recognize the power and importance of employee participation in management processes. The second reason is the erroneous but lingering belief in the value of financial incentives. Managers still hope to find incentives that will work. The third reason encompasses a number of serious problems with employee compensation. There is a misplaced hope that a gainshare bonus will solve or at least provide some relief to the problems with basic compensation. A brief review of incentives and basic compensation will help explain these problems and thus put financial GainShares in a better perspective.

Incentives

For ages kings and kahunas, masters and managers, and other assorted bosses have used reward and punishment to motivate people. Popular jargon uses the crude carrot-and-stick metaphor of donkey driving to identify this traditional notion about motivation. First, dangle a carrot in front of the donkey to get the beast to move. Then, when that doesn't work, apply a stick to the animal's backside.

Variations on this crude carrot-and-stick method have been used consistently on humans, from the building of the pyramids to staffing modern corporations. In the past 100 years, however, carrots and sticks have lost their usefulness as managerial tools. Both have become obsolete but for different reasons. Managerial sticks have simply been taken away. Carrots still exist but have become so expensive that business and other organizations can no longer afford them.

Little by little the actions of democratic governments and the labor movement have whittled the manager's punishment stick down to about the size of a popsicle stick. Today's managers have virtually no power to punish employees. Even the ultimate punishment, job loss, doesn't frighten people into doing good work. It upsets people, true, but it does not motivate them to work. As recently as 50 years ago job loss was a serious matter, providing the manager with an effective threat. Today job loss is troublesome, but it is not a tragedy, and, therefore, it is not an effective threat. Popsicle sticks in the hands of managers don't worry people into being better workers. In fact, when managers use punishment nowadays, employees resent it rather than fear it. The impact of a weak threat is the loss of trust, credibility, and greater animosity but no performance improvement.

As for carrots, organizations just can't afford them anymore. People in desperate poverty will do a great deal of work for a minimal reward. People on the edge of poverty will work for a moderate reward. As a person's basic needs become more satisfied, however, larger and larger incentives are needed to motivate. Average wages have now increased to a level where the cost of pure performance incentives is higher than any businesses can afford.

The 19th-century piece-rate incentives of Frederick Taylor paid employees bonuses of 50% to 150% of their very low, two-dollars-per-day base pay. People earning extremely low wages can be motivated to work harder and better for the prospect of doubling their income. Workers today average over $100 per day, including insurances and retirement benefits; no company can afford 50–150% bonuses on this level of base pay in today's environment.

There is even some question whether the most common of all incentives, the sales commission, is still an effective motivator. A specialty food manufacturer hiring a new salesperson for the San Francisco territory wondered if the company's sales compensation system was in line with the competition. The sales pay consisted of a $30,000 base plus a performance bonus that paid a minimum of $10,000 up to a maximum of $20,000. Two national search firms confirmed that to hire top people the company would have to pay $60,000 per year plus the usual car and other expenses. Both search firms explained that it made no difference how the pay was split between base, bonus, or commission as long as it added up to $60,000 at the end of the year. The search firms agreed that tradition dictated some split between base pay and bonus, but how it was split, or if it was split, was beside the point. This is insufficient evidence to announce the demise of sales commissions as incentives, but it is enough evidence to suggest some serious rethinking about incentive pay even for salespeople.

In 1990 *The Wall Street Journal* reported a survey in which 50% of the companies were using some form of incentive plan for salaried and hourly workers below the executive level. This was up from 40% in 1989. The survey also showed that another 6% were planning to adopt such plans in the following year. These plans included profit sharing, year-end bonuses, and other individual or group incentives, according to the survey. There is still a strong belief (or maybe a hope) in carrots, so managers keep looking for the carrot that will work. The survey also reported that one-third of the companies admitted that their incentive plans were ineffective in motivating people to identify with the company's goals and do better work.

Still, many managers claim that incentives do work and that workers on incentives outperform those who are not. These claims are undoubtedly true, but the carrot alone is not making the difference. Incentive plans usually focus narrowly on very specific performance results such as output, quality, attendance, suggestions, or safety. This focusing effect provides information and a concentration of effort that accounts for much of the performance improvement. Rather than motivate, incentives provide information that enables incentive workers to focus on the right results.

In relation to the turnaround needed to move organizations to the levels of excellence that will be the norm in the 21st century, small financial incentives are of no value. New motivators with substance will be needed. The motivation to do better work in GainManagement are participation and achievement, rather than dollars.

Problems of Compensation

Compensation is management's biggest and most chronic internal problem. It is also their most expensive one. Despite a great deal of effort, energy, and worry, solutions to the compensation problems have so far been elusive.

Strategic planning is one potential source of solutions that has not been tried to any great extent and may account for the persistence of the problems. So far compensation has not been subjected to any serious strategic thinking. Solutions tend to be too shallow or short-term, whereas the problem is deep and long-term.

The financial GainShares in the GainManagement process are not compensation in the usual sense any more than they are incentives. Recent experience with traditional gainsharing programs indicates that managers try to use gainsharing to help solve basic compensation problems. The problems with compensation must be resolved, but the financial GainShares will not do it. Until the basic problems with compensation are resolved, the temptation to misuse the financial GainShare will continue to diminish the potential benefit of GainSharing. Compensation problems can be grouped into three categories: rising labor costs, growing employee discontent, and poor administration. But the underlying cause of all three problems is the failure of management to think strategically about compensation and to plan it well.

Rising Labor Costs

Managers are very concerned about rising labor costs and their effect on declining productivity. Statistics have shown an ominous trend of increasing labor rates and declining productivity since about 1967. Articles constantly remind managers of the disparity between the unit labor costs of American and foreign goods. Hearing this criticism and reviewing their own statistics, managers have erred by only working on one half of the problem—rising labor *rates*. They have not adequately addressed the other half of the problem, which is *declining productivity*.

General wage increases were standard procedure through the 1960s and 1970s but were abandoned in the 1980s, a time when many new efforts were made to reduce labor costs. There were layoffs, freezes, reductions, lump-sum payments, and two-tier programs. Few of these were well planned or explained, and most resulted in more worker discontent.

As part of the trend to contain labor costs many performance-related incentives were also introduced. New profit-sharing plans were started, and established ones were modified to include quarterly or semiannual cash payments in addition to or instead of deferred profit sharing. Talk in compensation circles turned to things like contingency pay, pay at risk, and the old standard, pay for performance. There was a new wave of experimentation with incentive plans, mainly group incentives. Gainsharing, as an incentive, was part of this trend.

There are two things that did *not* happen as part of the effort to solve the problem of high labor costs. First, managers did not go back and analyze when and how labor costs went astray. If they had, they would have discovered that their current problems are the result of decisions made 10 or even 20 years ago. The routine annual cost-of-living increases begun in the 1960s compounded base pay to its current high levels. These practices also led employees to the belief that annual pay raises were an entitlement, not something that must be earned with increased productivity.

Second, managers did not see the other half of the problem—that productivity was not keeping pace with labor rates. The problem is not the rising labor *rates*; the problem is rising unit labor *costs*, which is a function of labor rates and productivity. A balanced solution to the problem of rising unit labor costs must include efforts to increase productivity. By treating only one of the causes and asking employees to take the brunt of the solution in their paychecks, managers are alienating employees, who are their best resource for solving the other cause, which is productivity.

Employee Dissatisfaction

It is no secret that employees are more dissatisfied than satisfied with their pay. Despite steadily increasing wage levels, employee dissatisfaction with pay continues unabated. During the 1980s pay increases did not keep up with the rate of inflation. Many observers cite this as the cause of employee discontent but there was just about as much dissatisfaction with pay and benefits during the previous two decades, when pay was running ahead of inflation and annual wage increases often hit double digits. Even though pay levels continue to rise, and many employees and their families enjoy a good living standard, there is always pressure for more. However, this desire for more income is not the cause of worker dissatisfaction with pay. The issues that bother employees are lack of clarity, lack of candor, inconsistency, and unfairness.

Lack of Clarity

Employees often do not understand the systems used to determine their pay. Few organizations do an adequate job of explaining their pay systems to employees. Decisions always seem to be arbitrary even when they are not. When employees do not understand the pay system, whether pay decisions are generous or stingy, there will always be some discontent. For the organization Eileen Smith's paycheck is a minor journal entry. For Eileen it is her livelihood. How pay is determined and everything else about it is a matter of extreme importance to Eileen and all of her coworkers. Managers' failure to recognize that employees need to understand their pay system is evidence of shallow management thinking on the subject.

Lack of Candor

There is an almost universal feeling among employees that the organization is not candid with them about matters of pay. Explanations about profit and budgets and how wages and increases are decided are seldom adequate. Some organizations say nothing, others give out economic data that no one understands and few believe. In the absence of sound analysis and strategic planning managers have tended to base their decisions on industry patterns and the consumer price index. Beginning about the time of the 1979–1981 recession, U.S. companies broke with industry patterns and national trends. International competition was becoming more intense and profits were being seriously eroded. For the first time in two or three decades managers were forced to base compensation decisions on the company's ability to pay increased wages.

Profit is and should be the only basis for these decisions because the profitability of the company must be protected for the survival of the business. However, management is not able to tell employees candidly that profit is the principal reason because of the distorted understanding that employees have of profit. Managers have failed to properly explain profit as a critical need of the business and all of its constituents, including employees. They have, by their neglect, caused the misunderstanding that profit is for the shareholder and not for the employees. Because employees believe that their paychecks are in a tug-of-war with shareholders' profits, managers go to great lengths to avoid this conflict when they talk about wages. This failure to be candid not only causes employee dissatisfaction over pay but also adds to the mistrust that exists between management and the employees. Several years ago, as the workers were filing out of an automobile plant to go on strike, a machinist was heard to comment, "I don't know why there has to be a strike. All we are asking for is a nickel an hour. They have lots of money. Surely they can let us have a nickel."

Another candor issue concerns the secrecy that organizations try to maintain about individual pay. Some examples of the secrecy border on the bizarre. One major automobile company once had a policy of not telling individual employees the starting rates and maximums of their salary ranges. This policy was in stark conflict with the company's pay-for-performance program. Employees were confused when they were told they could increase their pay with better performance but were not told to what level their pay could go. Employees often subvert management's efforts at pay secrecy by openly discussing pay among themselves. Management argues that individual pay levels and pay decisions are confidential, but employees view the secrecy issue as a basic lack of candor. In addition, many employees interpret pay secrecy as a lack of willingness by management to be accountable for pay decisions.

Inconsistency

Employees are dissatisfied when they see inconsistencies in pay administration.

Some managers have high standards and demand high performance for raises; others have loose standards and give good increases even for mediocre performance. Some don't rate performance at all and give everyone the same increase regardless of performance. This is discouraging to the better performers, who in time will let their performance slip or may leave, hoping to find an organization that really does pay for performance.

Unfairness

From their perspective employees see inequities in the way people are paid in organizations. They are most unhappy with the growing gap between executive pay and the pay of other employees.

Marie's name came up for her annual pay review each December 1, her anniversary date. On December 1, 1990, she was told by her manager that her increase would be 3%. "Why so small?" asked Marie. "I've talked to others, and most have received 6% increases. Is there something wrong with my performance?"

"No," said the manager, "your performance has been great. I had you in the budget for a 6% increase, but sales are off in the fourth quarter and everyone has to cut spending. I have to cut your increase to 3%."

"What about the ones who got 6% earlier this year?" asked Marie.

"They were lucky," replied the manager.

Marie left work early that day saying she didn't feel well. That night she began to update her résumé.

In 1990 an AFL-CIO paper entitled "Excessive Executive Pay" stated, "While the compensation of corporate executives soared, worker pay lagged behind inflation." Lest these complaints be dismissed as so much union rhetoric, *Industry Week* reported a poll of middle managers in which 62% said that top management pay was too high. About this the magazine said: "Exorbitant executive pay is crippling morale and creating a high level of cynicism throughout industry." "Crippling" and "cynicism" express some very strong feeling.

This problem is approaching scandalous proportions. It is attracting criticism from shareholder activist groups and inquiries from congressional committees. In May of 1991 it was even a topic for *Nightline*, the ABC in-depth news hour. The lack of management response of these criticisms is more evidence of management's failure to recognize the strategic significance of pay issues. The dissatisfaction caused by this felt inequity erodes teamwork and the confidence of workers in their leaders. It also leads workers to believe that the rules of the game are to get as much as you can. No organization can excel when its members are more interested in manipulating the organization for their personal gain than in developing the organization for performance. The example that many employees receive today from their senior managers is most unhealthy.

These problems of employee discontent persist because there are no mechanisms in place for employees to air their concerns about lack of clarity, lack of candor, inconsistency, or inequity. Individual negotiations and collective bargaining have achieved some acceptance in American business culture, but complaints about clarity, candor, inconsistency, and inequity have not. More often than not such complaints are ignored or dismissed as unimportant. As a result, this discontent lies beneath the surface of almost every organization's compensation programs, preventing compensation from being effective.

Poor Administration

Most organizations, especially large ones, go to great lengths to set up elaborate pay administration systems. These include job descriptions, job evaluation, pay grades, salary increase guides, wage surveys, and performance reviews. There are manuals and forms and training and detailed budgeting and decision-making processes.

These systems are for the most part well designed, rational, and capable of being well administered. There are staffs of competent specialists who work hard to assist managers with wage administration and to maintain the integrity of their systems. The fact remains, however, that most salary systems are poorly administered from the perspective of the employee. Some of the problem is in the systems, but most of it is in the way managers apply the systems.

One administrative practice that demonstrates this weakness is that of "pay for performance." The phrase is so common as to be a cliché and, as practiced, is about as meaningful. Every organization claims to have a pay-for-performance program. Most consist of some form of a performance appraisal to rate an employee's performance according to predetermined standards of performance. This performance rating is used to determine the size of the employee's next pay raise. If all of the performance ratings are accurate, the typical pay-for-performance program works approximately as follows:

Performance	Average Percent Raise	Average Increase @ $600/Week Weekly
Above average	6%	$36
Average	4	24
Below average	2	12

This design does not provide an adequate pay differential for increasing levels of performance. It is highly unlikely that $12 motivates workers earning $600 per week to raise their performance from average to above average. In this example, after the annual increase the above-average performer is paid $636, the below-average one, $612. As pay for performance this is a feeble gesture that does not motivate people to high levels of performance.

In the previous example it was stated that *if* all the ratings were accurate, this would be how the system should work. But accuracy is a problem, too. Except for manual operations in the factory and office there are few valid standards of performance. We know very little about how to set standards for knowledge or service jobs. Most ratings are based on soft criteria and the subjective judgment of managers. This is a process that managers find very difficult and seldom do well. Every company has problems of inconsistent performance ratings from department to department. Some managers are tough, others are easy, and still others avoid ratings completely. Many managers first determine how much of a raise they want to give each employee and then write a performance review to justify that decision.

Moira Dolan, the quality-assurance manager for a carburetor plant, had just completed a very thorough training session about the company's new performance review and pay-for-performance program. In a follow-up interview she was asked her reaction to the training and the new program.

Interviewer:	How do you now feel about your ability to set meaningful performance standards and to evaluate the performance of your quality engineers and inspectors?
QA Manager:	For the first time I feel confident that I can develop performance standards for each of my reports. I also know how to rate performance against those standards and believe I can do it well. This training has been very helpful—one of the best I have ever attended.
Interviewer:	OK, now suppose that for whatever reason you have already decided to give one of your inspectors a 6% increase and the company's merit increase guidelines say that only performance rated "above average" can receive a 6% increase. You know that this inspector's performance has been barely satisfactory. How will you rate the inspector on the next review?
QA Manager:	Above average.
Interviewer:	Why?
QA Manager:	I have a department to run, and I have to keep people happy. These personnel programs don't fit every situation.

Another reason for poor administration is that managers are not held accountable for wage administration in their departments. There are budgets and budget accountability, of course, but no real account-ability for wage and salary administration. A department manager with 25 professional and clerical employees will have an annual salary budget of close to $1 million. If this manager were to be given a 6% salary increase budget, there will be an accounting for the $60,000. But there is never a reckoning about how well the $60,000 is spent in the interests of the company and its employees. If the manager does not get any complaints, it is assumed that the salary administration job was well done.

Even more serious, there isn't accountability for how the basic $1 million was spent. Did it go to reward performance that contributed to the success of the business? Could that same performance have been achieved for $800,000? This manager can spend $1 million for wages with very little accountability but most likely cannot buy a $1,000 software program without extensive justification.

Many managers simply do not have confidence in their com-pany's compension plans and feel they must devise their own rules to meet the needs of their department. In some cases this is because they do not understand the company's program, and in others it is because they do. In either event too many managers devise their own hiring rates and manipulate job evaluations and merit budgets to suit their needs regardless of company policy.

Another administration problem is the way organizations handle fringe benefits. There was a time when benefit programs were a fringe on total labor costs, but that time is long past. Still, many companies treat benefits as the petty cash item they were 50 years ago. Costs for health insurance, holiday and vacation pay, and other benefits have become a major expense. National statistics show that fringe benefits average between 25% and 40% of base pay. By treating benefits separately from wages employers have allowed employees to assume that benefits are free. As a result employees do not under-stand or support the many current cost-containment efforts.

In the 1990s there may be no compensation issue more fraught with misunderstanding and fear than the health insurance issue. The bitter 1990 strike in the West Virginia coal mines was not about wages; it was brought about because management tried to change the em-ployees' health care plan. The miners knew that management could not afford larger wage increases due to the financial condition of the coal business. However, they did not understand what this had to do with their health and welfare benefits. Health insurance and other benefits are labor costs just as much as wages are, and they should be planned, budgeted, and administered as a single cost. Only then will employees be able to understand the financial reality of benefits and the actions needed to control their costs.

As was stated at the beginning of this section, the underlying cause of many of these problems is the lack of strategic planning for compensation. The search for solutions must continue, but until serious strategic thinking is applied to offset traditional clichés and quick-fix solutions, little progress will be made. The knowledge needed to solve these problems is available. For instance, it is known that compensation is not a simple matter of base pay and a benefits package. It is also known that compensation must be more closely linked to the strategic needs of the business. In his book on this subject, Edward Lawler states that management spends too much time and energy on reducing labor costs and not enough on how to use labor costs to benefit the organization.[1]

There are many compensation components, and every component has some immediate, or tactical, purpose and impact. Every component should also have a long-range, or strategic, purpose because each has a strategic impact. Figure 7-1 lists the more common compensation components and their immediate and strategic purpose. To begin a process of strategic compensation planning an organization could construct a model such as this for its specific compensation components and specific business needs.

A model such as described would enable a company to analyze each major compensation component to determine how well it succeeds in fulfilling its immediate purpose and the extent to which it is having the desired strategic impact. Such analyses would help organizations to improve the structure and administration of compensation programs and avoid the fad trap of trying new ideas with little more than a hope they will work.

GainShares

GainSharing bonuses were omitted from the list of compensation components in Figure 7-1 for two reasons: The GainSharing bonus is (1) not an incentive and (2) not a compensation component in the usual meaning of compensation. Employee financial GainShares are only a minor part of the GainShares employees receive in an excellent

Figure 7-1.   Compensation strategies.

Compensation Component	Immediate Purpose	Strategic Business Impact
Individual Compensation:		
Base pay and benefits	Hiring and retention	A competent workforce
Sales commissions	Increased sales	Revenue and market share
Merit pay and individual incentives	Better individual performance	Productivity
Special bonus	Specific performance	Innovation, productivity
Long-range incentives, retirement, stock options	Retention of key personnel	A competent workforce
Management incentive plans	Specific annual business results	Market share, profitability
Group Compensation:		
Team rates	Cross-training, flexible workforce	Productivity
Small group incentives	Better group performance	Productivity
Deferred profit sharing	Retirement benefit	A competent workforce
Cash profit sharing	Better organization performance	Productivity
ESOP (Employee Stock Ownership Program)	Shared ownership	Profitability

organization. It is doubtful that even high-performing organizations will pay out large GainSharing bonuses, and small bonus checks do not motivate high levels of performance. Past experience shows that where gainsharing is considered an important incentive by managers and employees, the programs are fair-weather programs and work well only so long as there are bonuses.

Although workers can buy just as many groceries with a $100

GainSharing check as they can with a $100 paycheck, the GainSharing check in the GainManagement process has a different impact. The paycheck is expected, is consistent, and is based on the amount of time worked. (It also carries the taint of all the history of dissatisfaction and inequity described above.) The GainSharing check must be detached from all of these problems and set apart. It must *not* be expected, consistent, or based on time worked. The GainShare bonus must be seen as the application of the new principle of equity between company and employee as described in Chapter 5. It should be determined by management not according to how much or how little it will take to "keep 'em happy" but according to solid business results in a true spirit of "everybody wins or nobody wins."

The GainSharing bonus is similar to the compensation components in Figure 7-1 in that it does have immediate and strategic purposes. The immediate purpose is to reinforce GainMaking efforts. It is a reward for improved productivity, but much more important it is also feedback about how well these efforts are succeeding. Its strategic purpose is to support participative management, teamwork, and partnership. It is not an extra payment the organization gives employees when they have been "good." It is an equity share that employee partners *earn* as they participate and contribute to their organization's excellent performance. It is their partnership dividend.

This equity concept is essential to successful GainManagement. Past problems with compensation make employees skeptical at best, cynical at worst, that the company will be completely fair. Tradition and past experience cause managers to believe that they can still motivate employees to high levels of performance with financial incentives. The GainShare bonus must be planned, implemented, and communicated in a way that overcomes obsolete notions about motivation. Employees must experience fairness in their financial GainShares. Managers must learn that excellence is not a commodity they can purchase but something that will be freely given by full-fledged partners.

For financial GainSharing to have its full effect the problems with basic compensation need to resolved. When there are unresolved compensation issues organizations are tempted to use the GainShare bonus to supplement one or more weak components of their basic program. The folly of this misuse of GainSharing is that the basic pay problems don't get resolved and the immediate and strategic benefits of the GainShare bonus are not fully realized.

The Financial GainSharing Base: Minimum Profit

Before financial sharing can occur, there must be real gains in business or organizational performance in such areas as quality, market share, revenue, service, productivity, and profitability. Plans that pay employees for cost savings regardless of overall business performance may work in the short term as incentives for cost savings, but such plans are not GainManagement. The idea of a partnership means that everyone benefits or no one does. *GainPlanning* promises employees that they will participate as full partners, and it provides the structure and process for them to do so. *GainMaking* enables employees to participate as partners. They are given information about the state of the partnership and are challenged to excel. *GainSharing* fulfills the partnership agreement. Financial GainShares reflect the extent to which the partnership achieves financial excellence. Minimum profit must be the basis for financial GainSharing. When there is no gain in profit, there are no financial GainShares. When there is a gain, the shares reflect the extent of the improved profitability.

The financial GainSharing base can be no less than the minimum profit the organization needs to maintain itself and grow in its competitive environment. The first purpose of GainManagement is to create and maintain a healthy, growing organization. Before there can be GainSharing bonuses, the health of the organization must be secured.

In our book *Gainsharing and Productivity*[2] we said that the productivity base should be set at a point where prices, wages, and profits were all reasonably competitive. In GainManagement that guideline for profit must be revised. Reasonably competitive levels are still valid criteria to apply to prices and wages. It is easy to ascertain competitive levels for prices and wages, and the external comparison is valid. In a free-market economy competition is the primary force controlling prices and wages. But a competitive level is not a valid criterion for profit. Market competition is not the force that controls the level of profitability. Although competitors may temporarily affect the ability of the company to be profitable, *profit is primarily an internal matter in terms of both how much is needed and how much is made.*

How much profit a business *needs* depends on its current health, the risk level of the industry it is in, the strength of its competitive environment, and the company's growth objectives. How much profit a business *makes* depends on its internal productivity, product quality, market share, and other factors unique to each business.

The profit a company needs is the amount necessary to pay its obligations to shareholders and fund its strategic plan. As described in Chapter 5 (see Figure 5-1, step 2) the strategic planning process called for strategic objectives in eight categories, with the eighth objective being the profit required to implement the strategic objectives in the other seven areas. These profit requirements are the basis for strategic profit planning.

The following example is very much oversimplified, but it demonstrates the concept of minimum profit planning to support the company's strategic plan.

In 1990, when the Ajax Company had a $10 million capital base and $20 million in sales, management set two strategic marketing objectives: to increase market share and to double sales volume in five years. To accomplish those objectives the company must add $10 million (additional production equipment) to its capital base in order to support the $40 million sales goal. One of management's financial objectives is to fund future growth from current operations without any additional long-term debt. Therefore, to increase its capital base by $10 million in five years Ajax must average $2 million in profit over the next five years. The profit plan shown in the table will enable the company to reach its business objectives.

	Capital Base	Sales	Minimum Profit	ROI	Percentage of Sales
1990	$10,000,000	$20,000,000	$1,500,000	15%	7.5%
1991	11,500,000	23,000,000	1,725,000	15	7.5
1992	13,225,000	26,450,000	1,983,750	15	7.5
1993	15,208,750	30,417,500	2,281,313	15	7.5
1994	17,490,063	34,980,126	2,623,509	15	7.5
1995	20,113,572	40,227,144			

These figures show how current operations provide the profit Ajax needs to increase its capital base to reach its 1995 objective of $40 million in sales. The example, of course, is very much oversimplified. In actual practice there are many more variables to be considered than are shown. The example is only intended to show how minimum profit relates to the achievement of the company's strategic plan.

This minimum profit must be the basis for financial GainSharing, and bonuses should be paid only when the company exceeds its required minimum profit. The strategic planning process determined that the company must attain a market share represented by the $40 million sales level. To do less than this would limit the company's future and the job security of its employees. The achievement of strategic goals means a great deal more to a company than just a higher sales figure. The higher volume will provide promotions for present employees and new jobs for new employees. The greater market share will provide more security for current jobholders and investors and future economic security for retirees. *The reference point for setting the GainSharing base is not history or industry averages but the strategic future of the company.*

At the proper market share and profitability level the company will be able to serve its customers better. A company of sufficient size and profitability can afford the internal support services, systems, and equipment that create the efficiency and the quality work environment that are the mark of excellent organizations. When profit is too low, it acts as a demotivator for the company. There isn't money for the equipment and staff necessary for excellent operations. There is a lack of space and crowding that creates inefficiency. The marginally profitable company is slow paying vendors and has difficulty getting the supplies it needs. The unprofitable company usually has lower pay scales that lead to high turnover and prevent the hiring of excellent people. Only profitable companies are healthy enough to be excellent.

Profit is not and should not be the sole purpose of an organization. Profit does not dignify the work of a person or of an organization. The mission statement identifies the purpose that dignifies organizations. Profit is no more than a simple, direct measure of current performance and a requirement to provide the capital for future operations.

Minimum profit is similar in some ways to the employees' base pay. Employees need a good base pay to satisfy their basic economic needs, and the company needs a base profitability to satisfy the basic economic needs of the business. When both sets of basic needs are properly met, the conditions necessary for GainSharing are possible and will work effectively. The GainShare then functions as a bonus for both the company and the employees.

This minimum profitability is entirely unique to each business and cannot be determined by any type of competitive comparison.

Where valid data are available, checks can be made of profit in competing businesses for information purposes and to see how a company stacks up in its industry. No matter what this comparison shows, however, each business must determine its own minimum profit requirements based on sound strategic planning.

A good profit plan with a clearly defined minimum profit is critical to the successful use of GainManagement to achieve the company's objectives. First, using minimum profit to establish the productivity base is beneficial to the company because it places the business on a solid financial base that will ensure the company's growth and survival. Second, minimum profit is beneficial to employees in two important ways: as security and as information. Every employee's job security and opportunity to grow in a job depends on the success and growth of the business. Workers need to know the factors upon which their futures are based: that current success, measured by profit, is a condition of future opportunity. This clear knowledge helps employees take personal responsibility for their futures.

As information, minimum profit is a much easier concept for employees to understand than the confusing traditional statements about profit maximization. Communicating and explaining the company's strategic goals and minimum profit requirements will dispel the antagonism and mistrust that employees now feel about corporate profits. When the importance of profit is understood, employees will also understand why financial GainShares must be based on exceeding the minimum profit requirement. They will understand that minimum profit is just as important to them as to the company and its other constituents. Most of the automatic GainShares accrue to everyone at the minimum profit level. Beyond that point additional financial GainSharing is possible. With this understanding an organization can avoid the wasteful internal conflicts of the past and use its energy to make the pie bigger rather than fighting over the size of each slice.

Profit planning is not a precise science in many companies, so the actual process for determining an adequate minimum profit still involves a good deal of judgment and reasonable estimates. As long as this is done aboveboard and explained well, it does not cause mistrust. Here is where the new principle of equity for all partners is visibly applied. Mistrust grows out of past practices of concealing profit information from employees. More openness, better communications, and an honest admission that the numbers include some judgment, estimates, and even "guesstimates," creates trust and support. In companies where strategic planning and profit planning are not done well, management must take responsibility for learning and improving these management practices as described in Chapter 5. This is no easy step, but it is what must be done in organizations committed to achieving excellence and to establishing a rational base for financial GainSharing.

To get started in this process an organization does not need a precisely calculated minimum profit. Management can start by putting together a basic strategic plan. The cost of implementing the various strategic objectives can be estimated to calculate a starting point for a strategic profit plan. Each year the process can be refined so that within three to five years a sound profit plan can be determined. The more openly this is done and the more employees participate in the process, the better will be the acceptance of the results as a legitimate GainSharing base. Communicating and sharing this information will significantly increase employees' willingness and ability to contribute to GainMaking.

This minimum-profit concept is designed primarily for for-profit companies. Nonprofit organizations can use all of the features of the GainManagement process except, perhaps, the financial GainSharing. In some nonprofits it is possible to devise an appropriate financial GainShare as outlined above. In others a minimum profit cannot be calculated. Even without financial GainShares, however, the GainManagement process is a powerful process for achieving excellence because the nonfinancial GainShares are substantial and adequately motivating.

The Productivity Measurement

To improve productivity an organization needs regular feedback about productivity—at least a monthly scorecard. Employees need to know the results of their recent efforts and the extent to which greater effort is needed. Managers need a productivity scorecard to help them determine appropriate **Focuses** and **Charges.** A proper productivity measurement is one that includes all the factors that contribute to minimum profit.

The early gainsharing programs measured only the productivity of labor in determining gainsharing bonuses. In the 1980s many gainsharing programs were installed using multiple-factor measurements. These contained separate measurements and bonus credits for factors such as output, quality, labor efficiency, and safety. Almost all past programs used various types of partial productivity measurements, but these are no longer adequate to the productivity task facing most organizations. The productivity of labor can and should be measured, but labor productivity alone, or any other measure alone, is an incomplete solution to today's productivity problems and an incomplete base from which to pay GainShares. Productivity is more than output per hour; it is output compared to all of the resources, direct and indirect, used to produce it.

A common argument for partial measurements is that the GainShare must only be tied to things the employees can control. The term "line-of-sight" is frequently heard to mean that the Gain-Share should only reward productivity savings over which the employee has direct control. This is another example of System 3, consultative management, limiting the scope of employee participation. If there are ever to be major breakthroughs in productivity, management must expand employees' line-of-sight so that they begin to see not only their direct impacts but the many ways they impact productivity indirectly. All employees need to be educated about the whole business, not just the small part of it that surrounds their immediate work area. This is a major undertaking of considerable complexity and requires a serious commitment of time and resources. Businesses and other organizations have become so functionally specialized and concerned with departmental lines-of-sight that most employees are unaware of the whole. The waste, the missed opportunities, and the extra effort resulting from this lack of interunit understanding and coordination may account for as much as 20% of the total cost of some businesses. That 20% could go directly to the bottom line and be the difference between an average or mediocre business and an excellent one.

It is not enough that product designers come up with "gee-whiz" designs that look great in the sales brochures and annual reports; they must design products for manufacturability, too. Every engineering text supports this concept, but few engineers ever go out on the factory floor and actually talk to the machinists who must read their drawings and produce their designs. Line-of-sight for the accounting department means finding computer programs to complete the monthly recording and reporting tasks faster or with less labor. But total productivity also suggests that the accountants should be out talking to employees and managers to determine what information these people need or how well they understand and are able to use the reports now provided. Perhaps the way for the accounting department to improve productivity would be to increase its costs by $25,000 by adding an accountant to provide analysis and data that will enable the operations department to problem solve and reduce operating costs by $250,000.

Partial productivity measurements limited to line-of-sight will produce partial productivity improvements at best, or improvements in one area that impede productivity in another area at worst. The willingness of managers to adopt partial productivity measures for gainsharing programs shows how poorly productivity is understood and managed.

GainManagement assumes that employees are willing and able to learn about the whole business and to contribute to its total success. Given the right opportunity people would rather build cathedrals than lay stones. The information employees need is in the strategic plan, but they need to have it explained in ways they can understand. The **Focuses** and **Charges** help this process as do other formal communications, including the monthly productivity report and GainShare statement (see Figure 7-2).

The monthly productivity report and GainShare statement contains several important pieces of information:

- Total sales and/or income for the month
- Total expenses in categories important to the organization, i.e., labor, materials, energy, etc.
- Profit related to the minimum profit target
- Profit gains and GainShare information

In 1985 15 vice-presidents of a major East Coast public utility met to consider offering a gainsharing program to the unions in upcoming contract negotiations. It was explained that to use gainsharing they would have to develop a base productivity measurement to which the union would agree.

One vice-president commented, "How could we ever get the union to agree to a productivity measure? We can't agree on one ourselves."

The company decided to forgo proposing gainsharing during contract negotiations.

Figure 7-2. Monthly productivity report and GainShare statement.

NORTHWEST PLYWOOD CORPORATION
Monthly GainShare Summary

1. Sales		$778,924.00
2. Expenses		
Labor	$258,870.00	
Materials	359,774.00	
Other	77,243.00	
Total		695,887.00
3. Profit		83,037.00
4. GainShare Base (15% ROI) (7.5% of sales)		58,420.00
5. Gain		24,617.00
6. 20% to Reserve Fund		4,923.40
7. GainShare Pool		19,693.60
8. Employee Share - 50%		9,846.80
9. Participating Employees - 126		
10. Share Amount		78.15
11. Total Value of Reserve Fund to Date		$ 13,694.00

===

Key Productivity Trends - February	Profit Impact
• Sales price average decrease - $2.60	($59,500.00)
• Hardwood cost decrease - $1.32	$28,600.00
• Output up 124 panels per day	$23,100.00
• Rejects down from 5.4% to 4.8%	$ 7,600.00

▲ Key productivity trends or events that did or will impact productivity

The minimum-profit GainSharing base must be expressed in some form that allows for monthly tracking and for computing periodic GainShares. There are many ways to express the productivity base. The most common are dollars of profit, return on investment (ROI), and profit as a percent of sales. The simplest and most direct measurement is dollars of profit. The annual profit plan is divided into monthly or quarterly segments, which are used as monthly/quarterly targets. Profit in excess of the monthly/quarterly targets is to be shared. The profit number alone provides good information about gains or losses, but it does not show how the profit or loss occurred. This information is provided in the key productivity trends section of the GainSharing statement.

Return on investment is another way to express the GainSharing base. Return on investment is used here in the generic sense to represent the profit earned on the capital assets used by the company. There are many other measurements that serve a similar purpose, such as return on equity (ROE), return on assets (ROA), and return on net assets (RONA). ROI is especially useful in organizations where the productivity of capital is an important consideration. In organizations with a negligible capital base profit expressed as a percent of sales is an adequate alternative.

Return on investment is one of the best productivity measurement available today. It combines the data from the profit-and-loss statement and the balance sheet to provide information about the total economic performance of the business. It is the cumulative results of all the actions and decisions of every employee in the company.

> *ROI:*
> Sales minus expenses   = return
> Return divided by investment = ROI

In the ROI model an increasing return or profit means some combination of higher sales and lower costs. Higher sales are the direct work of marketing and sales employees, who determine prices, discounts, and volume of sales. Production and service employees affect sales indirectly by providing quality products and services on time, which are easier to sell and bring higher prices. Support-staff employees help marketing, sales, production, and service employees do their jobs more effectively by providing accurate information and services.

Reducing costs is the other half of improving return in ROI. This area is where the bulk of the GainMaking efforts are directed. Every employee in the company has some direct and much indirect impact on expenses. There are always opportunities to save time and material, find a better way, substitute a more economical material, improve quality, and meet schedules. In this area of cost reduction one resource can replace another.

In the early days of the Donnelly Scanlon plan it was discovered that labor productivity could be improved by increasing the pressure on the grinding wheels and producing more parts per hour. The problem was that this pressure significantly increased the wear and tear on costly diamond grinding wheels. The savings in labor productivity was not cost-effective when the added grinding wheel cost was figured into the equation. Only total factor productivity measurements prevent such problems.

The opportunity to improve the productivity of the company's capital resources is omitted from most current gainsharing programs. (Capital resources include plant, equipment, tools, machines, inventory, and working capital.) Making gains in this area means reducing unnecessary investment or getting a higher rate of return on the assets used. There are many opportunities for employees to make gains by conserving plant and equipment, tools and machines. A dollar's worth of oil today is much cheaper than replacing a $1,000 bearing next month. Costly inventories can be turned over faster and kept at the lowest levels necessary for plant efficiency and to meet customer needs. The popular JIT (just-in-time) program is a way to minimize inventories of raw materials and purchased parts by taking delivery "just-in-time" to put them into production. This reduces the capital dollars tied up in inventory and the space that would be required to store it. Many employees influence the purchase of inventories, from steel in the factory to paper clips in the office. They contribute to gains by ordering economically and increasing the turnover of dollars tied up in inventory.

The minimum-profit GainSharing base can be converted to a target ROI, as shown in the table and on line 4 of the productivity report in Figure 7-2. With current information about the status of the ROI employees approach problem solving with a total business perspective. ROI targets can also be used by the work teams to assess the cost-benefit of different solutions to problems they are solving. For example, a team considering a solution with a 5% ROI could be encouraged to look harder for a solution closer to the 15% ROI target. So many new inventions are coming to market these days, there is always a new machine or computer that can be used. Whether something should be bought and used can be determined by calculating ROI compared to the target.

ROI is a good way to present performance information to employees, but it isn't the only way. Some organizations or divisions cannot calculate a meaningful ROI—either their capital base is too small or the information is not available. In these cases a good productivity measurement can be provided using profit as a percent of sales. Minimum profit is converted to a percent of sales, which can be calculated and reported monthly. This is also shown in the table shown earlier in this chapter and in Figure 7-2. The other information in the monthly productivity report is quite similar and can be obtained from the same sources. The only difference in the profit-to-sales model is that the productivity of capital is not included in the measurement.

Sharing the Gains

The GainSharing productivity base defines the point where Gain-Sharing begins. The next issue to determine is how the gain will be shared. In *GainSharing and Productivity*, Chapter 7, we described how the four major gainsharing plans—Scanlon, Rucker, Improshare, and Profit Sharing—share productivity gains. The major emphasis in the early programs was that of fairness: that percent of the gains that would fairly reward employees for their greater efforts and new ideas. For instance, in Scanlon plans fairness was defined as paying 75% of the savings in labor costs to the employees. The company received the other 25% of the labor savings plus 100% of any other nonlabor savings. The assumption or hope was that there would be other nonlabor savings and that fairness would be achieved. While never stated as such, it would appear that fairness in these plans was defined as near equality. The equation could be stated as:

75% of labor savings $\approx$ 25% of labor savings + 100% of other savings

Rucker plans and Improshare use this same basic logic. No studies have ever been conducted of these experiences to determine if equality is achieved in practice, but there is general agreement that this approach to sharing has been fair.

What little has been said or written on this issue has always had a single perspective: Is the employee's share a fair share? But fairness is not a one-dimensional notion. The question of fairness in regard to the GainSharing must consider all parties. The GainShares must be fair to the company, to the employees, and to other constituents of the company as well.

Scanlon history includes an instance of a Canadian CEO complaining to Joe Scanlon that his company's plan was paying employee bonuses while the company was losing money. They had not designed the base properly, and the result was not fair to the company. In the long run it would not be fair to the employees either. Anything that is harmful to the health of the company will sooner or later be harmful to the employees who depend on the company for their present and future livelihood.

This inclination to consider fairness only from the perspective of the employees is an example of System 2 paternalistic thinking, which continues to hamper progress to more effective systems. This view of GainSharing reflects incentive thinking rather than partnership. In the past the fairness question was whether management was giving employees a fair share considering what they were being asked to do. *This is no longer the correct question.* The correct question, which GainManagement asks, is how to use the productivity gain to benefit all of the organization's constituents.

Basic issues of fairness are, or should be, resolved when the financial GainSharing base is derived from the minimum profit target. Minimum profit should be set at a level that provides a *fair* base pay to employees. Fair pay is defined as competitive for the locale, the industry, and the type of work. The free market determines base pay levels as it determines prices, and this is generally accepted as fair. The system is far from perfect, but it does work. For profit, fair is defined as the minimum profit that will allow the company to thrive, grow, and develop.

If employees' pay and company profits are both fair at the financial GainSharing threshold, what should be the basis for sharing financial gains between the company and the employees? There is no moral principle to apply because the moral issue of fairness was resolved in establishing the base. The question no longer is what *should* be done with the gain but rather what *can* be done with the gain. What does the farmer do with grain left over after the family has been fed and an adequate supply of grain has been set aside to plant next year's crop? The farmer can either declare a feast for the family and eat the excess grain or save the excess and plant a larger crop next year. A more likely alternative is to do some of each: Feast on some of the surplus, and save some of it to expand the farm for future feasts.

This analogy can be directly applied to the sharing of productivity gains. Some of the gain can be paid in cash to all employees, and some of the gain can be reinvested to accelerate the growth and development of the business. There should be an analysis of different sharing options to see which one offers the greatest overall benefit. How would it benefit the employees if the company paid out 25%, 50%, 75%, or even 100%? How would it benefit the company to retain 25%, 50%, 75%, or even 100%? There are benefits to both employees and company from any combination of payouts and retention.

Any payout to the employees from 25% to 100% is an obvious benefit to them because it increases their personal income. This is comparable to the feast for the farmer's family. Extra personal income also benefits the company by keeping experienced workers, who increase the company's ability to perform. Any amount retained by the company from 25% to 100% benefits the company by increasing its capital base. When the extra capital is put to work, the increased investment also benefits employees by providing more job opportunities, more promotions, and more job security.

This is a new concept for financial GainSharing, and each company must determine the best possible application of GainSharing funds. There is not yet enough experience with these plans to provide norms for how this issue should be decided, but a few predictions can be made. When an organization has done a good job of strategic planning and has determined its minimum profitability level, this profit level will be very high, most likely higher than the company's historic profit level. This new level of performance will be such a reach that when it is attained the company will want to celebrate and feast on the achievement. Success will also stimulate the organization to reach for even higher levels of performance. The decision to share gains 50–50 is predictable: pay out half of the gains to employees, and reinvest the other half in additional growth and development.

There are, of course, many ways to use these extra funds. One company decided to limit monthly cash bonuses to 15% of pay and apply shares over the 15% to the employees' ESOP accounts. Some of the GainShare pool could be used to create a fund to retrain displaced workers. Sales prices could be reduced to increase market share. Once organizations break out of traditional incentive thinking about GainSharing, the possibilities are intriguing. A true partnership can finally stop the age-old tug-of-war over wages and profits and get serious about managing the business so that everybody wins and all are joined in a common pursuit of excellence.

Other Financial GainSharing Issues

There are GainSharing issues to be addressed in addition to the GainSharing base and the sharing ratio. These are the issues of:

▲ Distribution method
▲ Who to include in financial GainSharing
▲ Frequency of payout
▲ Reserves for loss periods
▲ Ceilings
▲ Form of payment
▲ When and how to adjust the base and sharing ratio

There is a fair amount of detail about these issues in Chapter 7 of our book *GainSharing and Productivity*. The following section will discuss how to approach these issues in the GainManagement process.

Distribution Method

In GainManagement the GainShares are distributed in equal dollar shares to each employee. This is a change from traditional gainsharing plans, which distribute gainshares to employees as a percentage of pay. In the past only about 10% of the plans paid in equal dollar shares. The argument that percentage of pay recognizes individual differences in skill levels and ability to contribute to productivity improvements has prevailed in past gainsharing programs. A review of some experience in actual GainManagement installations may help to explain this shift from percentage of pay to equal shares.

One GainManagement design team decided on equal shares using the Robin Hood approach: taking from the rich and giving to the poor. Their analysis showed that the bulk of the workforce, those paid near the average, would receive just about the same amount of money under either the percentage-of-pay method or equal shares. The team held a lively debate and concluded that they needed to improve the compensation of new hires, who were paid only slightly above minimum wage. The company was having difficulty recruiting and retaining people at that low wage and the design team wanted to do something to alleviate that problem. The decision to use equal shares lowered the financial gain paid to the more highly paid executives and professional employees, but it increased the financial gain to the lower-paid new hires.

In three other installations the same decision emerged from each debate. However, rather than the Robin Hood approach they applied the Super Bowl bonus analogy. Every player on an NFL football team negotiates his own salary based on personal skill and performance, so there are huge differences in individual salaries. However, when a team wins the Super Bowl, every player on the roster, even those who did not play in the Super Bowl game, receives an equal share of the bonus money. Some players on injured reserve have been voted shares by their teams. The argument is that it takes the whole team to get through the season and the playoffs and win the Super Bowl. Salary pays for individual performance, and the Super Bowl bonus pays for team performance.

After thoroughly debating the issues all three GainManagement design teams decided to share the gains equally. Their reasons were that base pay rewards individual performance and that there needs to be a special reward for team performance. Except for equal Gain-Shares the design teams saw no other reward in their companies' basic compensation packages for teamwork.

The Robin Hood argument is weak because GainShares should not be used to remedy other compensation problems. When there are compensation problems hurting the company's productivity, they should be resolved independent of the decisions about how to distribute the GainShares.

The Super Bowl argument is the premise for equal shares in GainManagement. The goal in GainManagement is to develop a one-team mentality where everyone contributes what they can to achieve the organization's goals. Base pay rewards people differently based on individual skill and contribution. Distributing GainShares as a percent of pay also reinforces individual performance more than team performance. The GainShare should reinforce teamwork and team performance. Equal shares does this best.

Another advantage to the equal shares method is that it avoids the question of whether the company's base pay program is internally equitable. For percent of pay to work the company's base pay system must be reasonably equitable. When GainShares are distributed based on current pay rates, any problems of inequity are magnified. Compensation administration is not a precise science, and every company has some problems of internal equity. Distribution of equal shares prevents base compensation from contaminating financial GainShares. Compensation problems must still be resolved, but by using equal shares those problems can be separated from Gain-Sharing.

Fair Labor Standards Act

In any type of bonus program where the payout is tied to performance the FLSA provision of time and one-half for overtime must be observed. According to the law a bonus increases the hourly rate for nonexempt employees, and overtime premiums must reflect the bonus. In plans that pay GainShares as a percent of actual pay this provision of the law is automatically covered. When a company elects to use equal shares, they must recalculate all overtime premiums paid to reflect the amount of the GainShare. A simple way to deal with this is to adjust the sharing ratio from 50–50 to 51–49. The company retains an extra 1% and uses that to pay the overtime premiums to the nonexempt employees. Unless there is a high rate of overtime, the amount of money is negligible and this method is a simple expedient. When overtime is a major factor, there is no simple solution, and using the percent-of-pay option may be the most practical alternative. Perhaps one day the law will change to support the ideal of equal shares.

Whom to Include in Financial GainSharing

In GainManagement every employee participates in financial Gain-Sharing because the idea of one team is both a goal and an important part of the process. GainManagement will not realize its full potential if anyone—senior managers, field sales people, or part-time employees—is excluded from full participation.

In the past 30 years gainsharing programs have compromised on this issue. Joe Scanlon always insisted on full participation by everyone, and early Scanlon plans followed his lead. Later programs, especially in large companies, excluded senior management, field sales, and others. Senior managers were excluded from many gainsharing programs because they were on their own bonus program, and salespersons were excluded because they were on their own incentive plan, commissions. Rucker plan experience was similar to that of Scanlon plans. Improshare plans were designed to include only blue-collar workers. This tendency to exclude top management and only include lower-level employees is more evidence of how System 2 paternalistic ideas influence the design of gainsharing programs. In GainManagement everyone must participate in a team effort to make gains, and everyone should share in the gains that result.

Equal shares simplifies the issue of including executives and commissioned salespersons. With the equal share option for distribution there are no obstacles to including both groups.

Frequency of Payout

Distributing the GainShares is an opportunity for both communications and a distribution of money, so there are two issues: how frequently to communicate performance information, and how frequently to pay out financial GainShares.

The answer to the first issue is simple: the more frequent, the better. For total organization performance monthly is the minimum and usually turns out to be the most practical interval.

Most organizations do some type of financial closing each month, providing the information needed to inform the company of overall productivity results and significant trends. For instance, there may have been only a slight increase in overall productivity, less than was planned. Incoming orders may be slowing and inventories rising; there may be a backlog in shipping or a shift in product mix. All these data about ongoing performance should be communicated to the company for problem solving and action. There should be a comprehensive information report at least monthly. See Figure 7-2 for an example of a monthly productivity report, especially the key productivity trends at the bottom of the page.

Frequency for the payment is another matter. Monthly is by far the most common interval and is recommended over other options.

The true value of the monthly GainShare payment is not the money but the information. Not everyone will read and understand a monthly financial statement, but everyone will read and understand a check and the way it indicates an increase or decrease in productivity.

Especially in the beginning, when employees are still unfamiliar with such things as productivity, order backlogs, and product mix, the monthly check communicates results very clearly. And when the monthly **Focus** and **Charge** are announced, everyone understands clearly, as the team leader explains, "Last month's GainShare checks would have been $50 instead of $35 if we had reduced rejects by 10%, which is this month's **Focus**."

The only other serious option for payment of GainShares is quarterly. Combined with monthly information statements, quarterly payments are frequent enough to keep people interested. They also have the advantage of being three times larger than monthly payments. A $100 check once per quarter does have some appeal over monthly checks of $33. Semiannual and annual payments, even though the checks are much larger, are not recommended because they are too distant from day-to-day activities to influence ongoing performance and understanding.

Some business experience wide productivity fluctuations from month to month, resulting in gains one month and losses the next. This is especially true in the manufacture of large capital equipment with a long in-process time. There are months of high costs and low shipments followed by a month of equally high costs but very high shipments. Quarterly payments smooth out fluctuations and are, in such cases, a practical alternative.

In deciding frequency the first consideration should be given to the information value of the payment. Other issues can then be brought in to satisfy the needs and preferences of the company and its people. Sometimes companies find that they must make some adjustments to their accounting procedures to accommodate the decision about frequency of payments and information statements.

Reserves for Loss Periods

Productivity fluctuates from time to time in varying degrees in all organizations. It is not uncommon for productivity to rise above the base for one or more months and then sink below the base in following months. If shares are paid in months when productivity is above the base, losses must be recovered in months when productivity drops below the base. There are two preferred ways to deal with fluctuating productivity in GainManagement.

1. The reserve technique involves withholding an amount from each payment and creating a reserve account, or as some refer to it, the balancing account. Reserves are accrued from month to month as GainShares are earned. In months where productivity is negative (actual costs exceed the cost allowed by the productivity base, or profits fall below the target), an amount equal to the loss is deducted from the reserve. The size of the reserve deduction, from 10% to 30%, depends on the size of the anticipated fluctuation. An analysis of past experience will indicate the proper deduction. Reserves are accrued to a predetermined safe level. Once the safe level is reached, the deductions are stopped and all the shares are paid out as earned. When losses occur, a withdrawal is made from the reserve account and reserve deduction resumes until the safe level is again reached.

2. The continuous accrual method eliminates the need for reserves. Productivity gains and losses are simply accrued continuously, and shares are paid when the account shows a positive balance. Losses, when they occur, must be made up before any further shares are paid. This process continues from month to month and year to year. Any adjustments required by audits are made on a current basis.

Deciding which of these methods to use in dealing with inevitable fluctuations requires an analysis of past productivity performance. Where fluctuations are not severe, either method should work quite well. When anticipated fluctuations may be great, consideration must be given to protecting the company's interest and maintaining the employees' interest. Paying out shares during the first half of the year only to suffer greater losses during the second half will harm the company and defeat the purpose of GainManagement.

Major fluctuations in the GainShares and no-bonus periods have been problems in gainsharing programs that have been used as incentives. Problems such as extended no-bonus periods are best dealt with openly. Unpleasant surprises and false expectations must be avoided. Experience has shown that people can deal with difficult organization problems intelligently if they are kept well informed.

Because GainManagement places greater emphasis on GainMaking than GainSharing, these problems are easier to handle. Clear goals and open communications lead to more realistic expectations. Higher levels of participation give workers more confidence that they can overcome adversity.

Special care must be taken when starting up a GainManagement process because it may be difficult for GainMaking to exceed the minimum-profit level early in the process. It is likely that deficits will occur for several months. For this reason the financial GainSharing feature should not be activated until the threshold is reached. In this way deficits are not accrued until the organization reaches the threshold. Building up a large deficit in the first months of a new process could be demoralizing to the organization.

Ceilings

The idea of a ceiling on GainShares is a holdover from traditional incentive plans. Some of the early piece-rate and similar plans were improperly administered and paid what management felt were excessive or runaway bonuses. For this reason ceilings are customarily added to incentive plans to prevent the payouts from getting too high. In the early discussion of GainShares the notion of a ceiling is apt to come up. The GainShare is not an incentive, and ceilings are not appropriate to GainManagement. The productivity base should be set at a level where the company is receiving an adequate level of profit. Any excess is extra to the company and the employees and there should be no limit to how high either the company or the employee share should be allowed to go.

Form of the Payment

GainShares have almost always been paid in cash, but there is an opportunity here for experimentation. There are some tax advantages to payments in the form of merchandise, vacation trips, and ESOP or 401k contributions. Most companies starting GainManagement are so involved with planning the process, training, communications, **Focus, Charge,** and problem-solving meetings that there is little time or energy for additional experimentation. But there are opportunities for alternative forms of paying the GainShare, which should be explored at an appropriate time.

Adjusting the Base and Sharing Ratio

It is to be expected that the GainSharing productivity base and/or the sharing ratio will be adjusted to accommodate changing business conditions and new strategic plans. The inevitability of such changes makes it necessary to review the base and the ratio each year to see if changes are needed. Everyone in the company should understand that the base will be changed whenever necessary in order to keep the company operating at the minimum level of profitability. As part of the annual plan review changes should be made when it is necessary to do so. The need for change will come directly from the strategic planning process. It is quite possible that minimum profit will change every year. To avoid suspicion that someone is tampering with the base the need for change must be thoroughly explained to all employees so that they will know what to anticipate.

The sharing ratio is also subject to change if and when circumstances require. Changing the ratio will occur much less frequently than changing the base. The ratio should only be changed when a different sharing ratio will allow the company and the employees to take advantage of some new opportunity.

Summary

The GainSharing element in GainManagement goes beyond traditional gainsharing in several important ways. In GainManagement:

- ▲ All constituents share in the organization's performance gains.
- ▲ Employee GainShares include job security, personal growth, promotions, a better quality of work life, participation, and a financial GainShare.
- ▲ The financial GainShare is a partnership dividend, not a paternalistic incentive or an alternative pay component.
- ▲ The base for financial GainSharing is the minimum annual profit needed to fund the organization's strategic business plan. Partial productivity bases, such as labor-only bases, are

not sufficient for today's organizations and do not support total participation.

▲ Shares are distributed to all employees in equal shares to reinforce teamwork and team performance.

The GainSharing element must be designed to pull the organization into a single team with one set of goals to which all are committed and in which all participate.

Notes

1. Edward E. Lawler III, *Strategic Pay* (San Francisco: Jossey-Bass, 1990).
2. Robert J. Doyle, *Gainsharing and Productivity* (New York: AMACOM, 1983).

III

How to Plan and Implement GainManagement

Implementing the GainManagement process is a major undertaking for most organizations and must be carefully planned and executed to ensure success. The following chapters present a step-by-step procedure for implementation.

First: An investigation is made to determine if GainManagement is an appropriate process for the organization (Chapter 8).

Second: A design team is appointed and studies both the GainManagement process and the needs and potential of the organization (Chapter 9).

Third: The design team adapts the process to fit the specific circumstances of the organization (Chapter 9).

Fourth: The GainManagement process is installed and begins to operate (Chapter 9).

Fifth: The process is regularly evaluated and continually developed (Chapter 11).

Because education and training are so important to a successful implementation, Chapter 10 presents a summary of the training needed to support GainManagement.

Chapter 8

Investigating GainManagement

GainManagement is a sound, basically simple process, but it is not an easy process to install or a quick fix. GainManagement creates significant change in the way most organizations work. Success in this venture requires that an organization commit time, energy, and resources to implement the process. Before starting down this path an organization must be committed to seeing it through. The necessary commitment should only be made after a serious investigation of the GainManagement idea and a thoughtful analysis of the needs of the organization.

An organization considering GainManagement needs to conduct a serious investigation of sufficient scope to allow management to decide, with full knowledge of the work and risks involved, whether or not to pursue the process. The investigation must examine the nature and details of the GainManagement process and analyze the needs of the organization and its people. GainManagement is a solution, an answer. When both GainManagement and the organization have been sufficiently studied, it should be clear whether or not GainManagement is the right solution or answer to the needs of the organization. As a secondary benefit the study also provides information that enables the organization to decide key guidelines for the design and implementation of the process. ·

GainManagement, like its gainsharing predecessor, will appeal primarily to small independent organizations that have traditionally been the first to innovate organizationally. However, recent trends suggest that larger multiunit organizations are also looking for new approaches to solve their problems of productivity and quality of work life. GainManagement has worked and will work in larger organizations, but only at the plant or unit level.

Small, independent organizations need only a single study to determine if and how to implement GainManagement. Major corporations, on the other hand, must conduct studies on two levels. A corporate-level study is needed to determine the feasibility of GainManagement for general or specific corporate application. Local studies are conducted by individual units to determine whether or not and how to implement the process in a specific plant or other unit. Corporate studies as a rule are more formal and comprehensive than local studies or studies by independent companies. Whether formal or informal, comprehensive or simple, all studies must be thorough enough for the situation and circumstances of each organization. GainManagement is not a trivial pursuit. It is a process for excellence that will create high expectations in some employees, and anxiety in others. It must be approached seriously and this calls for a careful study and a thoughtful decision.

Corporate Management Feasibility Study

The corporate management feasibility study is usually conducted by one of the corporate staff departments or a special task force. A mixed task force ensures that the perspectives and interests of operating managers as well as key staff departments such as finance and human resources are thoroughly considered.

Every organization has its own specific concerns, which should be specified and clarified for or by the feasibility task force. The issues and questions for this GainManagement study generally include the following:

- ▲ What are the productivity, competitiveness, or quality-of-work-life problems that call for a major response such as Gain-Management?
- ▲ What are the potential benefits of GainManagement to the corporation, to local units, to employees, and to other constituents?
- ▲ Is the basic concept of GainManagement consistent with the values, policies, strategies, and goals of the corporation?
- ▲ How will GainManagement fit with other employee-relations, labor-relations, and management programs?

▲ Will accounting and information systems departments be able to support GainMaking and GainSharing?

▲ What are the proper GainManagement units, and what changes in organization structure might be needed to establish GainManagement units?

▲ What changes in base compensation programs might be needed before implementing GainSharing?

▲ What changes in other corporate policies might be needed to take full advantage of GainManagement?

▲ What risks can be anticipated if some units use Gain-Management and others do not? What if the units are in the same community or close proximity? Are those risks acceptable and manageable? Will the risks be offset by the potential benefits?

▲ How much uniformity in the units' application of Gain-Management will be necessary to utilize the process effectively?

▲ What policies, rules, and/or guidelines should the corporation issue to ensure the successful use of GainManagement and to minimize adverse impacts?

▲ How much corporate coordination and administration will be required? How will this be accomplished? Will additional staff be needed?

▲ How should GainManagement be introduced in the corporation?

▲ Will pilot programs be used? How will pilot locations be selected?

▲ What GainShare base productivity formula makes the most sense for the organization's operations?

▲ What other options are there to address problems in productivity, competitiveness, and quality of work life? Have they been adequately studied?

Whether performed by staff or by task force this study usually proceeds through a sequence of data collection, analysis, evaluation, deliberation, and conclusions. During the data-gathering step the members of the task force learn about GainManagement theory and practice by reading, attending seminars, holding conferences with consultants, and visiting experienced companies. Once the members are adequately informed about GainManagement, a list of issues specific to the organization or company is drawn up. Data about these issues are collected as needed, and each issue is deliberated until an appropriate conclusion is reached. The study concludes with formal recommendations that are presented to top management for approval. All this may result in the adoption of an official position, or it might produce additional issues to be studied and decided. Once all issues have been resolved, the official position should be communicated to operating units for their guidance and action.

When the decision is in favor of GainManagement, some organizations issue a simple statement encouraging its use and granting total autonomy to local divisions, plants, and offices. More often, though, large organizations provide more direction to their divisions or plants and issue a formal statement. (An example of a multidivisional corporate policy is shown at the end of this chapter.)

An outline for the corporate policy statement follows:

☐ Policy

- A basic statement of support for the GainManagement concept—from very strong support to no objections
- Whether use is mandatory or optional
- The reasons for supporting its use, i.e., productivity, competitiveness, quality of work life, employee involvement
- The benefits expected from the use of GainManagement for the corporation, division, employees, customers, and other constituents

☐ Procedures

- Corporate approval required, and how to obtain it
- Need for a local feasibility study
- Process to be linked to specific business objectives
- Relationship and coordination with other corporate programs, including union contracts, compensation, etc.

☐ GainManagement features to be arranged in two lists: (1) required and (2) recommended but optional

- How to design the process—by whom
- Who participates in the process and in the GainShares
- Employee-involvement structures
- Employment security
- GainShares—measurement, sharing ratios, frequency, distribution method, deficits, and changes

- Structure and use of the GainManagement council
- Accountability—who, what
- Education and training required
- Communications, records, reports
- Audits and ongoing development
- Union involvement in planning and operations

A comprehensive statement of policy will enable local units to move forward with confidence to design the GainManagement process suitable to their needs. It is important that the feasibility study stop with feasibility issues, however, and not preempt decisions to be made later by the local design team. Local ownership of the process is critical, and this ownership develops during the design process. When corporate staff does too much, it limits the opportunities for the local units to design and own their own customized GainManagement Process.

Local Management Feasibility Study

Local managers, whether of an independent company or a division of a large corporation, must conduct their own feasibility studies. Compared to the corporate study, which is for feasibility, the purpose of the local management study is to decide whether or not to use GainManagement and, if so, how to move ahead with planning and design.

Experience has shown that local management is more comfortable conducting a quiet, management-only feasibility study to determine if a GainManagement program is advantageous to the organization. Managers prefer to avoid raising expectations until feasibility has been established. They fear that once momentum develops it will be difficult to stop even if the study shows that the organization is not ready for GainManagement. This management feasibility study is desirable and recommended because GainManagement will have its biggest impact on managers, who must be sure they are ready for the change.

The study is conducted by the entire top-management team. Unlike gainsharing, which has often been applied to hourly employees under the guidance of the production manager and the personnel manager, GainManagement involves employees at all levels and should be guided by the senior managers.

The local management feasibility study examines many of the same issues as the corporate study, but with a different perspective. The corporate study looks at GainManagement in the abstract to determine a policy. The local study looks at it from the perspective of dealing with here-and-now business and people issues. Though many of the questions are the same, the point of view is quite different. There are some other questions that only apply to the local study, including:

- ▲ Will GainManagement address the immediate and strategic issues—productivity, competitiveness, and quality of work life?
- ▲ What will it cost to implement GainManagement, including management and staff time, training, communications, and consultation?
- ▲ What is the anticipated cost-benefit ratio?
- ▲ Are the local managers, employees, and union ready for this change?
- ▲ Is there sufficient corporate support and direction?

Like the corporate study this local management study follows the process of data collection, analysis, evaluation, deliberation, and conclusions. At the end of this chapter are three exercises to guide the local management group through its study of the organization's needs.

The local feasibility study will result in one of three recommendations:

1. GainManagement is not feasible for the organization, and other methods should be considered to deal with productivity, competitiveness, and quality of work life. This recommendation should also explain why GainManagement is not feasible and why other approaches are felt to be more appropriate.

2. GainManagement is feasible for the organization—but not now. This conclusion should also explain when or under what conditions GainManagement is to be reconsidered.

3. GainManagement is feasible and should be pursued now. This recommendation should include guidelines about how to proceed, such as:

▲ An invitation to the union to conduct its own feasibility study and join in the design process

▲ The appointment of a joint employee-management or union-management design team to begin the design process, including the timing and a budget for the design

▲ Guidelines or limitations that the investigating team feels must be observed by the design team

▲ How management will communicate the decision to pursue GainManagement to the organization

These recommendations conclude the feasibility study and the assignment of the task force. Some members of this group are often assigned roles on the design team and in the ongoing administration of the GainManagement process. The members of the investigation team are a knowledgeable resource and should be used in any appropriate continuing role.

Union Feasibility Study

Where there is a labor union and management has decided to pursue a GainManagement program, the union should conduct its own feasibility study. This study can be done by the local, regional, or international office, depending on the union's internal structure. It may also be conducted jointly by two or more unions having contracts with the company.

The experience has been that unions do not conduct thorough feasibility studies. Local unions tend to examine fragments of information and take positions for, cautiously for, or against management's proposals. The prospect of developing a successful joint labor-management program is greatly enhanced when the union conducts its own feasibility study similar to the management study. The additional perspective of the union can enhance a joint labor-management project. The union needs to explore similar data and work through a similar agenda but from their particular perspective. The union should focus its attention on how GainManagement would benefit not only the employees as members of the union but also the union as an organization.

Chapter 12 presents a detailed outline of the principal elements of the union feasibility study. The systematic analysis of an agenda as described there would enable the union to participate as an informed party and contribute to the joint effort. The lack of such a study places the union in the position of always having to react to management initiatives, often without adequate information or a well-developed position. Joint labor-management projects will never be more than moderately successful as long as management continues to initiate and the union only reacts. The way out of the reactive mode is for unions to do their homework. When a union is present, a successful GainManagement process will be one in which the union is a knowledgeable and strong partner.

Feasibility Study Checklists

GainManagement offers a solution to problems of productivity, competitiveness, and quality of work life. The most pertinent and most difficult questions to be answered during the feasibility study are those about the needs of the organization. It takes both information and integrity to probe such issues as:

- ▲ The extent and nature of productivity and competitiveness problems
- ▲ The extent and nature of quality of work life problems
- ▲ The strengths and weaknesses of the organization

The information necessary to answer these questions is not always readily available, and the information that is available is sometimes unreliable. Even with sufficient accurate information it is difficult for management to admit that there are problems of low productivity and employee dissatisfaction. However, progress and the pursuit of excellence demand accuracy and honesty in assessing current conditions. It takes vision and courage to set a course for excellence. The road to mediocrity is safe and comfortable and doesn't require much soul searching. Guidelines and checklists will not completely overcome the lack of sufficient and accurate information or make the job more comfortable, but they do break the task into pieces. Both judgment and honesty improve when applied to specific components of productivity and employee satisfaction. This makes the job more manageable and should increase everyone's confidence in the analysis.

The checklists that follow are presented in the form of exercises to be completed by the task force as it deliberates the pros and cons

(*Text continues on p. 230*)

Checklist 1—Competitive Analysis

How we compare to our competitors in each of the following:

	Better	Worse	Don't Know
Technology, patents			
Market position			
Market share			
Customer base			
Products			
Services			
Strategic business plan			
Financial resources			
Managers			
Management systems			
Workforce			
Union support			
Productivity			
Plant and equipment			
Profitability			
Administrative systems			
Research and development			
Distribution/sales			
Marketing/advertising			
Other local issues			

Summary:
1. What are our principal competitive strengths?
2. In what areas are we competitively weak?
3. In what important areas do we lack competitive information? Do we need this information before we proceed? How can we obtain the information we need?

Conclusions:
1. How will the GainManagement process enable us to build on our competitive strengths? overcome our weaknesses?
2. What other actions should be taken to strengthen the company?

Checklist 2—Organization Analysis

What are the strengths and weaknesses of the organization?

	Is a Strength	Needs Improve-ment	Don't Know
Communications			
Coordination between functions			
Decision-making practices			
Organization of work			
Absence of red tape			
Goal clarity			
Job challenge			
Job clarity			
Rewards			
Job security			
Concern for people			
Employee involvement			
Employee commitment			
Managerial leadership			
Employee/labor relationships			
Individual performance			
Team effectiveness			
Teamwork and cooperation			
Other			

Summary:

1. What are our important organizational strengths?
2. What important elements of the organization need improvement?
3. In which important areas do we lack sufficient information? How can we obtain the information we need?

Conclusions:

1. How will the GainManagement process enable us to build on our organizational strengths and strengthen the areas of weakness?
2. What other actions should be taken to strengthen the organization?

Checklist 3—Perfomance Analysis

Assuming that excellent performance is the organization's goal, the following force field diagram facilitates an analysis of the forces that are currently helping or restraining the pursuit of excellence. Each of the listed forces, plus others unique to the organization, should be analyzed to determine their strengths. To achieve excellence the helping forces need to be strengthened and the restraining forces weakened or eliminated.

CURRENT PERFORMANCE → → →	EXCELLENT PERFORMANCE
HELPING FORCES	RESTRAINING FORCES
Pressure from customers →	Lack of vision ←
Pressure from competition →	← Lack of strategic goals and plans
Pressure from investors/debtors for higher earnings →	← No systematic improvement plan
Pressure from community or consumer groups →	← Lack of productivity measures
Market opportunity →	← Inefficient plant and equipment
Spirit of performance →	← Poor organization
Desire for growth →	← Lack of skills for change
Desire to improve QWL →	← Complacency
Desire for higher pay →	← Lack of trust in leadership
Desire for security →	← Fear/resistance to change
Other →	← Other

Summary:

    1. Which are the strongest helping forces? How strong?
    2. Which are the strongest restraining forces? How strong?

Conclusion:

    How will GainManagement strengthen the helping forces and weaken or eliminate the restraining forces?

of using GainManagement. They are presented not as forms to be filled out but as concepts to be adapted for use by each investigating task force. They can be used by a staff or resource person to collect information and present it to the investigating task force. They can also be completed by individual task force members and form the basis for the group's debate and deliberation about Gain-Management.

With a thorough understanding of the GainManagement process and the organization analysis represented by these checklists, a management task force should be able to make a well-informed decision regarding GainManagement.

The following is based on an actual example of a corporate GainManagement policy developed by a medium-size, multidivision manufacturing company:

Lorien Forest Products, Inc.
GainManagement Policy

November 1990

Statement by the President, LFP, Inc.

Lorien Forest Products, Inc., strongly believes in the worth of the individual and his or her ability to make contributions to the overall excellence of the organization. For these reasons we are committed to a GainManagement process for the purpose of making the corporation and each location more competitive, productive, and profitable. Division Managers are directed to take an active, visible role in developing, implementing, and nurturing a Gain-Management process in their division that achieves the active participation of all employees. All employees are to be actively involved in the GainManagement process. LFP expects each employee to participate fully, contribute his/her ideas, and benefit from the results.

/s/ T. R. Beard
President, LFP, Inc.

Purpose

The purpose of GainManagement is to increase product quality and productivity, and to improve the quality of the employees' worklife through employee involvement in the decision-making processes affecting their jobs.

Structure and Accountabilities

1. GainManagement requires corporate approval prior to implementation. Details of the process—including general approach, objectives, method of measurement, funding, sharing, and payout—must be included in requests for approval.
2. Annually the General Manager and staff are to develop objectives, both short-range and long-range, for the GainManagement process at their location. These objectives are to be communicated to all employees and are to be reviewed periodically to ensure that they are being accomplished. The Gain-Management objectives will be one of the overall objectives that the manager includes in the "white book." The division manager's annual performance evaluation will be based on accomplishing those objectives.
3. Participative management is to be adopted as the principle of management in all areas.
4. All employees should be involved in the process to some extent since the major purpose of Gain-Management is to tap the division's total human resource capability.
5. The Plant General Manager with support from Corporate Personnel is primarily responsible for the overall success of the GainManagement process.

Features

Education and Training

All employees will be given the necessary training and education to function actively in the GainManagement process. This training includes, but is not limited to, employee orientation, problem-solving techniques, participating in effective meetings, basic management skills, participative management skills, and a basic understanding of the GainSharing bonus calculation within each location. Through the Corporate Personnel Office, Division Personnel Managers are to be trained to conduct GainManagement, participative management, and supervisory and employee skills training in-house.

Compensation

The GainShare bonus is not to reduce an employee's base wage. Nor should the presence of GainSharing preclude future pay increases. It has always been Lorien Forest Products' philosophy to pay a fair and competitive wage to its employees regardless of other opportunities.

Participative Structure

1. All employees are eligible from date of hire to participate in the GainSharing bonus.
2. The General Manager and staff will develop a productivity improvement **Focus** for the plant on a monthly basis. The Superintendent, with the assistance of the supervisors, will develop a **Charge** for each work team in support of the **Focus.**
3. Each location will maintain a log of their action plans and suggestions that tracks the number, cost, benefit, and resolution time of each idea. The Personnel Manager, as coordinator, will be responsible for the following coordination tasks:

    • Administration of the Idea Log
    • Scheduling of meetings, elections, and training

- Training, conducting new employee orientations, and conducting or arranging for special training as needed
- Communications including the newsletter and bulletin boards
- Assisting in the annual audit
- Ex-officio member of the GainManagement Council
4. Attractive and informational newsletters and bulletin boards will be developed at each location to communicate, educate, and recognize accomplishments (group and individual) resulting from the Gain-Management process, including the following topics:

    1. GainManagement Council meetings summaries
    2. Updated Idea Log
    3. Announcements of meetings, rosters, and agendas
    4. Business information
    5. Information on GainShare goals and actual results
    6. Monthly **Focus**
    7. **Charges** for each work team
    8. Key business trends
    9. Significant action plans and suggestions
    10. Safety notes
    11. Educational articles about GainManagement
    12. Message from the General Manager

Bonus Formula

The development of the bonus formula will be a cooperative effort between the corporate office and each location with final approval from corporate.

1. A base return on investment will be developed for each location.
2. Distribution of the bonus will be based on a percent of each employee's gross pay for the month in which the bonus was earned. The bonus will be distributed on a monthly basis.
3. A reserve fund will be set up for each location for

those months when profit does not reach the base ROI. Ten percent of each GainShare pool will be set aside into this reserve fund. This reserve fund will be charged when profits fall below the base ROI. Reserve fund deductions will be made until the division reserve fund maximum is met. A series of low ROI months could cause the reserve fund to develop a negative balance. When this happens, the negative balance will be carried until it is repaid with the gains in the months when the ROI level has been exceeded.

4. Cash bonuses will be limited to 15% of base pay. When bonuses exceed 15% of the employee's annual base pay, the excess will be paid into the employee's ESOP account.

5. Lorien Forest Products intends that the above formula guidelines are permanent, but recognizes that conditions may require that they be revised.

Summary

The careful planning required to implement GainManagement begins with one or more investigation studies to determine feasibility.

Smaller, single-unit companies usually need only one study to decide whether or not to pursue GainManagement. Where there is a union the union conducts its own investigation.

In large multiunit organizations there are two levels of investigation studies. Corporate studies look to overall feasibility and usually result in a policy and procedures statement. With corporate approval local units still need to do their own investigation to decide whether or not to use GainManagement.

This chapter contains several lists of questions and issues to be investigated, three checklists to help the investigation team, and an example of a corporate GainManagement policy statement.

Chapter 9

Designing the GainManagement Process

When the investigation described in Chapter 8 concludes that GainManagement is feasible and appropriate for the organization, the hard work of study, design, and startup begins. The Gain-Management process cannot be designed and installed overnight. There are many details to adapt to the special situation and characteristics of each organization. GainManagement is a powerful process when it is well designed and there is a conscientious effort to apply it. It is absolutely critical that all of the managers and the majority of the employees start the GainManagement process with a commitment to use it to improve performance and quality of work life.

Organizations successfully utilize GainManagement when they understand that changes must be made and they have a clear vision of the human and business results they seek. This calls for serious study and detailed planning by a carefully selected design team. The work of this team has three phases:

1. Design team studies GainManagement and the organization.
2. Design team designs the GainManagement process features.
3. Design team educates the organization and guides them through the startup process.

GainManagement Design Team

The design team is a group of employees representing the entire organization. There are operating details to be designed, which must be customized for those who will use the process. Once designed, the process will need a broad base of support throughout the organization. A team representative of the whole organization is ideal for customizing the design and obtaining the support required for a successful startup.

The members of the design team are selected and invited to participate in designing the process by the management group that conducted the feasibility study and authorized GainManagement for the organization. Where a union is involved in a joint project with management, the union appoints its own representatives to the team. The managers and, where applicable, union leaders who did the initial investigation understand the design team tasks and are, therefore, the only ones with sufficient information to choose those employees who are most capable of conducting the important work of designing the GainManagement process. Elections for representatives to the design team would be preferable but are seldom practical because the employees lack sufficient information to be able to vote intelligently. It is simply expedient to have the investigating team select the design team. Design team representatives are selected using the following criteria:

- ▲ Enough members to represent all functions, levels, and shifts
- ▲ Members who are influential and respected by their peers
- ▲ Members who are good communicators
- ▲ Members to represent differing perspectives: female and male, senior and new employees, line and staff, hourly and salaried, and so on
- ▲ Members from different organization levels: management, supervision, professional, technical, administrative, skilled, unskilled
- ▲ Members with special expertise in finance and human resources
- ▲ Members willing and able to devote time to the study and design tasks

The typical design team has 10 to 15 members representing a diagonal slice of the organization. Each member represents one or more specific employee groups within the organization and is expected to maintain close communications with his or her group throughout the design process. Each member receives a formal invitation accompanied by a complete explanation of what is involved and why he or she was selected.

When the design team is fully staffed, the members meet with management (and union leaders)* to receive a formal commission to proceed with the design of the GainManagement process. Management (and the union) conducted the feasibility study and decided on GainManagement as the way for the organization to achieve certain strategic goals for excellent performance and quality of work life. This decision that GainManagement is right for the organization must be communicated by management (and union leaders) to the design team as their commission or charter. The design team must accept the challenge to design a GainManagement process that will enable the organization to achieve excellence. The design team then works through three distinct phases: study, design, and startup.

Phase 1: Study

The design team study phase typically takes three to six months and covers two principal topics: the GainManagement process and the needs of the organization. The design team must become very knowledgeable about the concept, details, and operation of the Gain-Management process and about the competitive status, current performance, and strategic goals of the organization. These two knowledge bases are necessary for the design team to customize the GainManagement process to the special needs of the organization. There is no one-size-fits-all GainManagement process. There are basic elements and common features, but each organization must adapt the process to itself. The key word is *adapt*. The design team should not *adopt* a GainManagement process that worked for some other organization; it must *adapt* the process to the unique needs of their organization.

The GainManagement study goes into much greater depth than did the earlier feasibility study investigation. The design team must go beyond an awareness of the various features of the process to an intimate knowledge of the how and why of each feature. The team must also understand the interaction of the features and how they combine to create the total GainManagement effect. This is accomplished by studying not only specific GainManagement literature but also other related material about employee involvement and high-performance organizations. Several recent books are excellent sources

*Because unions are not always involved, their participation will be noted in parentheses.

of the kind of information the team will need for study: *Strategic Pay* by Edward E. Lawler III (Jossey-Bass, 1990); *Leadership Is an Art* by Max De Pree (Doubleday, 1989); *The Fifth Discipline* by Peter M. Senge (Doubleday, 1990); *Well Made in America* by Peter C. Reid (McGraw-Hill, 1990); and *Productive Workplaces* by Marvin R. Weisbord (Jossey-Bass, 1987).

The team establishes a study plan based on the time allotted for the study and on the depth of study to be done, then follows the plan closely. The overall study can be made easier by assigning parts of the study to subgroups of the team, who complete their part and report to the full team. The members are encouraged to discuss and debate concepts and techniques of organizational effectiveness and to develop their own approaches about what to do and how to do it. In organizations experienced with other participative-management or employee-involvement programs this study includes an analysis of the successes and failures of their own past experiences.

Visits to other organizations are an excellent way for the design team to learn about GainManagement. Organizations with successful programs are usually willing, within reason, to host visits. Experts from other organizations and consultants can be brought in to help the team do this study. As the design team learns about the features and techniques of GainManagement, there will be occasions when the team will make preliminary design decisions. Issues or features will be encountered that the team will want to be sure to do or to avoid in its own program. Throughout the study these design decisions, whether tentative or firm, are recorded for later use when the team begins to design. Keeping a to-do list avoids having to stop and debate design issues prematurely and preserves good ideas for when they are needed.

The second subject for the design team study is the organization. A few senior members of the team may have enough information about the organization to customize the design, but the rest will not. Everyone on the team must have complete information about the needs, opportunities, and expectations of the organization. Some information, such as strategic goals, may have been provided by top managers when they commissioned the design team. But now more information is needed—about sales, customer satisfaction, competitive activity, production, quality, finances, compensation, employee satisfaction, and internal and interunit operating problems. The team also needs to know about organization and departmental plans for the future.

Some of this information can be provided by team members who, because of their jobs, have access to the necessary information. Other information is obtained by having department managers or specialists make presentations to the team. Sometimes design teams conduct surveys to obtain information about employee satisfaction and organizational climate.

These two studies about GainManagement and about the organization run concurrently. One meeting may concentrate on Gain-Management and the next meeting on a presentation by the vice-president of sales. When the design team completes its study and has sufficient information and understanding about Gain-Management and the needs and opportunities of the organization, the team moves on to the design phase.

Communications Between the Design Team and the Organization

Beginning with the study phase and throughout the design phase, it is very important that the design team maintain close, open, two-way communications with the rest of the organization. Team members are expected to communicate regularly with the groups they represent to offer information about the work and progress of the design team and, in return, get reactions, comments, and questions from their groups.

This communication is done by having design team members hold ten-minute briefings with their groups following each meeting of the design team. The information they provide in these briefings can be supplemented by posting minutes of team meetings on bulletin boards and in break areas. The purpose of this process is to establish two-way communications between the design team and the rest of the organization. At the start of each design team meeting, members give summary reports of the reactions, comments, and questions from their groups.

The closer this linkage between the design team and the organization, the more the organization will have ownership of the Gain-Management process when the design is completed and is ready to be installed. If there are obstacles to the success of GainManagement, the design team must learn about them early in order to take steps to resolve them before attempting to install the process. As the design moves along and employees are kept well informed of the work of the design team, understanding and support should grow among the employees of the organization. The exercise shown in Figure 9-1, to be completed several times during the study and design phase, helps the design team to take the pulse of the organization. Each team member assesses his or her own group, and the team consolidates the information into an overall assessment. Where problems are

Figure 9-1.   The understanding and support matrix.

STRONG SUPPORT

	Quadrant 1	Quadrant 2	
F U L L U N D E R S T A N D I N G	**Support With Understanding** People in this quadrant cause the change and enable it to progress smoothly to its logical conclusion.	**Support Without Understanding** People in this quadrant are mainly cheering spectators. They don't help the process actively because they don't know enough. They do help the process passively by going along. They need more information.	N O U N D E R S T A N D I N G
	Quadrant 3	Quadrant 4	
	Opposition With Understanding People in this quadrant are the informed opposition. They have a different insight and should be given careful consideration and the opportunity to present their case.	**Opposition Without Understanding** People in this quadrant may be reactionaries, but they should be listened to with patience and understanding, since their opposition may add insight. They also need information.	

STRONG OPPOSITION

Summary:

	Department or Group	Number	Percent
Q1 Good support and good understanding	_____	_____	_____
Q2 Good support but low understanding	_____	_____	_____
Q3 Low support but good understanding	_____	_____	_____
Q4 Low support and low understanding	_____	_____	_____

indicated, the team decides on an appropriate action for one group or for the entire organization.

Getting this two-way communication process started is always difficult because the design team members are uneasy about their lack of information early in the study and design phase. After a few meetings it becomes easier, but getting started requires some extra effort. Taking a few minutes at the end of each design team meeting to decide what to communicate helps all of the members. Two-way communications are so important to the eventual acceptance of GainManagement by the organization that extra effort must be taken to ensure that information flows smoothly in both directions.

Phase 2: Design

The specific details and techniques of the GainManagement process were presented in Chapters 5, 6, and 7 and will not be repeated here. This section will summarize ten separate design tasks and describe the procedure for completing the design.

1. *GainManagement Goals.* GainManagement is a process for excellence, not just a new technique for employee involvement. The first step in design is to specify the goals for this process. The goals for GainManagement, which are derived from the goals in the organization's strategic plan. The purpose of GainManagement is to help the organization to perform and to achieve its strategic objectives. The structures, meetings, and other GainMaking processes are means, not ends, so GainManagement development begins with the performance goals of the organization. The goals of GainManagement should be expressed in several statements such as:

Productivity:	"Improve after-tax ROI from 17% to 20%."
Volume:	"Increase output to 500,000 board feet per day."
Quality:	"Zero defects, no field returns or claims."
Delivery:	"100% on-time delivery."
Market Share:	"Increase to 37% in three years."
New Markets:	"Enter northeastern supermarkets witin two years."
New Products:	"Two new products per year."
Profit:	"Increase average profits to 12% of sales."
Finances:	"Finance growth without increasing debt-to-equity ratio."

Plant and
 Equipment: "Build and occupy new plant in three years."
Stores: "Open 14 new stores in next four years."
Organization: "Achieve and maintain an overall satisfaction in-
      dex of 4.50 on annual organization survey."
Safety: "Reduce lost-time accidents to zero."

The design team identifies a specific list of strategic goals similar to these. The success for the GainManagement process is the extent to which it helps the organization to perform and to reach its strategic objectives.

2. *Employee Involvement.* The work team structure is designed to establish effective problem-solving work teams. Some restructuring may be needed to subdivide groups that are too large and to group the correct resource people into logical work teams. "Orphans" are identified and assigned to teams. Job descriptions with team mission statements, accountabilities, and performance standards are prepared or put on a schedule to be developed early in the startup phase. Teams must be encouraged or helped to develop performance-feedback procedures to enhance the work team's problem-solving capability.

The meeting calendar is designed to fit into the organization's current meeting structure whenever possible.

The idea-processing system, including forms, idea log, authority levels, and coordination and approval processes, is detailed. Goals are set for the number of action plans and suggestions and the time within which to resolve them.

3. *Team Leadership.* The GainManagement process requires the strong and competent leadership described in Chapter 6. The design team also identifies GainPlanning management practices for special emphasis and recommends appropriate changes to job descriptions for managers and employees. Details of the GainPlanning management practices and a sample job description are included in Chapter 5.

4. *Training.* Training is needed to support team problem-solving activities, just as leadership training is needed to support participative management. The design team prepares a schedule and a detailed training plan identifying which employees need what training. Detail about the various training programs and guidelines for preparing this training schedule are covered in Chapter 10.

5. *Communications.* There are several specific communications materials and activities to be designed. An employee orientation program is prepared to explain the total GainManagement process to all employees during startup. This same program will be used to orient future new hires. An employee handbook briefly but fully explaining the GainManagement process is essential. This handbook is prepared by the design team and presented to all employees at the orientation meeting.

A newsletter may be designed and published. Bulletin boards are usually installed early in the study phase to facilitate communications between the design team and the rest of the organization. The use of posters, graphs, charts, and other attractive displays improves the quality of the bulletin boards and enhances their value as communications tools. The design team also designs the processes of getting good information to the team leaders for their weekly information meetings.

A contest to name the organization's GainManagement process adds interest to the whole startup effort. In addition, many organizations find good descriptive names for their programs this way.

6. *Documentation.* To ensure consistency and to provide a base reference point for ongoing development, the initial Gain-Management process is documented in a policy and procedures manual. The manual is accessible to all employees but is used primarily by the GainManagement council for process development, to resolve questions about the process, and as the basic source of information and training about GainManagement.

For development purposes certain records of GainManagement activities must be maintained, including communications, **Focuses** and **Charges,** meeting notes, and records of action plans and suggestions. These records are used for tracking, analysis, and development. The design team decides what records to maintain and designs the necessary forms, procedures, and documents.

7. *GainSharing.* There are several GainSharing design decisions to be made. The GainShares for the organization's several constituents must be described so they can be communicated and tracked. The financial GainSharing base is designed in conjunction with the management team, which has the profit plan information needed for this decision. The other financial GainShare design decisions to be made include: the sharing ratio, whom to include in GainSharing, the distribution method, frequency, reserves, and others as presented in Chapter 7.

8. *Implementation Plan.* The design team prepares a complete startup plan to include the following:

- ▲ Obtaining formal approvals from management and employees, and where applicable from corporate management and the union(s)
- ▲ Schedule for employees' orientation meetings
- ▲ Startup dates for work team problem-solving meetings
- ▲ Schedule of training to precede startup, such as leadership and problem-solving training
- ▲ Additional training to be scheduled during the first year.
- ▲ Action plans to correct any special organizational problems that must be resolved prior to startup or within the first few months
- ▲ When financial GainShares will commence

9. *GainManagement Council.* The design team becomes the GainManagement council as soon as the process is formally installed. The team prepares and presents for organizational approval the charter and procedures defining the scope, operation, and maintenance of the council. (Details about the GainManagement council are in Chapter 11.)

10. *Development Plan.* The formal plan for the continuous development of the GainManagement process is the final design task. The design team should specify the goals to be used to evaluate the success of the GainManagement process, the procedures for the ongoing review and evaluation, and the timing and procedure for the annual audit. (Details of the GainManagement development plan are in Chapter 11.)

The Design Procedure

The design of a GainManagement process is a big job and must be done well for the process to get off to a good start. The organization must allow sufficient time for the team to complete a careful study and a good design. Design teams are often overwhelmed by their assignment when it is first presented to them. One design team described its task as like trying to eat an elephant. The first thing the team must do is prepare a work plan or a project plan listing tasks, deadlines, and resources. Once the total project is broken down and assigned to individuals and groups, the job becomes more manageable. The elephant can be eaten—one bite at a time.

Most design teams divide themselves into three subgroups and divide the ten design tasks among them. These subgroups then work out the details of their assigned tasks and present their recommendations to the full design team. A typical division of labor of the design team includes GainSharing, GainMaking, and communications subgroups. Tasks not assigned to one of the subgroups are completed by the full team. Other employees or consultants can also be used to work on these design tasks.

The study phase should be completed before the design is started, but it is not necessary to complete all ten design tasks before installing parts of the process. For instance, some of the training can be designed and implemented while the team continues work on other design tasks. The work of the design team can be spread out over several months as the process is phased in. Decisions about how

---

A multiplant West Coast manufacturing corporation decided to implement GainManagement throughout the corporation, but to phase it in over five years. The company started the process by preparing GainSharing minimum-profit targets for one plant, expanding to the other plants over a two-year period. As GainSharing targets were established for each plant, department suggestion committees were also established to solicit and process employee suggestions and to problem solve specific Focus and Charges.

Next GainManagement councils were established at each plant to monitor the GainManagement process and advise management on work-community policy issues.

Once these basic structures were established, the company began a steady program of upgrading each element of the process, using the annual audit to guide decisions about the intensity and direction of their development. In the development phase some plants moved to involve more employees by training them in problem solving, and by adding work team structures to replace suggestion committees. Other plants chose to concentrate on System 5 leadership and management training.

All plants continue the annual audit and execute an annual GainManagement development action plan.

to schedule and phase in the design tasks are unique to each installation, and it is up to the design team to establish a schedule reflecting the priorities and capabilities of the organization.

Phase 3: Startup

Startup is when the GainManagement process is formally installed and begins to function. As mentioned above, this can be phased in over several months or several weeks. Whichever approach is used, there are five major startup tasks.

- Leadership approval and support
- Orientation for all employees
- Training for managers, team leaders, and team members
- Problem-solving meetings
- GainShares

Leadership Approval and Support

The management team (and the union) that commissioned the design team must give final approval to the design before it is installed. This may be only a formality, but it must be observed. Local management (and the union) will have participated directly or through representatives in the design process, so all should be familiar with the design. Regardless, a presentation should be made to company (and union) leaders, who must express their approval of the design and their support for the process. This formal approval is best done in a letter signed by the senior manager (and the union president), which becomes one of the formal GainManagement documents and can be reprinted in the employee handbook.

If top managers (and union officials) have not followed the design closely, this is their opportunity to become fully informed and express their acceptance and support. If corporate approval is required, this is the time to get it. (The same holds true if local unions must obtain regional or international union approval.)

The nature of these approvals is also important. Their approval must show a commitment by the leadership to use the Gain-Management process. Passive acceptance is not sufficient. People at all levels in the organization must know that their leaders want the process to be successful and will help to ensure that success. When the GainManagement process develops momentum, as ideas for change flow freely and bonus checks are written, some problems requiring management action may emerge. If top management is then surprised or hesitant, the whole process will stumble and fall. An enthusiastic approval by the leadership based on a thorough understanding of the plan is the first step in a successful implementation. It is better to delay the installation than to proceed in the face of any doubts or reservations by the leadership.

When approaching top management (and union leaders) for approval, the design team must be sensitive to their concerns. It is impossible to predict everything that may happen once GainManagement is installed and begins to function. There will be a tendency for leaders to be conservative and protective until experience shows that the process is safe. This is one reason for the continuous development plan, which spells out when and how the process will be changed to correct the problems that will inevitably arise. Top management is responsible for organization results, and union officials are responsible for protecting the interests of their organization and their members. All will look for assurances that their interests are protected. The design team must anticipate these concerns and present a proposal that will be acceptable. Design teams that encounter problems in this approval step may have to go back to the drawing board and make changes to obtain leadership approval.

Orientations

After the process has been endorsed by the organization's leaders, it must be communicated to and accepted by all of the employees. This is accomplished through a series of employee orientation meetings. Even though employees will have been briefed by their design team representatives throughout the study and design phases, there is a need for them to receive a comprehensive explanation of the completed design.

Orientation for Managers

Depending on how the communications have been handled up to the point of startup, there may be a need to hold special orientation or training sessions for all managers. As the GainManagement process begins to unfold, managers, especially first-line managers, experience the most intense change. GainManagement requires managers to make the break from authoritarian or consultative management practices to full participative management. It is not easy to change years of habits, so managers usually need special help during startup. The leadership training discussed in Chapter 6 will help them to understand and learn the daily practices of participative management.

Managers are also expected to know and understand the GainManagement process thoroughly and to support it enthusiastically. Immediately following the installation employees will direct their questions about the process to the first-level manager rather than to the design team members. When the managers are able to respond to these questions, they feel more ownership of the process. When employees receive good answers, they sense the managers' commitment and are thus encouraged to support the effort.

Before any manager or team leader is confronted with employees' questions the design team must conduct an orientation/training session for all leaders to make sure they fully understand the following:

- ▲ The reasons why the company decided to adopt the Gain-Management process
- ▲ The business and quality-of-work-life goals for Gain-Management
- ▲ The role and responsibilities of leaders in the process, and how their performance will be measured
- ▲ The responsibilities of work team members for the process
- ▲ The details of GainSharing: GainShares for all of the organization's constituents, the financial GainSharing base, sharing ratio, and method, and how to read and interpret the Gain-Share statement
- ▲ Monthly meeting calendar
- ▲ Team action plan and suggestion quotas
- ▲ Team leaders' responsibilities for processing team action plans and employee suggestions

This orientation/training session must be more than just an information session in which the team leaders are told about the process. To be effective this session must provide an opportunity for the managers to express their doubts, fears, and hesitation in a

During the third month of one rather successful Gain-Management startup a team leader made the following statement to his team at their regular weekly information meeting: "I think this whole program is a crock. It will never amount to anything, and I, for one, flatly do not support it." This statement made its way to the manufacturing manager, who immediately summoned the team leader for a discussion. The leader acknowledged that he had made the remark and that those indeed were his sentiments.

The manager pointed out that there had been ample time and many opportunities for the team leader to voice his objections and reservations during the study and planning phases and during the training and personal coaching he had received. There was still an opportunity to discuss his reservations so that he could receive whatever help he needed to implement the program. The manager pointed out that a decision was made by the entire company to proceed with the program, and as a team leader and manager he now was responsible for the success of the program in his department.

At that point in the discussion the manufacturing manager, in very colorful language, told the team leader his options were to support the program or leave the company.

supportive atmosphere. None of the managers can be expected to be instant System 4 or 5 leaders. It must be explained that they will be given time and help to develop the new practices and skills. However, they must also know that they *are expected* eventually to become System 4 or 5 leaders.

Orientation for Employees

This presentation is made by senior management (union leaders), and members of the design team. A simple structure for this presentation is to distribute copies of the new GainManagement employee handbook and present the information as it appears in the handbook. For instance:

A senior manager (with a union leader) presents:

- ▲ The business and quality-of-work-life goals for the Gain-Management process

▲ Management's commitment to use GainManagement and to allocate resources to ensure its success
▲ Management's expectation that all employees will actively participate and their promise to be responsive to employee participation
▲ The employment security policy

Design team members present the remainder of the orientation.

A design team member from the GainMaking subgroup presents:

▲ GainManagement goals
—100% participation
—Two action plans from each monthly work team problem-solving meeting
—Two individual suggestions per work team each month
—Other goals
▲ Work team structure
▲ Calendar
▲ **Focus** and **Charge**
▲ Monthly team problem-solving meeting
▲ Action plans
▲ Suggestions
▲ Forms and the idea log
▲ Idea processing system
▲ Team authority or spending levels

A design team member from the communications subgroup presents:

▲ Weekly information meetings and agenda
▲ Bulletin boards
▲ Newsletters
▲ Sources for other information

A design team member from the GainSharing subgroup presents:

▲ GainShares for all constituents
▲ Company financial status
▲ GainShare base and how it was decided
▲ Sharing ratio
▲ Distribution of financial GainShares
▲ Frequency and reserve fund
▲ Monthly productivity and GainSharing statement

Other information presented by design team members:

- ▲ GainManagement policy manual
- ▲ Training plans
- ▲ Roles and responsibilities
- ▲ GainManagement council
- ▲ Development plan

These orientation meetings work best when presented to single work teams or at most two or three teams with no more than 25 employees in attendance. In smaller meetings employees have better opportunities to raise their questions.

Early gainsharing experience advised an employee vote to determine acceptance of the program.[1] This is still an option to be considered but should not be necessary if the design team has communicated adequately throughout the design process. The design team provides information as it develops to help employees understand the design. Problems with the design need to surface well in advance of the formal startup. The design team encourages a response to the design as it develops; thus, the program they present at the orientation meetings already has the basic support of the organization. If there is opposition during the orientations, the design team must determine the source of the problem and find the proper way to resolve it. Problems encountered at this stage call for one of two possible solutions: a better explanation to reassure employees that the process is beneficial to them, or a change to the design that will make the process more acceptable.

The design team must also be prepared for a certain amount of skepticism or even cynicism no matter how good the design or the communications. It is important to separate normal grousing from real opposition. The skeptics will usually agree to a request to go along and give it a try. Real opposition calls for action as described above.

Training for Managers, Team Leaders, and Team Members

The orientation meetings described above are to explain the GainManagement process and how it operates. Beyond a knowledge of the process there is a need to develop specific skills for operating the process. The design team will have prepared an overall training plan, some of which occurs during installation. Other training to increase GainManagement skills continues well beyond startup.

Focus and **Charge** training and team problem-solving training for managers and team leaders must be completed prior to the first team problem-solving meetings. In addition to their orientation employees receive an introductory session to prepare them for the problem-solving meetings.

The schedule and details of the team leadership training, the **Focus** and **Charge** training, and team problem-solving training, as well as the other training that comes after startup, are found in Chapters 6 and 10.

Problem-Solving Meetings

When an organization has been talking about employee participation for the several months of the study and design process, pressure builds to start the process. Team problem-solving meetings are the most interesting and visible piece of the new GainManagement process, and the teams are anxious to get them started. Once the organization has accepted the design and everyone has been to an orientation, the **Focus** and **Charges** should be selected and work teams should hold their first problem-solving meetings.

GainShares

An important startup activity is the GainSharing announcement. Interest in GainSharing runs very high in the beginning. Most of the details about the GainShares, including the financial GainSharing base, are explained at the orientation. The only remaining formal startup activity is an official announcement of when GainSharing will begin.

In GainManagement the GainSharing base is set at a high level of performance—often higher than the organization's current level of performance. It may take several months of active GainMaking before GainShares are earned. Rather than accumulating losses in the beginning, the GainSharing is not officially activated until the first positive GainShare is earned. This information needs to be communicated in a way that encourages the organization to make productivity gains.

GainManagement Coordinator

Some organizations appoint a full-time GainManagement Coordinator, for others a full-time position is unnecessary. Generally this decision is influenced by the size of the organization and the complexity of the process. Larger organizations, with more than 300 employees, are more likely to use a coordinator. Smaller organizations assign coordination duties to one or more employees as additional responsibilities. Controllers and personnel managers are the ones most often given coordination assignments.

The tasks to be performed are included in the coordinator's job description illustrated in Figure 9-2. If a full-time coordinator is not appointed, these tasks must be assigned to several employees.

This coordinator position should not duplicate other resources already available in the organization. For instance, if the organization has a training department, it will conduct the training mentioned above. The GainManagement coordinator need only schedule and help plan training activities.

If a full- or part-time coordinator is used to perform these activities in support of the GainManagement process, it is important that this position not diminish the responsibility of general managers, department managers, or first-level managers to provide active leadership for the GainManagement process. Giving a coordinator the title of "manager," as in "GainManagement Manager," should be avoided to prevent the incumbent from assuming inappropriate influence over the process and to keep others from expecting too much from the coordinator.

Summary

In the study and design phase of the GainManagement process the idea comes to life through the efforts of the entire organization. Everyone from the top managers to the newest new hire has the opportunity to participate in the design of the program. This is a time-consuming part of the installation, but the time spent on these activities pays huge dividends.

The design work begins with a study of GainManagement and of the organization. The design team then customizes every feature

Figure 9-2.   Job description for GainManagement coordinator.

GAIN MANAGEMENT COORDINATOR

Basic Purpose: To support the GainManagement process by providing administrative, expediting, training, and coordination services to all team leaders, employees, and teams.

Principal Accountabilities:

1. Idea Processing—Records, logs, transmits, expedites, and tracks all suggestions and action plans.
2. Scheduling—Plans regular and special meetings, training, orientations, and representative elections.
3. Training—Conducts and/or coordinates training activities for the GainManagement process, including employee orientations.
4. Communications—Prepares and posts meeting minutes, maintains and distributes employee handbooks, maintains GainManagement bulletin boards, and facilitates the flow of all information necessary to the process.
5. Secretary and ex-officio member of the GainManagement Council—Prepares agendas and reports, prepares and distributes minutes and records of all meetings.

---

of GainManagement to the special needs and opportunities of the company. When this is complete and approved, startup commences.

Startup is a busy time, but it is also an exciting time because a good deal of work will have gone into the design and everyone will be eager to get started. There is a great deal of information and understanding to be transmitted at startup. Nothing should be assumed or taken for granted; everything must be explained thoroughly and patiently.

Note

1. Robert J. Doyle, *Gainsharing and Productivity* (New York: AMACOM, 1983).

Chapter 10

Training for GainManagement

There will be many changes in the organization that chooses Gain-Management as a process for excellence. Changes will occur in organization structure, jobs, roles, responsibilities, principles, practices, relationships, and communications. GainManagement is a new process that will facilitate these changes, but it takes people to make the process work. Employees in every category will need new knowledge and skills to use GainManagement effectively.

The investigation, design, and startup activities to implement GainManagement in a medium-size organization can usually be completed within one year. The training and development needed to increase the knowledge and skills of employees in an organization committed to excellence never ends. Every achievement of excellence creates a new horizon of excellence calling for more knowledge and skills. The pursuit of excellence using the GainManagement process requires nothing less than a commitment to continuous learning. Organizations should learn from the example of professional athletes and musicians. The New York Philharmonic is an excellent orchestra and the Portland Trailblazers are an excellent basketball team because they all practice, they learn, and they develop continuously. Organizations choosing GainManagement must also learn and develop continuously.

The decision to use GainManagement must include a commitment to training and development for all employees and work teams. Necessary training includes knowledge and skills in leadership, teamwork, problem solving, innovating, managing conflict, collaborating, cooperating, analysis, diagnosis, implementing, influencing, contributing, strategic thinking, planning, controlling, and cost analysis, to name quite a few. These subjects are organizational knowledge and skills that have been neglected in training programs concentrated on professional and technical knowledge and skills. For excellence training must include a balanced diet of organizational and technical training.

The changes and new responsibilities introduced with Gain-Management produce a variety of reactions among employees, ranging from anxiety to curiosity. One team leader admitted to sleepless nights and nausea in anticipation of his first weekly information meeting. Few experience such an extreme reaction, but many who have never held information meetings or led problem-solving meetings are nervous. Employees are skeptical about team problem solving and the organization's willingness to use their ideas. Training and experience are the answers to these concerns. Training provides the knowledge and basic skills to get started. Experience, carefully analyzed and put to use, leads to proficiency.

All organizations have training and development needs that become more apparent as the GainManagement process unfolds. A thorough training-needs analysis, and a well-designed training policy and plan, fortifies the whole GainManagement process and ensures steady progress to excellence. This chapter presents the training and development activities required for a successful launch of the GainManagement process and the most likely programs for ongoing training and development.

GainManagement Training for Startup

There are four specific training activities to support the startup of the GainManagement process:

1. Team leadership training and development
2. How to set the **Focus** and **Charges**
3. How to solve problems in teams
4. How to read and interpret the GainShare statement

The design team plans and schedules these training activities to occur at appropriate times as part of the startup plan.

System 5: Leadership Training and Development

As described in Chapter 6 team leadership supports the whole GainMaking process. Team leadership supports increased participation in all five areas of work but, in particular, the areas of designing work processes and strategy and goals. Team leaders who only know the authoritarian management practices of Systems 1, 2, and 3 need to learn new skills and become proficient in the participative management practices of Systems 4 and 5.

All managers from the CEO to first-line managers not only need training to help them understand the leadership practices of the new GainManagement process but also a process to help them develop the new skills of participative management. Since the days of T groups in the 1960s there has been an undercurrent of criticism directed at organizational leaders and their practices of leadership. Many of the participative leadership training programs, often called labs, did not succeed in changing the practices of management. Some experts concluded that effective leadership in conventional organizations was not possible, so they turned their attention to changing structures. In the late 1980s so-called leaderless work groups or autonomous work groups became popular. GainManagement takes the approach that leaders are essential to organizational effectiveness, but the way leadership is practiced must change. The Gain-Management process radically changes but does not diminish the leadership role of either the first-line managers or other managers. On the contrary GainManagement requires very strong and competent leadership.

The strength of participative management is a very different kind of strength from that of authoritarian management. The strength of authoritarian management came from the organization's power to reward and punish, which in turn derived from its ability to give or withhold the satisfaction of the employees' basic economic needs. The strengths in participative management derive from the leadership skills of developing people and teams and motivating them to achieve and excel. To make managers effective in authoritarian systems it was only necessary to appoint them to a position of authority and provide some basic training in techniques and administration. The strength of the authoritarian manager derived from the power of the organization, not the skills of the individual manager.

In GainManagement it is essential for managers to understand leadership and develop effective leadership skills. Training is insufficient if it only provides a list of behaviors to avoid: don't discipline, don't order people around, don't make all the decisions, don't be authoritarian. Also it is not enough just to tell managers to be more of a coach and mentor, to empower workers, or to be supportive. Leadership is a discipline with very specific leadership practices that can be described, measured, and learned.

Team leaders and managers need a full explanation of the four major leadership responsibilities described in Chapter 6—that is:

1. Develop people.
2. Build teams.
3. Guide work.
4. Promote goals.

Leadership practices can be explained in a classroom setting, but team leadership skills can only be developed on the job. This calls for a development process based on a continuous assessment and feedback of the manager's leadership practices on the job. Feedback provides managers with the information they need to evaluate and analyze their daily leadership actions and set priorities for continuous skill development.

Although leadership is difficult to define, there is no mistaking the effect of good and bad leadership. A leadership survey, completed by members of the work team, is a practical method for assessing leadership practices. Leadership surveys can assess the performance of both the team leader and team members in each of the four major leadership responsibility areas. These assessments are used to set goals and prepare action plans for leadership development. Subsequent surveys measure progress and are used to reset goals and plan continuous improvement. An entire organization can

---

Tony wanted to be a good team leader in the participative management system, but he complained that he just didn't know what was expected from him. In the absence of good instruction he tried his best, but it was difficult and he became frustrated and sullen. His frustration was incorrectly interpreted as a lack of commitment, and disciplinary action was taken against him. Tony became angry and left the company feeling that he had been treated very unfairly.

learn to develop effective participative leadership practices by the combination of knowledge training and survey-guided skill development.

Because team leaders have such a critical role in a successful GainManagement startup, it is desirable to begin System 5 leadership training two to three months before the GainManagement startup. The first round of training and leadership surveys is completed at least two months before the first team problem-solving meetings. Beginning this training early has another practical benefit in the design and startup procedures. The active involvement of employees completing leadership surveys helps sustain employees' interest while the design details are being completed. The leadership training, survey completion, and development activity also provide a preview of things to come, which helps convince some of the skeptics that real change is imminent.

Another aspect of System 5 leadership is that team members share responsibility with the team leaders for the leadership of the team. Team members are responsible for supporting the formal leader, for providing leadership to each other as members of the team, and for helping to develop effective team leadership skills within the team. This sharing in the leadership is another form of participation. GainManagement is not a paternalistic or permissive process to make employees feel good about the organization. It is a process to enable employees to act responsibly within the organization as full partners. When employees are requested to participate in the assessment and development of team leadership, they also begin to learn about their responsibility for the success of the organization.

How to Set the Focus and Charges

The **Focus** and **Charges** serve two important purposes. First, they extend the strategic and operating planning process to a monthly event that links the GainManagement process with the real business of the organization. Past gainsharing programs have tended to be partial programs directed at blue-collar labor productivity alone rather than the whole business. GainManagement is a mainstream process concerned with the whole business. Second, the **Focus** and **Charges** provide specific targets for monthly team problem solving and innovation.

The **Focus** and **Charge** is a new experience for most organizations and is introduced prior to the first round of problem-solving meetings. A training program to explain the what, how, and why of the **Focus** and **Charge** is needed. Separate training programs can be conducted explaining the **Focus** to top management and the **Charges** to the team leaders, but a combined training session has some decided advantages in dealing with such a new feature.

A combined session for top management and all team leaders ensures that everyone receives the same information and that all levels of management have the same understanding of the relationship of the **Focus** and **Charges.** This training is designed and scheduled so that management actually decides the **Focus** for the first month as part of the training program. The best time for this training is two weeks prior to the startup of the first monthly work team problem-solving meeting.

By observing top management deliberating and deciding the **Focus** team leaders understand better how the **Focus** is determined. This understanding helps the team leaders explain the **Focus** to their teams. After the **Focus** has been decided, the training session moves on to the **Charges.** Following an explanation of the **Charges** each major department manager discusses and decides on **Charges** with each of their team leaders. These **Charges** will be used in the problem-solving meetings. Team leaders learn from their own **Charge**-setting activity and from observing other team leaders go through the same procedure.

During the **Charge**-setting phase of the training top management is given the opportunity to observe what happens to their **Focus** when it goes to the next level. It is common in this training for senior managers to discover that their first-line managers know and understand very little about the organization's goals and plans. This often prompts them to schedule additional training to provide the team leaders with more information about the organization's mission and strategic operating plans. As the team leaders learn more about the organization and its goals, they communicate more with their team members, and everyone's awareness and understanding of the business grows.

How to Solve Problems in Teams

The team problem-solving meeting is the most visible and active of the startup activities and of the continuing GainManagement process.

From the very beginning most teams find their monthly problem-solving meeting interesting and challenging. As they develop proficiency and see their results, it becomes a major event each month.

Getting started requires formal training for team leaders and team members. Many employees have never participated in team problem solving and few managers have led team problem-solving meetings. The method used in GainMaking is a highly structured and disciplined approach that is new even to those who have been involved in other participative management programs. Team leaders need a complete explanation of the structure and method of the meeting, and some practice in the technique. They must learn how to encourage employee participation without dominating the meeting. They must learn to lead the team to two action plans in a well-run, one-hour meeting.

Team members learn the process of team problem solving from their team leaders as they participate in the actual meetings. To help them get started they are given an introduction and explanation of the meeting structure and process and their role in it. Their participation determines the outcome of the meeting, and they need to understand their responsibility for the process prior to the first meeting. A practical procedure is to schedule the first problem-solving meeting for one and one-half hours and to provide training for the team members in the first half hour of the meeting.

It is absolutely critical that the team leader and the team succeed in the very first attempt. For this reason the training program includes having a coach guide each team through their first few meetings. The coach meets with the team leader to prepare for the meeting, then attends the meeting and helps the leader and/or the team, as necessary. Following the meeting the coach completes an evaluation and reviews the meeting with the team leader, offering specific tips to help in running subsequent meetings.

In GainManagement the coach is not a meeting facilitator, as in some currently popular group problem-solving programs. The coach maintains a low profile so as not to preempt the team leader's role in the meeting or with the team. Leading team problem-solving meetings is one of the more important skills that team leaders must develop. Coaching must support leaders, not replace them.

Some team leaders pick up the process very quickly, others need more help. As the team members learn the process, they help to keep the meeting on track and productive. Most team leaders and members are amazed by what they can accomplish in a well-structured one-

> The team had just completed its first GainManagement monthly work team problem-solving meeting. Before the meeting Ellen, the team leader, had been nervous about the meeting. Yet, at the end of the meeting the team rated the meeting one of the best they ever had. They had decided on two very good action plans, and the meeting ran over the allotted hour by only five minutes.
>
> After the meeting Ellen said: "I am amazed. Six months ago we tried to solve this same problem. We met for half a day, and all we did was talk about the problem and blame top management and data processing. We never did get it solved. Today we solved most of the problem in just one hour. Everybody seemed to enjoy the process, and there wasn't any complaining—just good problem solving. I still can't believe how easy it was!"

hour meeting. Then, as their action plans are implemented, they enjoy the new experiences of achievement, involvement, and influence. As these experiences continue, the team leaders' and team members' skills and enthusiasm for the process grows rapidly.

As with leadership training problem-solving training should not be approached as a one-shot program but rather a continuous development process where each experience develops the skills a little more.

How to Read and Interpret the GainShare Statement

The explanations of GainShare statements at the orientation meetings are necessarily somewhat abstract, and generally only a few questions are asked. When the first monthly statement arrives, however, showing just how well the organization performed in the previous month and how much (or how little) of a GainShare check each employee is to receive, there will be a different reaction. In many organizations the first GainShare statement provides the employees with their first serious look at company financial performance. Thus, the early GainShare statements can be expected to release a flood of questions. Team leaders must be well prepared to answer most of these questions, demonstrating a level of understanding and proficiency that shows their commitment and support for the overall process. If they are unable to answer questions, it may appear to team members that they lack interest in the program. Even more important, each monthly GainShare statement provides an opportunity to educate employees about profit, productivity, and the operation of the business. Every advantage must be taken of these educational opportunities.

The training for the team leaders explains the concept and calculations of the GainSharing base, the sharing ratio and how it was decided, the reserves, and the meaning of the key productivity indicators. Typical questions are proposed during the training and answered to provide a model for the team leaders to follow. Special attention needs to be given to the problem of how to handle the bad news months when the GainShares decline or disappear. Finally, the team leaders should be given a "911" hot-line number to call for expert help when they need it. There will be some technical questions that only the experts can answer. This training is given just prior to distributing the first GainShare statements. Figure 10-1 recaps the training for a typical GainManagement startup.

Advanced Training

For the first several months of the new GainManagement process the organization is busy assimilating the startup training described above. Teams are working on problem-solving meeting skills, and managers are learning more about setting and communicating **Focuses** and **Charges** and team leadership action plans. As these activities become routine and employees begin to see real improvements in productivity and quality of work life, it will be time for a new phase of training and development. As has been said many times throughout the book, people are the only resource in the organization capable of growth and development. The growth and development of the human organization is the only certain path to excellence. Wise investments in the training and development of the organization's people always return good dividends. Taking advantage of the momentum created by the GainManagement startup increases the dividends from training and development.

Every organization has unique training and development needs and opportunities, the most common of which fall into five categories:

Figure 10-1.   Start-up training summary.

Timing	Training Event	Participants
2-3 months prior to startup, after the design team has completed the work team structure	Special GainManagement orientation for managers and supervisors	All team leaders
	Team leadership training	All team leaders
	Team leadership survey	All employees
The month prior to the start of team problem-solving meetings	**Focus** and **Charge** Training	Top management and all team leaders
	Orientations	All employees
Start of team problem-solving meetings	Team problem-solving meeting leadership	All team leaders
	Team problem-solving meeting participation	All employees
Just prior to distribution of first GainSharing statement (checks)	How to read and interpret the GainShare statement	All team leaders

1. Understanding the business
2. Advanced problem solving
3. Teamwork and cooperation skills
4. Trainer skills for team leaders
5. Individual skill development

Understanding the Business

Past gainsharing programs often reported that employees developed a better understanding of the business. This was considered an extra or side benefit of the gainsharing program. In GainManagement this is not an extra benefit, it is a major factor in the success of the process. For employees to contribute purposefully to the success of the organization they must understand what the organization is all about. Meaningful GainMaking is impossible when about 80% of the employees are shooting in the dark. There must be a comprehensive training effort to explain the business in detail to all employees. This represents a major undertaking and will take time and creativity to accomplish. It is especially important that organizations simplify the communications from functional departments and eliminate unnecessary professional jargon. What is needed are fewer buzz words and more straight talk. Educating employees about the business includes the following subjects:

- History of the organization
- Mission and strategic objectives
- The planning process
- Profit planning
- Budgets and the budgeting process
- The technology of the business
- Product service and knowledge
- Industry and competitor information
- Profit: dollars, return on investment, percent to sales
- The purpose of profit in the business
- Productivity—for teams, departments, and total company
- Understanding other functional departments

Advanced Problem Solving

The basic procedure for problem-solving meetings is easily learned. It is quite adequate as a starting point and as the basis for more advanced problem-solving. Many of the problems that teams tackle in the first several months are problems that have been around for a while. Not much analysis and diagnosis will be needed to identify causes, to brainstorm, and to find the first 50 action plans. Once the teams have picked the low-hanging fruit, however, they will need advanced problem-solving training to solve more complex or long-standing problems. Training such as the following will be needed and beneficial:

- Problem analysis and diagnosis
- Creative problem solving
- Work simplification and similar techniques

Teamwork and Cooperation Skills

The real strength of an organization is the teamwork within and among its many work teams. The GainManagement startup activities begin the process of strengthening teamwork. Additional training and development enhances and accelerates the growth of teamwork. Training is needed in the following areas:

- ▲ Team leadership—the startup leadership development process should be continued indefinitely
- ▲ Team building
- ▲ Interteam cooperation and conflict management
- ▲ Organizational communications
- ▲ Labor/management cooperation

Trainer Skills for Team Leaders

The evolution of management practices to higher levels of participative management requires that team leaders do more coaching and training than ever before. In the job description for participative leaders the ability to train employees has a higher priority than technical proficiency. The high level of employee participation envisioned in the participative management model presented in Chapter 2 does not happen automatically with the startup of the Gain-Management process. Employee participation develops over time, supported by a good deal of training, development, and experience. To accomplish this sizable training and development task the team leaders must become trainers. To do this they themselves must be trained, especially in the following areas:

- ▲ Techniques and methods of learning and training
- ▲ Preparation of training plans
- ▲ Presentation skills
- ▲ Special training in specific content areas

Individual Skill Development

Most of the training described so far has dealt with teams and leaders. These teams are made up of individuals—engineers, machinists, secretaries, accountants, and others—who must be skilled at their own specialties. Every person in an excellent organization must be excellent at his or her own job, just as every person in an excellent orchestra must be an excellent musician. This requires continuous training for every employee, and retraining where necessary:

▲ Continuous training in the employee's area of professional or technical competence
▲ Cost, quality, and timing standards for their job
▲ Cross-training to improve coordination, flexibility, and employment security
▲ Marketing or customer-awareness training

Summary

Dick Raymond, founder of the Portola Institute, is fond of saying that the long-term survival of an organization requires the continuous education, training, and development of people. People learn and grow in organizations, especially in modern cultures where organizations play such a large role in people's lives. As they learn and grow, people and their organizations become stronger, more competent, and more excellent.

There are four specific training experiences required to start up the GainManagement process: team leadership development, **Focus** and **Charge** training, team problem-solving training, and interpreting GainSharing statements. There are unlimited ongoing training opportunities available to accelerate the GainManagement organization to excellence.

Organizations interested in their future are committed to training. Organizations committed to training will be of interest in the future.

Chapter 11

The GainManagement Council

The GainManagement council is the most important structure in the GainManagement process. This council, though a direct descendant of the Scanlon screening committees and similar gainsharing structures, goes well beyond gainsharing. The council represents the whole organization and is responsible for the continuous development of the GainManagement process and for employee participation in policy making.

As soon as the initial design work is complete and the GainManagement process is installed, the design team automatically becomes the GainManagement council with two primary responsibilities:

1. To develop the GainManagement process
2. To decide work community policies

These are ongoing tasks, so the GainManagement council changes from a temporary design team to a permanent structure with continuing duties and responsibilities. In effect, the design team becomes the first GainManagement council, with the same members. The primary concern of the council during its first year will be to nurture the new GainManagement process, and the design team members are those who know best how things are supposed to proceed.

Organizing the GainManagement Council

During the first year, in addition to monitoring and troubleshooting the GainManagement process, the GainManagement council organizes itself for its permanent role. The council debates and decides its own charter, membership, and procedures.

Council Charter

For the council to function effectively and for the organization to use the council efficiently, there must be a council charter including a statement of the council's purpose and role in the organization. The charter is a statement by management and, where applicable, the union(s), establishing the GainManagement council and specifying:

- ▲ The purpose of the GainManagement council
- ▲ The representative nature of the council
  —its accountability to all employees
- ▲ the scope of the council's work
  —to guide, troubleshoot, maintain, and develop the Gain-Management process
  —to decide work community policy and procedures
- ▲ The council's authority
  —advisory: identify problems and opportunities for others to act upon
  —problem solving: identify and analyze problems and recommend specific solutions subject to the approval of management (and union)
  —decision making: identify, analyze, and decide solutions to problems with the GainManagement process or work community policy

Seldom do organizations have any difficulty with the Gain-Management council charter insofar as it concerns the development of the GainManagement process. They are only too glad to have the knowledgeable help that only this group can provide. Chartering the council to decide work community policy, however, is a sticking point for some managers. Authoritarian managers, accustomed to making all decisions, are hesitant about giving up real decision-making power because they have not learned to trust employees to make responsible decisions in this area.

As a compromise some organizations initially limit the council's charter on policy matters to an advisory role. This is a safe and practical System 3 position to take as a temporary expedient. It is compatible with the spirit of GainManagement, provided steps are taken to prepare the council for a greater role in work community policy issues. GainManagement council representatives must be educated about the situation and the needs of the organization so they learn to make informed and responsible decisions. At the same time managers must learn about the principles and practices of participative management so that they are able to trust employees to make sound policy decisions. Organizations that learn these lessons and extend employee participation to its highest level will realize the full power of teamwork. Then and only then will true excellence be possible. Drucker emphasized the importance of this step as early as 1976: "Plant and office are more than just geographic locations. They are communities . . . work communities. To make workers achieving they must also take substantial responsibility for the work community."[1]

When the organization has a contract with a labor union, care must be taken to ensure that the policy role of the GainManagement council does not conflict with collective bargaining and the contractual grievance procedure.

Membership

The second organizing issue for the GainManagement council is membership. Toward the end of the first year the original appointed members must begin to rotate off the council and be replaced with elected representatives. In organizing itself the GainManagement Council reviews its membership to ensure that all groups in the organization are properly represented on the council. They make whatever changes are needed to achieve proper representation.

The original members of the design team are appointed by the managers or union officers who understood the design challenge. After startup the whole organization knows the GainManagement process and the role of the GainManagement council. Not only will people be able to select their own representatives, it is critical that they do so. Participation through representatives is effective only if employees select their own representatives.

The original design team members should not rotate off the GainManagement council all at once. The development of the GainManagement process takes time and requires steady progress. The council guiding this process should maintain continuity over time. It is advisable for council representatives to be given staggered three-year terms. This would retain two-thirds of the council from year to year and provide the necessary continuity.

The process by which representatives are selected should be formalized and treated with great respect. It was common in past gainsharing programs that employees did not take seriously the election and assignment of members to productivity, screening, and similar committees. As a result these committees seldom developed into the powerful resource they could have. GainManagement is designed to increase the strength of all the organization's resources including the council. The first step is to treat the council with respect by including in the council's charter real authority to act. Employees will be more serious about electing representatives to a council with real authority than to an advisory board with limited authority.

The second step is to have a well-designed system of nominations and elections. Nominations are solicited at large by allowing people to submit an employee's name, including their own, in nomination. Bulletin boards, newsletters and the weekly information meetings are used to announce the solicitation of nominations and to remind employees of the duties, responsibilities, and role of the Gain-Management council. The objective is to nominate those who can do the job best. The best representatives are those who will understand and participate meaningfully in the work of the council and who are well known and able to communicate easily with their constituents.

Ballots should be prepared and a date and time set for the election. This is an important opportunity for participation and every effort should be made to have a large voter turnout. Short educational meetings may be conducted before the voting to emphasize the importance of the council and the election of competent representatives.

To ensure that the elected council members have the backing of a substantial number of employees, a procedure is used that the successful candidate receive votes equal to 50% + 1 of the *eligible* voters. This may result in runoff elections, but it prevents a person being chosen as a council representative by a small minority of the people voting. Effective employee representation is too important not to take these steps to ensure that most employees vote and that the elected council is truly representative of the employees.

Procedures

The GainManagement council establishes a variety of procedures for its work and for the organization to use the services of the council. Different councils will approach these tasks differently according to the culture and history of their organization. Some establish very precise and formal procedures, even to the point of adopting Robert's Rules of Order. Others minimize formality. This is a matter of style and choice, but some formal procedures are necessary to guide the work of the council, including the following:

- Leadership and functional roles—e.g., chairperson, secretary
- Meeting times and places
- Quorum requirements
- Visitors and spectators
- Decision-making processes, i.e., voting or consensus
- Agendas and calendar
  —Council-initiated: monthly meetings, GainManagement audit
  —Organization-initiated: policy problems or disputes

There also need to be procedures relating to how the organization uses the GainManagement council, such as:

- Election of representatives—regular and special elections
- Communications between the council and the organization: minutes, special bulletin boards, meetings, newsletter
- How individuals or groups bring GainManagement issues or work community policy issues before the council

As the council formalizes its role and work in the organization it needs to prepare a manual to guide its operations. This includes the charter, membership and election procedures, and council rules of order and procedures. Shortly after GainManagement starts up, the council should work through enough of these details to enable it to function efficiently. As council members become more experienced and their routines become more refined, additional procedures are added to the council manual.

Once the council has worked out a basic plan of operation, it should hold briefing for all employees to explain the continuing role of the council and how it will serve all employees and the organization.

Developing the GainManagement Process

Every design team works out the very best GainManagement process it can for its organization. This work is not completed with startup, however. As the organization uses the GainManagement process, there will be successes and failures; suggestions made and implemented and suggestions mishandled; meetings held, information shared, and problems solved; and meetings missed or not productive; team leaders trained and using better management practices and leaders, under pressure, slipping back into old familiar authoritarian practices. Technology, competitive threats, and market changes occur, requiring new strategic objectives and profit plans for the organization. Recessions will occur and wipe out profits and GainShares. Every change, both good and bad, creates opportunities for the organization. With experience both managers and employees discover opportunities not apparent in the beginning. New levels of participation and creative innovations impossible at the start of the program appear not only possible but essential.

Because bugs develop in the GainManagement process, because problems and opportunities occur, and because experience is the master teacher, the GainManagement process must include rigorous review, analysis, and development. GainManagement as a process is either getting better or it is getting worse. It cannot be maintained in neutral. The nature of the GainManagement process requires a constant striving for excellence. There is always another or better suggestion to be found. There are always opportunities to improve performance. Keeping an organization lean and in a state of high performance while aggressively pursuing excellence is a full-time activity.

The responsibility for the progressive development of the GainManagement process belongs to the entire organization, with leadership from the GainManagement council. As its designers the council members know how the process is intended to work. They helped to establish the goals and they designed the structures and procedures. They understand the complexity of the process and how to keep it simple and on track. If something is not working as planned, the designers have the background and the expertise to explain the proper operation or to make appropriate modifications. The designers also understand the power and potential of the process and how it can grow and mature.

One of the responsibilities of the GainManagement council is to prepare a development plan that includes the performance goals to which the GainManagement program is directed, and the procedure for ongoing review, analysis, and action. The goals for GainManagement are derived from the organization's strategic plan as described in Chapter 9. These are the real driving forces of the GainManagement process and the starting place for the development program.

The second part of the development program is the procedure for review, analysis, and action. The development procedure consists of two principal activities:

1. Monthly review of key GainManagement activities
2. Annual audit of the entire GainManagement process

Monthly Review

Each month the GainManagement council includes in its meeting a review of the key GainManagement activities from the previous month:

Focus:	Was it clear, specific, understood, challenging, and on time?
Charges:	Did every team have one that was clear, measurable, understood, and challenging?
Information meetings:	Did every team meet weekly and have an appropriate and interesting agenda? Did all team members attend?
Problem-solving meetings:	Did every team hold a problem-solving meeting? Were the meetings well attended and efficient, and did they produce two action plans in response to the **Charge?**

Suggestions: Did team members submit individ-
                          ual suggestions? Were they related
                          to the **Charge** or to other topics?
Idea log: Were action plans and suggestions
                          logged? Is the log complete, up to
                          date, and posted for all to see?
Processing ideas: Were action plans and suggestions
                          processed quickly? Are the resolu-
                          tions satisfactory? Are teams and
                          suggesters kept informed of prog-
                          ress?
GainShare statements: Are they on time? Understood? Do
                          they contain useful productivity in-
                          formation?

This monthly review is accomplished by having each member of the GainManagement council complete a checklist (see Figure 11-1) prior to the council meeting. Information for the evaluation comes from each council representative's own experience and comments from the employees they represent. Each member evaluates the previous month's performance of the key activities on a scale of 1 to 5. The individual evaluations are reported, discussed, and consolidated in the meeting. Areas of low performance are identified, and the council initiates appropriate corrective action. From this monthly review the council also tracks the trends for each activity and takes appropriate action when the trend analysis indicates a need to do so (see Figure 11-2).

During the monthly review the council also discusses any other matters considered to be relevant to the health of the Gain-Management process. In the first year there are many loose ends and specific problems with individual team leaders and teams. It is important that the council take prompt action to keep the process on track in these critical first months. Once the activities of Gain-Management become more routine, the amount of firefighting and troubleshooting declines, and the council is able to study the process for areas where performance can be developed to even higher levels.

Annual Audit

The monthly review covers the ongoing process and the activities of GainManagement. Toward the end of each fiscal year the council

Figure 11-1. GainManagement council monthly review evaluation.

Each month the GainManagement council reviews the key activities of the process. This checklist is completed by each member of the council in preparation for the monthly council meeting. In the meeting the checklists are consolidated and used for troubleshooting and to track trends.

Evaluate each activity and make notes about issues to discuss with the committee.

	SCALE:	Needs Improvement		OK		Excellent
		1	2	3	4	5
Monthly Productivity **Focus**		1	2	3	4	5
Notes: _____						
Team **Charges**		1	2	3	4	5
Notes: _____						
Weekly Information Meetings		1	2	3	4	5
Notes: _____						
Team Problem-Solving Meetings		1	2	3	4	5
Notes: _____						
Individual Suggestions		1	2	3	4	5
Notes: _____						
Idea Log		1	2	3	4	5
Notes: _____						
Processing Ideas		1	2	3	4	5
Notes: _____						
Gainshare Statements		1	2	3	4	5
Notes: _____						

conducts or commissions a thorough audit of the entire process. For objectivity, it is advisable that the council have the audit conducted by independent auditors from corporate headquarters, another division of the company, or outside consultants. The audit begins with a comparison of the organization's results with the GainManagement

Figure 11-2.   GainManagement council trend analysis form.

GainManagement COUNCIL

TREND ANALYSIS

Each month the GainManagement Council reviews these key activities. The scores for each activity, tracked month to month, will show trends that the committee should monitor and, as necessary, act upon. Scores for all council members are averaged each month and recorded in the appropriate block on this form.

	Jan	Feb	Mar	Apr	May	June	July	Aug	Sept	Oct	Nov	Dec
Focus												
Charges												
Weekly Information Meetings												
Team Problem-Solving Meetings												
Individual Suggestions												
Idea Log												
Processing Ideas												
GainShare Statements												

goals. It also reviews every feature of the process. From this in-depth audit the council prepares a specific development plan for the coming year.

The audit should include an analysis of the following features of the GainManagement process:

- ▲ Performance
  - —What changes, positive or negative, occurred in the organization's key performance measurements?
  - —What progress was made in the last year toward the organization's strategic goals?
  - —To what extent did the GainManagement process contribute to these results?
- ▲ Documentation and records
  - —Is the GainManagement process well documented in a policy manual and an employee handbook?
  - —Are there adequate records of team action plans, individual suggestions, meetings, and other important activities?
- ▲ Communications
  - —Are there effective weekly information meetings for all employees?
  - —Are there orientations for new employees? How effective are they?
  - —Are there special GainManagement bulletin boards and/or newsletters? How effective are they?
  - —Do performance feedback systems provide useful performance data for teams and the total organization?
- ▲ The GainManagement Council
  - —Is there a satisfactory charter and procedures for the council?
  - —How thorough and effective are the council's GainManagement development efforts?
  - —How well does the council handle work community policy issues?
- ▲ Leadership
  - —How well do top management and team leaders understand and perform their GainManagement practices and roles?
  - —Are **Focuses** and **Charges** properly set and used?
  - —Are ideas encouraged and used?
  - —Are leadership skills improving?
- ▲ Employee Involvement
  - —Are employees informed?

—Do they understand the information they get?
—Are employees encouraged to be involved?
—Do employees participate actively in team problem-solving meetings?
—Do they participate outside of the meetings?
—What is the quality of team action plans and individual suggestions?

The results of the audit are summarized and presented to the council, which studies the report, prioritizes the action required, and prepares a specific GainManagement development plan for the following fiscal year. In addition to taking appropriate corrective action based on the audit results the committee revises the GainManagement goals to coordinate GainManagement with any changes to the company's strategic plan.

This is also the time when changes, if necessary, are made to the GainSharing element. The strategic plan and, in particular, the profit plan may require a change to the GainSharing base. A new opportunity may make it desirable to change the ratio of sharing gains between the company and the employees. These and any other changes to the GainShares, such as frequency, reserves, and so forth, should be discussed and decided by the GainManagement council in its annual GainManagement review. When changes are made, they should be deliberated and communicated as carefully and as thoroughly as was the original design.

GainManagement is a dynamic process capable of growing with the needs of the organization and its people. However, this growth is in no way automatic. It will come only with experience and as the result of careful review, analysis, and planning for action.

Year-End Summary Report

When the council completes its review of the audit and of the GainManagement results for the year, it prepares ad distributes a summary report to all of the organization's constituents. The purpose of the report is to inform everyone associated with the organization of the progress made in developing the organization for excellence. The report includes:

- Summary of GainShares for each of the organization's principal constituents: customers, employees, shareholders, suppliers, community, etc.
- Progress made in the past year toward the achievement of the organization's strategic objectives
- GainMaking highlights from the past year, such as:
  —number of team action plans
  —number of individual suggestions
  —the results of the action plans and suggestions
     cost savings
     quality improvements
     other
  —special recognition for major improvements or ideas of special merit
- Audit highlights
- Training summary
- Other information of interest to the organization

This is the opportunity for the council to inform, give recognition, and reinforce the good efforts of the organization to use the GainManagement process for excellence. Each council must prepare and distribute a report that meets the needs of the organization.

Work Community Policy

The second primary responsibility of the GainManagement council is to decide issues of work community policy. People at work in an organization constitute a work community. There are issues and policies of concern to the work community that have little or nothing to do with the business of the organization. How they are handled, however, has a great deal to do with how well the organization performs its work. Work community policies create the culture or spirit of the organization whether the organization makes automobiles or ice cream. Effective policies create a good culture, a spirit of performance, and a commitment to excellence throughout the organization. Poor policies or a lack of consistent policy administration leads to alienation, cynicism, and poor performance. Involving employees in policy making is a way to make the process more effective. Employee input will improve the quality of the policies, and employee involvement will ensure employee acceptance and commitment to the policies. The GainManagement council is the most effective method for involving employees in policy making.

Chapter 6, GainMaking, presented the participation structure and leadership skills for involving employees in problem solving, innovation, work design, strategy, and goals—the first four areas of participation (see Figure 11-3). Here we will show how employees can be more involved in the fifth area of participation: policy making. This involvement is an important although indirect GainMaking activity. When employees participate in policy making, they experience more fairness and trust, feel greater loyalty, and become more responsible for and committed to the organization. Imposing policy on employees or setting policies with no involvement denies them the opportunity to become responsible and committed.

The policy issues of concern to the work community include hiring, firing, layoff, placement, displacement, employment security, promotion, training, educational assistance, safety, health, compensation, insurances for health, life, and disability, hours of work, vacations, holidays, retirement, leaves of absence, equal opportunity, affirmative action, job descriptions, drug and alcohol assistance, internal discipline, and personnel records. In addition to these common issues every organization has its own special policy issues.

Policies and procedures for these work community issues must be made and then applied consistently in the daily work of the organization. This creates opportunities for employee participation in

Figure 11-3.   Review of participation in management matrix.

STEP 1: Participation Opportunities

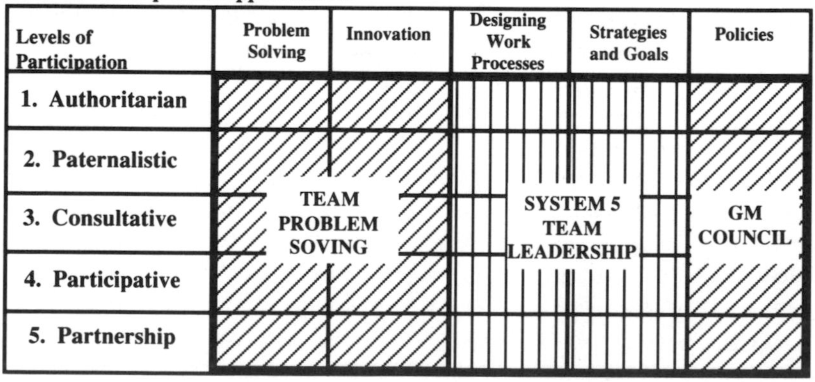

Levels of Participation	Problem Solving	Innovation	Designing Work Processes	Strategies and Goals	Policies
1. Authoritarian					
2. Paternalistic					
3. Consultative	TEAM PROBLEM SOVING		SYSTEM 5 TEAM LEADERSHIP		GM COUNCIL
4. Participative					
5. Partnership					

decisions concerning work community policy. Policy decisions are of four kinds:

1. Making the original policy
2. Applying the policy to a particular situation
3. Allowing an exception to policy
4. Changing the original policy

Every action and decision related to a policy is a policy decision in one way or another. The first and most obvious policy decisions occur when a policy is first decided. Most companies prepare formal written policy statements to record and communicate these decisions.

The most frequent policy decisions are made when applying a policy to a specific situation, employee, or group of employees. In a situation where a policy applies, the matter is settled in accordance with the policy.

In a few situations policies do not apply; when this occurs exceptions can be made to existing policy. When exceptions are allowed, they are made with the understanding that original policy does not change.

Finally, there are some situations that do not fit the policy and, on review, it is determined that the policy is not or is no longer correct. These latter cases provide the information to revise policy.

All four of these aspects of policy making afford opportunities for greater employee participation.

The GainManagement council is an ideal body for deciding policy issues related to the work community. The council is a permanent group and is representative of every level, function, and person in the organization. Representatives ensure that the needs and viewpoints of all employees are considered when policies are decided. This participation through the council representatives improves the quality and relevance of these policies.

The council also resolves conflicts and disputes over policy. Work teams and departments can only decide that a policy applies; they cannot make exceptions nor change policy. Policies apply to the entire organization, so exceptions or policy changes must be decided or approved by the entire organization. The practical way to do this is by vesting the GainManagement council with the authority to make and decide issues of policy.

At the time the GainManagement process is installed the council is seldom ready to take over all work community policy issues. First of all, the council will be preoccupied with specific GainManagement issues. Second, the members will need to become thoroughly familiar with current policies. In the beginning it is not necessary for the council to remake all of the organization's work community policies. A few may have to be adjusted to accommodate the startup, especially the employment security policy, but most can be accepted as they are. Then, as time and circumstances dictate, the council becomes more involved in making and modifying policy. Another reason for moving gradually in this area is that the first council, though representative, was appointed only to complete the original Gain-Management design. Making or deciding work community policies was not part of their original charter. As the original members are replaced by elected members, the council becomes more truly representative of the organization and comes to see itself as more responsible for work community policy issues.

Another reason for going slowly on expanding this policy role of the council is that in the beginning management is hesitant about turning over some work community policy decisions to the council. This is especially true of those issues with dollar signs such as compensation and benefits. In time and with experience the council can gradually increase its involvement in this area.

The use of the GainManagement council in setting work community policy issues and resolving disputes and conflicts is a bold move in the direction of workplace democracy. It is a gradual and sometimes painful development but a necessary one. Organizations cannot meet the new requirements of excellence without the full enthusiastic commitment of all their members. Commitment can only occur when workers are responsible, and responsibility cannot fully develop without a high level of participation. Workplace democracy is synonymous with a high level of worker involvement and participation. Although the impact of this involvement must reach every employee, the most practical way to involve employees in policy issues is through representative bodies such as the GainManagement council. And for the council members to work most effectively they must be given full decision-making authority. This does not have to happen all at once at the startup of the GainManagement process; it should be a gradual learning-and-doing development. Developing the council into a strong, capable structure should be included among the organization's strategic human resources objectives.

In a North Carolina manufacturing company the council's involvement in work community policy started this way:

Barbara was holding her monthly team problem-solving meeting. The team's **Charge** was to reduce the reject rate from 11.4% to 10%. The team listed several causes for the problem, then, surprisingly, selected "worker apathy" as the cause to brainstorm and solve. As their solution they recommended a change in a job bidding procedure they felt was unfair. At first Barbara was confused as the team seemed to be ignoring their **Charge**. Then it became clear that the team was sending a message to management: "If you want us to be concerned about rejects, you must be concerned about us."

Barbara's team did not have the authority to resolve this issue because it was a companywide policy. The team's recommendation was submitted to the GainManagement council. Within two weeks the council developed a new job bidding procedure, which was submitted to management and the workforce. There was overwhelming approval for the new procedure, and it was adopted. Barbara's team and the rest of the employees were very satisfied, and top management was pleasantly surprised by the whole process, the resulting new job bidding procedure, and the reaction by the employees to the whole event. As a result management encouraged the council to become more involved in similar work community policies.

Three months later top management again selected redoing rejects as the Focus. This time the team developed two excellent action plans that reduced rejects.

Managing Conflict

No organization can exist without conflict. There will always be different opinions, perceptions, and understandings. In an organization aggressively in pursuit of excellence conflict is not only normal, it is an important condition for creativity. When people are striving for excellence and conflict arises about the best way to achieve it, the odds of finding the best way improve significantly.

The key ingredient for success is to maintain everyone's focus on achieving the organization's objective. Wasteful arguments and conflicts that have nothing to do with the organization's goals should be avoided as much as possible. The GainManagement process keeps the organization focused on achievement, and the GainManagement Council resolves those work community issues that waste energy.

There are three basic ways organizations resolve conflicts:

1. *Force (win/lose):* This method, used in authoritarian management systems, is where a stronger party imposes a solution on a weaker party. Legitimate objections are not heard, which limits the quality of the solution and causes resentment and antiorganization feelings. Resolving conflict by force is completely inappropriate for a modern high-performing organization.

2. *Negotiation:* Win some/lose some. This is used where the parties are equal in power or agree not to use force. Solutions are usually found in a middle ground or some compromise between the two conflicting positions. Both parties to the conflict get something and give up something. Thus, negotiated solutions are seldom better than half right, but they are very common. They settle for inadequate resolutions rather than digging and finding the best solutions.

3. *Consensus* decision: Win/win. This method, appropriate to GainManagement, analyzes and debates an issue until a solution is found to which the conflicting parties agree. This is the only process that consistently yields the "best" solutions—best for the organization and best for the conflicting parties.

The GainManagement council must model consensus conflict resolution and encourage its use throughout the organization. To do this the council and the organization should learn the following perspectives about conflict management:

- ▲ Conflicts should be allowed and encouraged to surface easily in the organization. Suppressing conflict only intensifies it.
- ▲ Conflicts should be resolved quickly and as close to the point of origin as possible.
- ▲ The correctness of the solution, not the status or power of the parties, determines the outcome.
- ▲ Conflicts should be resolved in relation to common goals. (Another reason why a universal understanding of the organization's strategic goals is so critical.)
- ▲ Solutions must consider the needs of the total organization, not just the needs of the parties to the conflict.

When organizations charter a GainManagement council to resolve policy issues and other disputes, they not only create an effective way to deal with work community issues, but they also find that disputes actually decline. Knowing that it is easy to appeal an issue to the council, everyone pays closer attention to policy and makes decisions more carefully. Team leaders and managers do not want their decisions to be on the agenda of the next council meeting. Also, when mistakes are discovered, they are resolved more quickly for the same reason.

Summary

GainManagement is a process for increasing the strength of the organization and focusing all of that strength on the achievement of the organization's goals. It is a process that requires and enables every employee to be responsible for and committed to the organization and its goals. The GainManagement council, which is broadly representative of the entire organization, is the principal structure for developing the full potential of the GainManagement process. The council should be chartered to monitor and develop the GainManagement process and to decide work community policies and conflicts.

Notes

1. Peter F. Drucker, *Management: Tasks, Responsibilities, Practices* (New York: Harper & Row, 1973).

IV

Unions and GainManagement

GainManagement, like its gainsharing predecessor, is applicable in both union and nonunion settings. However, where a union is present, it must be a full partner in designing, implementing, and maintaining the process. Chapter 12 presents some of the issues that unions and managers must consider when working on a joint project.

Chapter 12

Unions and GainManagement

GainManagement has its roots in the labor unions. Joe Scanlon was president of his United Steel Workers of America local when he introduced his Scanlon plan in 1938. This started the evolution leading to the GainManagement process of today. His leadership from 1938 to 1956 led many unionized companies into participative management and his particular brand of gainsharing. His contribution and convictions provided a strong foundation on which to build.

Scanlon's practical, real-world results undoubtedly contributed to Douglas McGregor's Theory Y concept. McGregor acknowledged Scanlon's work as the practical application of Theory Y.[1] Unions are convinced that they are essential to the success of gainsharing programs. Joe Scanlon "fully understood that no plan to enlist the cooperation of workers could succeed unless it was rooted in a strong union, one able to negotiate on equal terms with the employer and with the power to enforce adherence to the terms of the contract."[2] Organizations without a union are just as convinced that it would be impossible to build a program within the union environment. Neither position is entirely correct or incorrect.

GainManagement works in union and nonunion organizations, but the presence of a union does provide an additional dimension to the process. Although union membership declined in the 1980s, in 1990 unions represented 17% of the workers in the United States. There has been speculation that unions will rise again toward the end of the 20th century as organized labor defines a new vision of services to the American worker.

The perspective of adversarial combatants fighting for a larger piece of a fixed pie no longer serves unions or organizations. Social, political, and economic changes are forcing unions to devise new strategies and develop new skills in their relationships with management. Similarly, management is moving to an awareness that a partnership with labor is a better strategy than conflict. The simple fact is that both labor and management must perform well to make organizations succeed in today's competitive environment and to meet the rising expectations of workers. Labor and management must become partners in planning, making, and sharing gains for there to be true gains in organizational performance and in the quality of work life.

Partnership means more than a union cooperating with a corporation. It means people participating in a venture in which they share a common fate and while doing so satisfy their personal needs and achieve their individual goals. The GainManagement concept, structure, and training go beyond the notion of just cooperation. Every employee has an opportunity to be involved in the long-term and short-term management of the business so that the needs of all concerned are met.

This chapter provides some perspective and guidelines for unions and organizations as they consider GainManagement. Each group must be sensitive to the concerns and responsibilities of the other in order to do a credible job of investigating, planning, and designing a program that will meet the needs of all. Earlier chapters presented in considerable detail the needs, concerns, and responsibilities of management and the organization. This chapter presents the concerns, viewpoint, and issues of the unions. The mutual understanding of both sets of concerns forms the basis for a joint union/management GainManagement process.

There is a growing union interest in all types of gainsharing, participative management, and quality-of-work-life programs. Unions and unionized organizations are trying new programs in growing numbers and with mixed results. These mixed results cause many companies and unions to remain skeptical. For unions the primary concern is that many programs fail to recognize the legitimacy, authority, and interests of the union as an organization. One union opinion states: "A local union really has only two options for facing the challenge [of participative management]. . . . It can force the company to drop the program altogether. Or it can decide to participate fully, organize its members, and press the limits of the program so that it really addresses the quality of work life, and builds rather than undermines the union."[3]

Many unions do not support employee-involvement programs because they have had bad experiences with them. Employee participation programs have been used as a tactic by union busters to break unions and dissolve the power base of unified employees. Managers have used the involvement techniques to persuade employees that they do not need a union. Such uses of participation programs are not consistent with the goals either of organized labor or of participation programs.

Both union and management have good reason to oppose badly conceived or badly designed programs. But for sound programs that have the potential to make organizations more successful and make workers more secure and satisfied, there is only one option: This is for the union to put its effort into developing its own vision for the future and then helping to develop joint programs that will accomplish this vision. Unions that are clear about their goals for workers are prepared to help management develop realistic programs. They are also prepared to use their legal leverage to hold management accountable for the GainManagement process. This can be a positive force contributing to the success of the GainManagement process, a benefit to their members, and an advantage to the organization.

Union publications often present arguments opposing employee participation while at the same time suggesting ways to make such programs work. There seems to be ambivalence about this whole matter within union ranks. Unionists who take a militant anti-involvement stance are not looking at the opportunities that participation offers for the future; rather, they are reacting to frustrating past experiences. Considering that unions and their members are caught up in the turmoil of corporate reorganizations, technological change, economic deal making, and global market uncertainty, they must expand their abilities to represent their members. Rather than reacting to the negative past, unions must adopt a policy of "proactive militancy" to assure that their members are more secure and satisfied and that the organizations they work for are more successful.

The principles and practices of GainPlanning presented in Chapter 5 apply to the union organization as well as to companies. One practice was the need for a clear mission and strategic goals. Proactive militancy requires that unions and their leaders create new missions and goals for labor. Union leaders are responsible for adjusting to new conditions and thereby improving their ability to represent their members and contribute to the evolutionary progress of a democratic society and a healthy economy.

Unions that have taken the time to clarify their own mission and goals prior to entering into involvement programs have had significant success. They have been able to identify program options that address problems of concern to their members. When unions participate as key players in these new strategies, their members develop a better appreciation of the role of the union in the workplace, the marketplace, and in society. Members also develop a better awareness of the union working in their behalf. Employees need the excellent organizations that GainManagement can create, and the unions need to embrace participation as a strategy that will serve the needs of unions and their members.

In Chapter 1 the point was made that management systems must catch up with the changing needs of the workers. The same is true for unions. Without changing their fundamental check-and-balance role in the overall process, the unions must adapt to the rising expectations of the worker. The unions have played a major role in helping workers satisfy their Maslow Levels 1, 2, and 3 needs. Now it is time for them to support the workers' efforts to satisfy Levels 4 and 5 needs. These higher-level needs are the substance of the new mission for organized labor.

As organizations move to more participative systems, the unions must examine some of their own organizational practices. A union that develops a clear, new proactive mission finds it easier to push decision making down to the members in the workplace. A union struggling to preserve the old mission is threatened by participation and finds it difficult to loosen its control of decision making from the union hall. Clarity of mission and careful advance planning will make these changes easier and more successful.

Management has a bias in favor of the organization's goals. Thus, many current programs are tipped toward productivity and the improvement of organization performance. Quality-of-work-life goals, while stated, are seldom given equal priority with productivity improvement. Therefore, the traditional check-and-balance role is appropriate for the union in these new programs. Balance is the key. The union will not help the process by insisting that the program be tipped away from productivity and toward quality of work life. The workers' job security depends on strong organizational performance. The union must support the organization's drive for performance while insisting on quality-of-work-life goals to give the whole

GainManagement process the necessary balance. Also, by working for the proper balance of productivity and quality-of-work-life goals, the union can insist that management do likewise.

Unions must develop and clearly communicate these new objectives to their members as well as to the employing organizations. Then they will be able to consider all employee-involvement programs and selectively support those that will benefit their members. They can avoid past problems of going along blindly only to be forced into opposition after the damage has been done. Union leaders who are clear about their objectives are in a much better position to resolve conflicts between labor's goals and management's goals.

Union Experiences With the GainManagement Process

GainManagement is built on the premise that workers' capabilities and needs are constantly growing. This basic premise is consistent with a new vision and mission for unions, combined with their historical role of bringing democratic ideals and processes into the workplace. In the following section we will review past union activities and current interests and trends as they apply to GainPlanning, GainMaking, and GainSharing.

GainPlanning

Historically, unions have taken a reactive role rather than a planning role in the affairs of the organizations where they represent workers. They do some planning in anticipation of the next collective bargaining contract, but this tends to be short term. They review the last contract and the immediate situation facing the industry and the organization, trying to anticipate opportunities to improve wages, hours, and working conditions. Unions have made very little formal effort to exert direct influence over the GainPlanning principles and practices described in Chapter 5.

In their advocate role unions have opposed management practices they felt were unfair or abusive to workers, but this has always been remedial, not planned, and certainly not strategic. Although the collective bargaining process does influence the future, what

happens at the bargaining table is not planning. Bargaining is reacting to the past and finding a compromise between the organization's
position and the union's position.

Regardless of past experience there is a role for the union in
planning, and there has been some movement in this direction. In
the 1989 negotiations between the Communications Workers of
America and U.S. West there was agreement to establish a structure
for joint planning throughout the three years of the contract. Rather
than negotiate a set of hard-and-fast rules to be administered over
the term of the contract, objectives and processes were established.
Objectives for serving the needs of the company's customers as well
as meeting the needs of union members were jointly approved.
Processes were established for involving union members in workplace
changes. In addition processes to continually adapt worker involvement to the goals of the business were approved. This agreement
confirmed a partnership between the union and the company as both
parties entered a new era of rapid change and new challenges. This
partnership provides an ongoing process for the resolution of issues,
for information sharing, and for joint goal setting. It is a new way to
resolve issues of contracting work, technology development and
deployment, employment security, and other organization changes
brought about by changing technology and the changing marketplace.

The General Motors Saturn operation provides an example of
involving a union in advance planning for the production of automobiles. The company and the United Auto Workers decided not to call
their experience a joint project because they felt that the word *joint*
implied two groups, and they wanted the rhetoric to signify one
team. The Saturn project began with 99 GM employees and UAW
members forming a study center to explore the possibilities of a
cooperative project. The memorandum of agreement between the
UAW and GM creates a labor/management Strategic Action Council
(SAC) that "will have particular concern for long-range goals and the
health of Saturn, with particular emphasis on planning. . . ."[4]

These experiences exemplify a growing role for labor unions in
the planning process. The result of this trend will be the eventual
elimination of the destructive adversarial relationship between labor
and management. The growing proactive partnership promises benefits to both labor and management far in excess of a situation in
which labor simply cooperates in the plans of management.

GainMaking

The roots of union participation in GainMaking go back to the Scanlon plan. A 1946 *Life* magazine article about the Scanlon plan at Adamson Steel Company describes how suggestions increased for improving welding techniques. It explained that welders who formerly waited for materials began helping with loading and unloading.[5] At Adamson Steel this union involvement in GainMaking began when Cecil Adamson went to the headquarters of the United Steel Workers of America in Pittsburgh. He told union leaders the shop wasn't working well and asked them what they wanted and how the company and the union could begin to work together to satisfy their individual needs.[6]

It is in GainMaking where unions and union workers have had experience and where they can have the most immediate and significant impact. As described in Chapter 6 the workers are the major resource available for GainMaking. However, union skepticism about participative management also applies to GainMaking. Traditionally the unions' position has been that workers' experience and expertise are one of the few resources that the company does not control. Unions fear that once worker expertise is given to the company, it can never be taken back. On the other hand sharing of money, authority, freedoms, and involvement can all be rescinded by the company. In one union cartoon a man is shown thinking that if the paint shop were closer to the shipping dock, "they wouldn't need two men . . . one of whom is me. So remember, you are not paid to think." There is a basic lack of trust in management's fairness that prevents many unions from embracing participation.

Unions know that workers are capable of improving the productivity of almost any organization. However, they need assurances that workers' interests will be respected in productivity-improvement programs. "Few workers arrive at the assembly line out of a life-long ambition to put together a Toyota Corolla. They work because they need a job. They need to be paid decently so they can support their families, increase their pleasure during leisure, see that their children get a good education, and participate in community activities. They work to live, rather than live to work. Within this context workers want their jobs to be safe and to fill various personal needs. Some of those needs converge with the corporation's needs, some do not. At the point where the needs diverge, does the corporation encourage the worker's need for personal growth, or respect the worker's commitment to his or her family?"[7]

This is one very important reason why the principle of equity for all partners is essential to a successful GainManagement program. Partners must be certain that the interests of all partners are acknowledged and respected.

Another agenda item for unions approaching participative management programs has been to negotiate for more worker control of their work. Operating issues of performance, productivity, market share, and such have not yet been given serious attention. The union wants to help the worker gain more authority in the workplace. This union thrust is very much in tune with the changing workforce; Maslow's Levels 4 and 5 include the workers' need to have more control of their work and more authority in the workplace.

GainSharing

Unions have been involved in every type of gainsharing plan, including Scanlon, Rucker, Improshare, and Profit Sharing. The following paper, written in 1980 by Reginald Newell, research director of the International Association of Machinists, was originally reprinted in *Gainsharing and Productivity*.[8] Although it is not an official union policy statement, it is still a comprehensive summary of union views on gainsharing. While the paper describes some of the employee-participation aspects of these plans, it is clear that the unions, just like management, view past gainsharing programs primarily as financial incentive plans.

Profit Sharing and Group Incentive Plans

For years American industry has attempted to tie workers' earnings to levels of output or productivity, rather than reimbursing an employee for specific skills, job functions, etc. Historically, this has been done through a variety of individual type incentive systems. Companies have assumed that the incentive principle operates best by giving each individual an opportunity to perform and paying him for extra performance. Individual incentives have major application where workers exercise control over their output. As mechanization increases, however, there is reduced need for the traditional individual incentive systems.

Whether because of technological change or the general opposition of American labor to pitting one worker against another, individual incentive plans have been on the decline. This is evident in the fact that in 1967, 26 percent of IAM members were covered by some type of incentive system. In the first quarter of 1979, this percentage had dropped to 20. As a consequence of this decline, more and more American companies are attempting to introduce plant-wide or group incentive programs.

There are basically two (2) different approaches to plant-wide incentive (production bonus) plans. Profit sharing is one type of collective or plant-wide incentive payment system. The other general type is based upon some measure of production, cost, or sales, rather than profits. Of this second type, the most commonly used systems are the Scanlon Plan and the Rucker (Share the Production) plan. Under both, workers receive a bonus for savings in labor costs.

These types of plans are not new, and some have been around since World War II. They are, however, undergoing a revival for two reasons. First, the nation is being bombarded by the press concerning the relatively low productivity growth of the 1970s. We are supposedly facing a "productivity crisis." Secondly, under the so-called "voluntary" Carter wage and price guidelines, offsetting increases in productivity is one way an employer can exceed the seven (7) percent pay standard and remain within the guidelines. Thus, industry is looking at both old and new ways of increasing productivity and group incentives are at the top of their list.

The purpose of this article is to review the IAM's position on profit sharing and discuss the two most common types of group incentive systems.

Profit Sharing

The IAM has, through the years, maintained a suspicious regard of profit-sharing plans. This opposition is based upon several points which include difficulties experienced on the part of the employees having their hopes built up that they would receive a bonus at the end of a prescribed period, only to have their hopes end when no bonus payments are made. Also, profit-sharing plans were frequently introduced by employers as a means of circumventing a wage increase that would be received by employees at each pay period, with the vague and uncertain prospects that a bonus would be paid six months or a year later.

If it is used in connection with pensions, profit-sharing plans are the least desirable of any form of retirement programs. This position is due largely to the fact that the employees of a company have no guarantee whatsoever that during a particular year the company will earn sufficient profits to add any credits to the individual employee's retirement fund. In other words, the money used to provide retirement benefits depends upon the company's ability to earn a profit. Since there are so many factors involved in the company's ability to operate profitably during a particular year, over which the employees have no control whatsoever, we consider it unfair to the employees to operate under such a plan. If business conditions are such that for a period of several consecutive years or several years within a different period of time the company does not make a profit, the employees would receive no credit toward their retirement fund.

It is true that some sincere employers have used a profit-sharing plan to the benefit of the employees; however, such cases are, unfortunately, the exception and not the rule. That is the reason why the IAM has opposed profit-sharing systems over the years. There have been instances in the past when profit-sharing plans, which were made to appear very attractive, were put into effect during a period of prosperous business, but when the period of prosperity ended, the employer insisted that the plan must work both ways since their business fell off and gross earnings were reduced. The experience of the IAM on the subject has also been the experience of other unions.

Naturally, there are occasions when, despite the IAM's position on profit sharing plans, our negotiators have no choice but to accept them. When this happens, it is our duty to make sure that we negotiate the best possible plan.

Types of Plans

Profit-sharing plans may take the form of (1) current distribution plan, (2) deferred payment plan, or (3) a combination of [the] two. Most current distribution plans provide for annual payment in cash. The amount distributed under distribution plans is deductible for income tax purposes by the employer, and is taxable income as far as the employee is concerned.

Under deferred payment programs, a portion of the profits is placed in a trust fund and invested in stocks or bonds. Individual payments eventually are made from the fund in the case of death, disability, retirement, or separation for some other reason; or, in some cases, an employee may direct that part of each year's contribution be used to purchase life insurance or an additional pension. Some deferred plans permit borrowing or withdrawal for medical expenses, financial hardships, education of children, or any "worthy cause." In an increasing number of cases, distributions are permitted as a supplement to unemployment benefits.

When faced by a company proposal regarding a profit-sharing plan, the first thing to be examined is the wage structure. If it is up to standard, then a profit-sharing plan becomes slightly less objectionable. In too many cases, however, a profit-sharing plan is introduced as a means of covering up the very low wage structure. If this is the case, one should steer away from any profit-sharing plan.

Another question that should be answered is whether the company can be relied upon to furnish accurate financial statements. If it does, and meets all the other criteria, then one should not turn down a profit-sharing plan out of hand. If the employees can make real gains, the profit-sharing plan should, at least, be explored.

Scanlon Plan

Like profit-sharing schemes, the Scanlon Plan is affected by the economic success of the company. Because company sales will have a great effect upon bonuses, it may be expected that the plan will look very appealing during period of heightened economic activity but may lose its appeal during periods of economic contraction. This is especially true in industries in which demand fluctuates greatly. Bonus payments may disappear entirely during periods of slack demand when labor costs tend to be higher, in relation to the value of output, than they would otherwise be. The Scanlon Plan is of necessity streamlined to the individual needs of the company where the plan is in effect. However, basically the plan is a group incentive rather than an individual incentive.

At first glance, the method of determining savings appears complicated and may have some varieties. Basically, the ratio between total payroll and sales value of production (net sales plus inventory) during some historical period is adapted as a norm or standard of labor cost. This ratio or percentage is then applied to the sales value or production for the month in question. The difference between the resulting figure and the actual payroll constitutes the savings in labor cost for the month. Thus, if the historical norm is 35%, in any month in which products worth $100 have been produced at a payroll cost of $30, the savings amount to $5 ($35 minus $30). Part of the savings, generally 25%, is put aside as a reserve to cover those instances where actual labor costs may be greater than the norm in any particular month. The rest is split, 25% going to the company and 75% being paid out immediately to participating employees. At the end of the year, if the reserve is greater than all of the deficits incurred during the year, the remainder is shared by the company and employees in the same proportion as the monthly payments.

The total savings to be distributed to employees may be calculated as a percentage of payroll and the percentage thus obtained applied to each employee's earnings to determine his share. Thus, if the share of savings going to all employees is 5% of the total payroll for the month, each employee will get 5% of his earnings for the month. However, under some plans, where the norm is also defined in terms of the ratio of labor costs to sales value, the total amount going to labor is divided by the number of hours worked, and a uniform increase in wage rates is paid to each employee for each hour worked.

Role of Committees

Theoretically, the rise in productivity, leading to lower labor costs, is a result of higher morale, a greater sense of participation, and better motivation rather than a speedup in the usual sense. Allegedly, the rise in efficiency is brought about chiefly by suggestions as to how time and effort can be saved. These suggestions are processed by joint Production Committees for each department and an overall Screening Committee. The committees, whose function it is to encourage, develop, and implement suggestions, are of central importance in the Scanlon Plan.

The above may sound complicated, but in reality is quite simple, provided that the management and labor have a complete trust in one another. (This is very important because if there isn't complete trust, the plan cannot be effective.)

With regard to the IAM's view of the Scanlon Plan, the following observations are offered:

1. In spite of its somewhat unique nature the Scanlon Plan is purely and simply a work measurement and wage incentive plan. Disputes will arise during the life of the agreement and during negotiations, where the Plan is in effect, just as is true with any other work measurement and wage incentive plan.

2. Under an individual incentive plan each operator works at his or her own pace depending on personal preferences. Workers tend not to be too concerned when fellow workers "goof off." This is not the case under a group incentive plan such as the Scanlon Plan. A good deal of "self-policing" takes place. Indeed, one of the primary objections to any group incentive plan is its inherently divisive effect upon the work force. We believe that it is unhealthy for workers to be placed in a position of policing fellow workers.

3. The Production Committee and the Screening

Committee, while they are not in theory a substitute for the grievance committee and the bargaining committee, may in fact assume a more important role in the eyes of the membership. It is easy to speculate about the impact of such an eventuality upon the local union.

4. Legitimate grievances may go unprocessed and unsolved because workers will hesitate to disrupt the production process. That is, grievances take the aggrieved and the steward away from their respective workplaces thereby adding to labor cost without increasing production.

5. During contract negotiations, in addition to all the other issues which must be resolved, there must be recalculations of the productivity ratio. If the recalculated ratio does not accurately and fully reflect the impact of improved wages and fringe benefits, the members of the bargaining unit will end up paying for their own bonus.

6. There is an assumption under any system, be it individual or group, that incentive earnings are as much a part of gross earnings as base pay. Therefore, it is common practice to use average incentive earnings as the basis for computing vacation pay. Under the Scanlon Plan bonus earnings do not apply to vacation pay. This means that workers incur an earnings penalty when they take their vacation. It also means that the more senior the worker the greater the penalty. The union, in essence, negotiates against itself. In the process of trying to obtain longer vacations for its members it, in effect, negotiates reduced gross earnings.

7. It is generally accepted that the more direct and immediate the relationship between a worker's effort and ingenuity and the resultant incentive payment or bonus the more effective the system. The relationship between a worker's productivity and the bonus, under the Scanlon Plan, is very remote. Not only that, but many factors beyond the worker's control, including production processes, demand, management efficiency, and quality of materials help determine the extent of savings. Total sales, for instance, may be affected by seasonal demand for the product or by the marketing skills of the firm. Since most low to middle income families budget their income to the

hilt it is difficult to make adjustment for unexpected declines in income. Yet that is precisely what can happen under the Scanlon Plan.

8. One way to increase the bonus is to reduce the size of the labor force while maintaining output and sales at previous levels and while leaving the productivity ratio unchanged. From the company's point of view this would obviously be desirable. In the short run it may be desirable for the worker. But the concept of a fair day's work which emerges under such circumstances may be untenable in the long run. Remember, under the Scanlon Plan *all* jobs are on incentive. There are no indirect labor jobs which older workers can turn to, as would be the case under individual incentive standards, when incentive jobs are too strenuous.

9. Finally, for the Scanlon Plan to be of any benefit to the employee, the broadest base of employee participation must be sought. All work units must be represented by the production committees so that problems, which could divide workers, may be thoroughly discussed. It goes without saying that workers' representatives should be appointed or elected through the union. These representatives should have access to company records that are used to establish or adjust bonus ratios.

Rucker Share-of-Production Plan

The Rucker plan is similar to the Scanlon plan in philosophy but is based upon much more sophisticated analysis. A historical relationship is established between total earnings (including indirect compensation) of hourly rated employees and production value created by the company. If major changes in products or production process occur, the plan is re-engineered. Because of the careful analysis that goes into the original ratio, adjustments occur less often than in a Scanlon plan.

An economic engineering audit of several years of past operation is conducted, including a detailed study of approximately two years, broken down by monthly operating results. Production value added by the company is sales value of output less cost of raw materials purchased and related costs such as supplies and power. A standard productivity ratio is calculated which expresses the amount of production value required for each $1.00 in wages paid including benefits. The productivity ratio also determines production shares, that is, the share of production attributable to labor and the share due the company. The analysis is conducted for each plant.

Assume that the company put $.55 worth of materials, supplies, and power into production to obtain a product worth $1.00. Value added or production value is thus $.45 for each $1.00 of sales value. Assume also that analysis shows that 40 percent of production value is attributable to labor. The productivity ratio becomes 2.5, and for a payroll (plus benefits) of $100,000 standard production value is $250,000. If actual production value for the month is $300,000, a gain of $50,000 is available for bonus and is distributed 40 percent to labor and 60 percent to the company. Labor's bonus share for the month is $20,000. Actually, 25 percent of the gain in any month is placed in a reserve account to offset months with poor results. The reserve account is distributed at the end of the year. The $20,000 bonus fund is distributed pro rata to individuals on the basis of their regular pay (including overtime and shift differential) for the month.

The plan is most often applied to production workers, but it may be developed to cover all the employees in the company. Analysis determines standard shares of production value for each group or team. A common arrangement is to determine the shares of the employee team (all hourly rated employees) and the company. The Rucker plan provides an integrated incentive to reduce costs of producing the same production value or producing a greater production value for the same costs. All savings go to the groups covered on the basis of their share of production value.

Employee committees are used to obtain and appraise suggestions for improvements in production costs. Typical "share of production" committees consist of worker representatives from each major department plus a lesser number of shop supervisors. Usually there are two chairmen, a top executive, and the union president. Committee members may serve terms of one year, or shorter periods may be specified to bring in new ideas.

Apparently these committees achieve results quite similar to those found under Scanlon plans. One study reports that committee members in successful Rucker plans are just as aggressive and critical of poor management as in Scanlon plan companies. It appears that the results and problems in Rucker plans are very similar to those existing in Scanlon plans. One difference may be that Rucker plans have been successfully added to existing individual incentive plans.

In summary, the IAM is very skeptical about any type of profit-sharing and/or group incentive plan. IAM negotiators are urged to avoid any system of indirect wage payment which is dependent upon factors over which the employee has little or no control. Instead, bargaining should center on obtaining single rates of pay for all job classifications. These rates should reflect skill level, labor market conditions, comparable rates of pay in the industry, the rising cost of living, improved productivity, and the need to increase a worker's real purchasing power.

Throughout the 1980s more companies turned to gainsharing and other so-called alternative pay plans in a general effort to control labor costs. Many of these plans were proposed in lieu of other pay increases and for that reason were opposed by the unions. Where they were installed, the union was often a reluctant partner. One union leader described it as follows: "The company gave us the option of profit sharing or plant closure. That's a Hobson's choice. The company is always willing to share profits when there aren't any. Three years from now, when there are profits, we will get our wages back." Another unionist, showing his gainsharing check, said he and his coworkers refer to their gainshares as "chump change" because they believe that management manipulates the numbers to be sure the bonus payouts aren't too large. It will be necessary to go well beyond gainsharing to overcome the built-up resistance and cynicism of many union leaders and members.

The Future of GainManagement and Unions

GainManagement will work well in a union environment because the principles of GainManagement are consistent with the goals of the labor movement. Unions benefit from improving organizational performance, and unions are committed to the personal well-being of their members. The GainManagement process includes the assumptions that improving productivity and improving quality of work life go hand-in-hand and that excellence is best achieved through the total involvement of the workforce in making gains.

For GainManagement to be most effective in a union setting both union leaders and management must be clear about their own objectives and supportive of each other's goals. The union is a separate entity with its own objectives, perspectives, issues, priorities, goals, and leadership. This is a reality that management must acknowledge, respect, and use effectively in the process. The organization also has objectives, separate from those of the union, that are driven by other constituents: customers, banks, shareholders, and owners. The union must acknowledge, respect, and support these objectives. In order to do a credible job of supporting the needs of each other labor and management must cooperate in investigating, planning, and designing the GainManagement process and overseeing its ongoing development.

Cooperation is essential to partnership, but it must be placed in its proper perspective. In the GainManagement process cooperation is not a goal, it is an essential skill and a means to the goal. The goal in GainManagement is to make the organization perform for all its constituents. Management will encounter union resistance if it presents cooperation as a specific GainManagement goal. Unions tend to view such goals as requests for the unconditional surrender of the union. Management must present the goal of the GainManagement process as the need to improve overall organizational performance—productivity, quality, market share, job security, employee participation, and quality of work life.

GainPlanning

GainPlanning can be brought to the negotiating table. The traditional collective bargaining table issues of wages, hours, and working conditions can and should be expanded to include psychological working conditions such as participation, communications, accountability, and decision making. In GainManagement the collective bargaining process should become a "collective planning process." The legal structure established over years of collective bargaining can be an energy source to make the GainManagement program work. However, this energy will not be fully utilized if the groups only meet once every three years. GainPlanning should be an ongoing activity throughout the course of the contract, as in the agreement between the Communications Workers and U.S. West mentioned above. The benefits from more frequent meetings are to maintain momentum and the ability to respond more quickly when unexpected situations arise. Conflicts are inevitable, and the ability to nip them in the bud is a great advantage. A collective planning process will be successful to the extent that all parties are equally skilled at planning, communications, and conflict resolution.

Involving union leaders in the planning stages presents the opportunity for them to suggest methods of moving toward the organization's strategic goals in ways that will allow the unions to develop their own objectives and people. For example, as new technology obsoletes old technology, there is a need to consider training and new opportunities for displaced workers. This is a primary union goal and with sufficient advanced planning these issues are more easily resolved.

Another advantage to union involvement is the additional legal leverage of the bargaining agreement for the fulfillment of the program objectives. Combining the strength of union leadership with that of line managers to ensure the commitment of the organization is a good insurance package. Both groups have considerable resources to keep the process on track and deliver mutually beneficial results.

Unions and organizations considering the idea of collective planning must be aware of the legal restrictions and freedoms that presently govern these activities. In the United States, national labor relations legislation requires the parties to negotiate wages, hours, and other conditions of employment. In addition unions and organizations are permitted to bargain any other subject so long as the activity is not illegal. However, the law does not compel bargaining these other issues, and it would be an unfair labor practice to strike or bargain to impasse over them. Cooperation in GainPlanning must be voluntarily undertaken, it cannot be compelled.

GainMaking

Three thrusts for GainMaking were described in Chapters 6 and 11: problem solving, leadership, and policy. All are opportunities for union involvement and support.

The union can encourage the participation of its members in problem solving and innovation. This is the first and easiest form of support. The union can also use its energy to nudge the process beyond System 3 consultation to levels where workers have real authority and control over their work.

One major corporation defined its policy as follows:

> The participative problem-solving process is a two-part process:
>
> 1. Development of alternatives to current practices can originate from the involved worker.
> 2. Decisions to act and commit resources reside with management.
>
> The system makes it possible for employees at all levels of the organization to develop alternatives to current practices. However, the decision to select among the alternatives and commit resources to implement changes is solely that of management at appropriate levels.

This is a System 3 policy: participation, but with authoritarian power close at hand. A policy such as this is not enough to support the GainManagement process. Management practices must be moved to Systems 4 and 5. The unions can help make it happen.

The union can also support the leadership development process and promote more active worker participation in team leadership, work design, and goal setting. Here is where the unions' major concern for employment security can play an important role. It is inevitable that jobs will change as work is redesigned for greater productivity. With diesel trucks and interstate freeways there just aren't any wagonmaster jobs available. Today, however, with proper training the wagonmaster is a dispatcher. The same must be done for other jobs that will be eliminated due to technology and other forces. As work teams find better methods and better work designs, their action plans must include retraining and/or reassigning displaced workers under a policy of guaranteed employment. The union, with its security orientation, can be an additional energy source to maintain this balance in the total process.

Finally, GainMaking calls for a great deal of training for all employees in leadership, problem solving, group process skills, new

Karen was president of Local 3-100 and a prime mover in bringing GainManagement into the company. As a leader in designing the GainMaking work team participation process she was chosen to be the company's first GainManagement coordinator. In the first few months suggestions began to bog down in traditional System 3 red tape. The employees began to complain that the work team meetings were a waste of time if nothing was to be done with their action plans.

Karen picked up a handful of delinquent action plans and suggestions and went straight to the president's office. She told the president in very clear language to cut the red tape or the union would withdraw its support for the program. Before the day was over the president summoned the Gain-Management council to deal with the problem.

At this meeting the council tackled the problem and developed a plan whereby each work team was given an annual $3,000 budget to implement suggestions. With this additional authority the suggestion backlog disappeared and the flow of new suggestions and action plans picked up.

Later both Karen and the company president said they were quite pleased about the way the problem was confronted and resolved.

job skills, and others. Unions have always supported training, and they can bring this interest to the process. GainManagement training in a union setting should include special training for union leaders to enable them to participate fully in the whole process. Collective planning suggests that bargaining committee members ought to have the same training as their management counterparts.

GainSharing

The full menu of GainSharing benefits for employees is completely consistent with union goals. Job security, promotions, workers' control of their work, a better quality of work life, and financial Gain-Shares are all benefits that unions have advocated throughout their history. Unions can and will support these goals. However, unions will always have a special interest in financial GainSharing stemming from their efforts to protect and to increase workers' wages.

One of the lessons from the 1980s was that for workers and their unions job security had a slightly stronger priority than wages. In the early 1980s, when unemployment was high and the U.S. economy was in a recession, many unions accepted gainsharing, profit sharing, lump sum, two-tier, and other so-called alternative pay plans and even wage cuts, when the alternative was unemployment. For a while it appeared that the unions would accept gainshares as a supplement to an otherwise competitive wage. But this did not last long. Within five years the unions were working hard to overturn earlier concessions and replace what they considered to be lost wages. The basic issues of fair and competitive pay are compensation issues and must be reconciled as such. Financial GainShares, to be effective, must be over and above basic compensation. This position is entirely consistent with union policy. Base wages will continue to be a subject for negotiations and collective bargaining. GainShares are income but not wages in the usual sense. As described in Chapter 7 GainShares provide a new opportunity to pay bonuses, expand the company, or some of each. The union should participate in the decisions about how best to use this opportunity.

GainSharing provides another opportunity for the union to provide balance as described earlier. During the design phase the calculations for the productivity base and the sharing ratio are usually done by the organization's accounting department, where the information and expertise reside. Lacking expertise, most employees are in no position to challenge, or even intelligently question, the calculations. And so they don't. Any weakness in the calculations will take months or sometimes years to surface. Unions, however, have experts and the strength to challenge, which can only help the process when both parties are committed to finding the best productivity base and the best application of the resulting gains.

Union Involvement in Establishing GainManagement

In the past GainManagement has always been initiated by management. It has happened and it is becoming more likely that progressive unions may also choose to initiate these processes. The critical first step in the GainManagement process for the union is to clarify union goals and objectives. Unions must do a better job of preparing themselves for involvement in these programs. They should not proceed with a plan they cannot fully support. Partial involvement or skeptical approaches will not help the union or the company; they are a waste of time and lead to more hard feelings. If the union prepares well before entering into the design phase of a program, it is in a much better position to help make the program succeed. The following is a recommended approach for a union to use when participating in the establishment of a GainManagement process.

Step 1: Convene a conference to work out the union's position on GainManagement well in advance of any anticipated activity. If the union is placed in a hurry-up-and-decide mode, they will not have sufficient opportunity to think through their own issues and make best decisions. Unions must accept the fact that management systems are moving toward greater employee involvement. It is in the union's best interests to do advance planning in order to respond to these new developments in a positive manner and in a manner that serves their membership. This is what is meant by proactive militancy.

The union conducts a formal feasibility study similar to that recommended for corporate management in Chapter 8. The questions for the union to address in this GainManagement feasibility study include:

▲ What is GainManagement, and what experiences have other unions had with the GainManagement process?
▲ Is GainManagement consistent with the union's values, mission, goals, policies, and strategic plans?
▲ What are the benefits to the union and its members from the GainManagement process?
▲ What are the risks to the union or its members in GainManagement?
▲ Is the security of the union at risk? How must union security be handled?
▲ What are the impacts of GainManagement on labor/management relations in general and the collective bargaining agreement in particular? Are these impacts acceptable?
▲ How does the union want to be involved in the planning, implementation, and development of GainManagement?
▲ What assurances do the members need that the process will be maintained and the GainShare calculated in accordance with the plan?
▲ How do GainShares relate to other compensation?

▲ What assurance do the members have that their ideas will not result in unemployment?

▲ Jobs will change. How will this be handled?

▲ What assurances must there be of commitment to training and retraining for job changes due to GainMaking?

▲ What resources must the company and the union invest in the development of the process and the development of the people?

▲ Does the union share in the cost of the training?

▲ What are the roles of union leaders and stewards?

▲ What are the methods for the sharing of financial and other performance information?

▲ How are changes to the process handled?

▲ What are the goals for quality of work life, and how will they be measured?

▲ How does the union participate in program planning and design?

▲ How much of the process must be negotiated and included in the contract or memorandum of agreement?

Unions are fundamentally representative organizations, so this study is conducted by elected officials including stewards. Stewards are close to the rank and file and thus are able to bring a broad member perspective to the study. The union team should be augmented with specialists, as needed, to ensure a thorough study. When the study produces a formal union position, it should be presented to the members for their approval. Where several unions represent the workers in a single company, they should establish a joint council and complete this study cooperatively. From this study a union policy statement should be prepared.

The example shown in Figure 12-1 comes from a joint labor/management effort similar to the GainManagement process. It is presented here as an example of a policy statement to which the union was an active partner. It demonstrates the principles that the union is an equal partner, that employee participation is welcome and expected, and that the new process will not conflict with collective bargaining. It also demonstrates that both the business objectives of the corporation and the objectives of the union are important and will be respected.

Step 2: Create a union steering committee to guide union involvement in the GainManagement process on an ongoing basis. This committee,

Figure 12-1. An open letter to employees.

U S WEST Communications and the Communications Workers of America believe that all employees have an interest in the long-term success of the corporation and the Union. Only by forming appropriate partnerships will we continue to provide quality service and enhance the quality of life at work for everyone.

The following premises support this philosophical belief:

- Employees are responsible, trustworthy and capable of making contributions when equipped with the necessary authority, information and training.
- Employees at every level will be expected to contribute and participate in decisions which improve their daily work, either individually or in teams.

The following principles will guide the Employee Involvement efforts:

- Employee Involvement is a joint Union-Management effort guided by the philosophy that the Union is an equal partner.
- Joint activities will continue to be encouraged, which means that a designated Union person and a manager will work together from the inception through the development, implementation and evaluation of an idea.
- Innovations which result from joint activities and experiments will not directly result in the layoff of any regular employee or negatively affect the pay or seniority status of any employee.
- Joint activities do not replace the collective bargaining process.
- Voluntary involvement by all employees is essential to the success of these joint ventures.
- The success of joint activities requires a safe climate which encourages initiative and experimentation. There is no one best approach to working together. Joint processes must evolve to meet the needs of all parties.

These principles and values are based on our continued joint commitment to the employees, customers and owners as well as encouraging equal opportunity, innovation, fairness and integrity.

A. E. Manseth	Walter F. Maulis
Executive Director	International Vice President
Employee Relations	Communications Workers of America
U S WEST Communications	District 7

Reproduced by permission of US WEST Communications and Communications Workers of America.

made up of those who conducted the feasibility study, continues to make policy, to educate and train members, and to review the activities from design to implementation to ongoing development in order to ensure that the policies and goals of the union are being met.

Step 3: Participate in the selection of members of the GainManagement design team. Once the union and the company agree to pursue GainManagement, they establish a representative team to design the process. The union participates fully in the selection of all members of this team.

Step 4: Educate union GainManagement design team members on the union's goals and perspectives. After the selection of the members of the design team the union should hold a training session to introduce the members to the union's goals, objectives, and concerns established in Steps 1 and 2. A similar presentation of the union's goals, objectives, and concerns should be made by the union officers to the management members of the design team.

Once the program has been installed, the union leaders must support the proper operation of the plan. They should voice their concerns about topics for the **Focus** and **Charges.** They should monitor the idea process, review and analyze the Idea Log, and offer support and suggestions to improve the whole process. They should review action plans to ensure that retraining and employment security issues are properly handled. They should observe training programs to ensure that union's goals for training are being met. When they observe deficiencies, they should initiate corrective action. The union represents a unique resource to guarantee the success of the Gain-Management process. Their legal status and the strength of their organization can be used to keep positive pressure on the organization to fulfill the commitments necessary to the success of the GainManagement process.

Summary

Unions are important members of many organizations that are moving toward higher levels of employee involvement. This trend to GainManagement contains a good news/bad news message for unions. It is good news because the goals of the unions are or can be entirely consistent with GainManagement. GainManagement has great potential for improving the working conditions of union members. The bad news is that some managers have misused these programs in the past, and there is the risk that this may happen again. Regardless of past experiences, however, unions must continue to explore partnerships with management for the short-term and long-range benefit of their members. Unions should oppose programs that do not meet the needs of their members and support those that do. To be in a solid position to make wise choices union leaders must do their homework. They must create new visions and reexamine their goals to be sure they are up-to-date with the evolving needs of their members. They must also become informed of the various approaches to employee involvement and preselect those that serve the needs of their members. With good planning the unions can become enthusiastic partners with management in implementing sound processes such as GainManagement.

Notes

1. Douglas McGregor, *The Human Side of Enterprise* (New York: McGraw-Hill, 1960).
2. Mike Parker, *Inside the Circle* (Boston: South End Press, 1985).
3. Ibid.
4. Memorandum of Agreement, Saturn Corporation, 1985.
5. John Chamberlain, "Every Man a Capitalist," *Life* (December 23, 1946), p. 93.
6. Ibid.
7. Mike Parker, *Inside the Circle* (Boston: South End Press, 1985).
8. Robert J. Doyle, *Gainsharing and Productivity* (New York: AMACOM, 1983).

Glossary

action plan Improvement idea developed by a work team in its monthly problem-solving meeting.

audit, GainManagement Annual in-depth review of the status of the GainManagement process, leading to a formal improvement plan to be executed in the following year.

authoritarian management Traditional or System 1 and 2 management.

collective planning process Ongoing collective bargaining between unions and management. Includes issues of development and collaboration in addition to wages, hours, and working conditions.

consultative management System 3 management. The transition system between authoritarian and participative management.

continuous learning Process of continually analyzing a person's or organization's experience, setting higher goals and growing.

Charge That specific piece of the monthly **Focus** assigned to each work team for problem solving.

equity Investment in dollars, labor, ideas, loyalty, and commitment of each of the organization's constituents.

Focus Monthly productivity improvement goal toward which all team problem solving is directed. The **Focus** is always tied to the organization's strategic and operating plans.

GainMaking All of the individual, team, and organizational efforts to improve productivity, performance, and quality of work life.

GainManagement Total process for involving all employees in continuously improving productivity, performance, and quality of work life.

GainManagement council Elected group representing all of the organization's employees. The council is responsible for the maintenance and development of the GainManagement process, for making or revising work community policies, and for resolving certain organizational issues and disputes.

GainPlanning Participative management principles and practices necessary to lead, motivate, and sustain the GainManagement process and GainMaking efforts.

GainSharing Equitable sharing of performance gains with all of the organization's constituents.

GainShares, Financial Monthly or quarterly employee share of financial gains in excess of minimum profit.

idea log Listing of all team action plans and individual suggestions for tracking, record keeping, and analysis.

job description Brief description of the work assigned to an individual or to a work team, including: (1) basic purpose, (2) principal responsibilities, (3) dimensions (revenue, budget, personnel), (4) key results expected, (5) scope of authority, (6) relationships and communications flow.

leadership, System 5 Highly developmental and participative leadership practices of GainManagement: Develop people, build teams, guide work, promote goals.

minimum profit Level of annual profit that will enable the organization to satisfy all current obligations and adequately fund strategic growth. Minimum profit is the basis for financial GainSharing.

paternalistic management Traditional System 2 management, authoritarian but sensitive to the needs of the people.

participative management System 4 management, highly participative.

partnership management System 5 management, highly participative but more egalitarian than System 4.

profit sharing Refers to a variety of programs that share profits with employees either directly, by current payouts, or into a deferred trust.

suggestion Improvement idea submitted by an individual employee outside of the monthly team problem-solving meeting.

team job description *See* job description.

team leader   Appointed leader of the team, usually a manager.

team mission statement   Clear, brief statement of the purpose of the work team. The "basic purpose" on the team job description.

work team   Basic working unit of a company or other organization, e.g., management work team, technical work team, production work team, clerical work team, etc.

Bibliography

Blake, Robert, and Jane Mouton. *The Managerial Grid*. Austin, Tex.: Gulf Publishing, 1964.

De Pree, Max. *Leadership Is an Art*. New York: Doubleday, 1989.

Donnelly, John F. "Participative Management at Work" (interview). *Harvard Business Review* (January–February 1977).

Doyle, Robert J. *Gainsharing and Productivity: A Guide to Planning, Implementation and Development*. New York: AMACOM, 1983.

Drucker, Peter F. *Management: Tasks, Responsibilities, Practices*. New York: Harper & Row, 1973.

Etzioni, Amitai. *An Immodest Agenda*. New York: McGraw-Hill, 1983.

Final Report and Testimony submitted to Congress by the Commission on Industrial Relations. U.S. Congress, Senate Doc 415, May 22, 1914.

Frost, Carl F., John H. Wakeley, and Robert A. Ruh. *The Scanlon Plan for Organization Development: Identity, Participation and Equity*. East Lansing: Michigan State University Press, 1974.

Hamel, G., and C. K. Prahalad. "Strategic Intent." *Harvard Business Review* (May–June 1989).

Herzberg, Frederick, Bernard Mausner, and Barbara Bloch Snyderman. *The Motivation to Work*. New York: John Wiley, 1959.

Kanter, Rosabeth M. "From Status to Contribution: Some Organizational Implications of the Changing Basis for Pay." *Personnel* (January 1987).

Kelley, Robert E. *The Gold Collar Worker*. New York: Addison-Wesley, 1985.

Lawler, Edward E., III. *Pay and Organization Development*. Reading, Mass.: Addison-Wesley, 1981.

———. *High-Involvement Management*. San Francisco: Jossey-Bass, 1986.

———, *Strategic Pay*. San Francisco: Jossey-Bass, 1990.

Lawler, Edward E., III, and Susan A. Mohrman. "Quality Circles After the Fad." *Harvard Business Review* (January–February 1985).

Lesieur, Fred G., and Eldridge S. Puckett. "The Scanlon Plan Has Proved Itself." *Harvard Business Review* (September–October 1969).

———, ed., *The Scanlon Plan: A Frontier in Labor Management Cooperation*. Cambridge, Mass.: The MIT Press, 1958.

Levering, R., M. Moskowitz, and M. Katz. *The 100 Best Companies to Work for in America*. New York: Addison-Wesley, 1984.

Likert, Rensis. *New Patterns of Management*. New York: McGraw-Hill, 1961.

Libert, Rensis, and Jane Gibson Likert. *New Ways of Managing Conflict*. New York: McGraw-Hill, 1976.

Maslow, A. H. *Motivation and Personality*. New York: Harper & Row, 1954.

McGregor, Douglas. *The Human Side of Enterprise*. New York: McGraw-Hill, 1960.

Moore, Brian E., and Timothy L. Ross. *The Scanlon Way to Improved Productivity*. New York: John Wiley, 1978.

Moore, Brian E., and Timothy L. Ross. *Productivity Gainsharing*. Englewood Cliffs, N.J.: Prentice Hall, 1983.

O'Dell, Carla S. "Gainsharing: Involvement, Incentives, and Productivity." AMA Management Briefing, 1981.

Parker, Mike. *Inside the Circle*. Boston: South End Press, 1985.

Peters, Thomas J., and Robert H. Waterman, Jr. *In Search of Excellence*. New York: Warner Books, 1982.

Peters, Tom. *Thriving on Chaos*. New York: Alfred A. Knopf, 1988.

"Productivity Sharing Programs: Can They Contribute to Productivity Improvement?" Staff Report, U.S. General Accounting Office, 1981.

Reid, Peter C. *Well Made in America*. New York: McGraw-Hill, 1990.

Sashkin, M. "Participation Is an Ethical Imperative." *Organizational Dynamics* (Spring 1984).

Senge, Peter M. *The Fifth Discipline*. New York: Doubleday, 1990.

Weisbord, Marvin R. *Productive Workplaces*. San Francisco: Jossey-Bass, 1987.

Weitzman, Martin L. "The Share Economy, Conquering Stagflation," *Harvard University Press*, 1984.

Yankelovich, Daniel, and John Immerwahr. "Putting the Work Ethic to Work." Public Agenda Foundation, 1983.

Index

[Page numbers in *italics* refer to illustrations.]